Illegitimate Freedom

Illegitimate Freedom: Informality in Modernist Literature, 1900–1940 is the first study of informality in modernist literature. Differentiating informality from intimacy in its introduction, the book discusses the informal in relation with sensory experience, aesthetic presentation, ethical deliberation or action, and social attitudes within modernist works. It examines these works for particular nuances of the word "informality" in each of its chapters in the following thematic sequence: informality that offers humour, interpretive freedom, and promiscuity as counters to self-absorption in works by Virginia Woolf; rebuttals to male priorities in liberalism through "feminine informality" in several short stories by Katherine Mansfield; contempt for colloquialism and intimacy, tinged with class-anxieties and crises of attitude, in T. S. Eliot's poetry; resistance to disgust in James Joyce's novels; and the fusion of irreverence, protest, and praise in W. H. Auden's writings before 1940. The book's conclusion considers the risks of informality through a discussion of what it calls "inverted dignity." The theoretical aspects of the book offer insights into Lockean liberalism, the ethical dimensions of what Hélène Cixous termed "feminine writing," relations of sublimity and domesticity, Sigmund Freud's arguments on humour and melancholia, and recent affect theory's—as well as Immanuel Kant's and Friedrich Nietzsche's—views on disgust, linking these with modernism. This wide range of engagement makes this study relevant for those interested in literary studies, critical theory, and philosophy.

Gaurav Majumdar is Professor of English at Whitman College. His publications include the book *Migrant Form: Anti-Colonial Aesthetics in Joyce, Rushdie, and Ray*.

Among the Victorians and Modernists
Edited by Dennis Denisoff

This series publishes monographs and essay collections on literature, art, and culture in the context of the diverse aesthetic, political, social, technological, and scientific innovations that arose among the Victorians and Modernists. Viable topics include, but are not limited to, artistic and cultural debates and movements; influential figures and communities; and agitations and developments regarding subjects such as animals, commodification, decadence, degeneracy, democracy, desire, ecology, gender, nationalism, the paranormal, performance, public art, sex, socialism, spiritualities, transnationalism, and the urban. Studies that address continuities between the Victorians and Modernists are welcome. Work on recent responses to the periods such as Neo-Victorian novels, graphic novels, and film will also be considered.

Music and Myth in Modern Literature
Josh Torabi

Materiality in Modernist Short Fiction
Lived Things
Laura Oulanne

Virginia Woolf's Unwritten Histories
Conversations with the Nineteenth Century
Anne Besnault

Illegitimate Freedom
Informality in Modernist Literature, 1900–1940
Gaurav Majumdar

For more information about this series, please visit: https://www.routledge.com/Among-the-Victorians-and-Modernists/book-series/ASHSER4035

Illegitimate Freedom

Informality in Modernist Literature, 1900–1940

Gaurav Majumdar

Unknown, "James Joyce with Nora, seated on wall in Zurich." Image from the UB James Joyce Collection courtesy of the Poetry Collection of the University Libraries, University at Buffalo, The State University of New York.

Routledge
Taylor & Francis Group
NEW YORK AND LONDON

First published 2022
by Routledge
605 Third Avenue, New York, NY 10158

and by Routledge
2 Park Square, Milton Park, Abingdon, Oxon, OX14 4RN

Routledge is an imprint of the Taylor & Francis Group, an informa business

Library of Congress Cataloging-in-Publication Data
A catalog record for this title has been requested

ISBN: 978-0-367-44462-4 (hbk)
ISBN: 978-1-032-11548-1 (pbk)
ISBN: 978-1-003-00989-4 (ebk)

DOI: 10.4324/9781003009894

Typeset in Sabon
by Deanta Publishing Services, Chennai, India

To Chetna Chopra

Contents

Acknowledgments

I have benefited from many kinds of help during the writing of this book. Invaluable suggestions and encouragement from Enda Duffy, Benjamin Boysen, Vicki Mahaffey, Gerri Kimber, and Aimee Gasston helped me form and reconsider its arguments. I am very appreciative of the patience, sensitivity, and courtesy of Michelle Salyga and Bryony Reece, the editor and editorial assistant for the book at Routledge.

I received financial assistance for this project from the office of the Provost and Dean of Faculty, with particular help from Associate Dean Helen Kim, at Whitman College, where I also received friendship and solidarity from Shampa Biswas, Bruce Magnusson, Jonathan Walters, David Schmitz, Paul Apostolidis, Libby Miller, John Cotts, and Tim Machonkin. My thanks to them and to my colleagues at Whitman's English department. I would like to thank Elizabeth Vandiver and David Lupher, especially, for generous gifts that helped this project.

The warmth, verve, and brilliance of Nicole Simek and Zahi Zalloua have transformed cautious collegiality into longstanding familial relations for me—that's a startling recognition, N. and Z. Similar recognition extends to other dear friends, whose generosity and hospitality have been crucial during the composition of this book: Siddhartha Mukherjee, Vivek Ramachandran, Sarah Sze, Siddhartha Sivaramakrishnan, Prabha Nagaraj, Krishna Nagaraj, and Jim Harder.

Several exceptional, dear students have buoyed me during my work for this project: I would like to acknowledge, with particular pride, Bryn Carlson, Tess Carges, Josh Tacke, Catherine Fisher, Philip Stefani, Chelsea Kern, Hayden Cooper, Peter Feehan, and Rohan Press.

Carmen Truyols, Anuj Majumdar, Kirti Chopra, and Amarjit Chopra have given me strong, idiosyncratic support and, more unwittingly, insights into dynamics of the informal. Vijay Chopra remains a model of affectionate informality for me.

Pinaki Chatterjee has gifted me beautiful, if sometimes beautifully exasperating, friendship. Chetna Chopra has gifted me love and support for this project that I could not have imagined.

The frontispiece image appears courtesy of the UB James Joyce Collection from the Poetry Collection of the University Libraries, University at Buffalo, The State University of New York.

Introduction

Informality as Illegitimate Freedom

Informal expressions flicker. They point to fluctuations in relationships, language, emotions, bodies, conventions, perspective, and the very possibilities of association. They mark colloquialism, camaraderie, curses, taunts, festivity, flirtation, repose, and intimate or intensely personal sensations. When recognized, their instability and evanescence signal the instability of existence itself and unsettle us. When not, they can lull us into a sense of familiarity and comfort. We face them in our daily negotiations with forms and norms, as both are shaped and reshaped in these encounters. Jostling norms, informality reminds us of the limitations and instability of norms, if not of life itself. As Marlow tells us in Joseph Conrad's *Heart of Darkness* (1902), "We live in the flicker" (106).

Modernist literary works embrace, and recoil from, informality in complex responses to it. In particular modernist forms of writing, philosophical strains, or tendencies, the informal is a condition of openness: a gambit for self-fashioning, as well as relations of various kinds. In other works, its inclusion signals class-anxieties, contempt, and melancholy, if not a Freudian melancholia. In all forms of literary modernism, it provides a means for cultural criticism. As it explores literary engagements with the informal, this book considers both support for informality and resistance to it in modernist works, studying informality as an aesthetic, social, and political model. I will mainly address the following questions here: How does literary modernism depict and theorize attitudes, relations, and sociability in its depictions of behaviour and situations at odds with norms? To what kinds of socially and discursively dominant conditions does modernist informality respond? What are the implications of modernist radicalization of aesthetic, social, and personal relations? What means of interaction does such radicalization give us?

Informality is a crucial—but neglected—aspect of modernist poetics. In the last two decades, theoretical work on affect—strong instances of which include Lauren Berlant's work on intimacy and "national fantasy"; Sianne Ngai's work on ugly feelings and the affective shaping of aesthetic categories; Adam Phillips and Leo Bersani's dialogue on intimacy; and Sara Ahmed's inquiries into the role of emotions in cultural politics—has

DOI: 10.4324/9781003009894-1

catalyzed the humanities' interest in affective processes and structures that define the intimate. Although several scholars have produced critical and theoretical studies of intimacy, the relations of informal attitudes with modernist literature itself have not received book-length attention. (I will differentiate informality from the more widely discussed notion of intimacy, below.) Broadly defined, informality is a condition that does not accord with standardized form or prescribed behaviour. It remains a topic explored only by implication in modernist studies and one without an essay-length, much less book-length, examination.

If informal conditions contrast or challenge norms, they resist normalcy. As such, they are not generalizable into uniform rules or states of behaviour. Dismissing the word "generalization" as "worthless" for its "military sound" alone, the narrator of Virginia Woolf's "The Mark on the Wall" (1917; revised version, 1921) expresses her objection to generalizations as follows:

> Generalizations bring back somehow Sunday in London, Sunday afternoon walks, Sunday luncheons, and also ways of speaking of the dead, clothes, and *habits*—like the habit of sitting all together in one room until a certain hour, although nobody liked it. There was a rule for everything. The rule for tablecloths at that particular period was that they should be made of tapestry with little yellow compartments marked upon them ... Tablecloths of a different kind were not real tablecloths. How shocking, and yet how wonderful it was to discover that these real things, Sunday luncheons, Sunday walks, country houses, and tablecloths were not entirely real, were indeed half phantoms, and *the damnation which visited the disbeliever in them was only a sense of illegitimate freedom*. What now takes the place of those things I wonder, those real standard things? Men perhaps, should you be a woman; the masculine point of view which governs our lives, which sets the standard, which establishes Whitaker's Table of Precedency, which has become, I suppose, since the war half a phantom to many men and women, which soon—one may hope, will be laughed into the dustbin where the phantoms go, the mahogany sideboards and the Landseer prints, Gods and Devils, Hell and so forth, leaving us all with an intoxicating sense of *illegitimate freedom*—if freedom exists ....
>
> (86; italics mine)

Sharing the view from Walter Pater's *The Renaissance* (1873) that "our failure is to form habits," Woolf argues against habituated life, numbed by formal domestic routine, early in the passage (236). Standardization and the masculine point of view ("What now takes the place of those things I wonder, those real standard things? Men perhaps, should you be a woman ...") are the forces of propriety and a normalization of reality in the passage. Woolf's solution to them is an "illegitimate freedom"—liberation from the appropriate, non-standardized expression, a perspective that does not seek the sanction of the proper.

Her text hints at its own preferences early, when its narrator recalls a moment when the prior owner of the house in which she sits

> was in process of saying that in his opinion art should have ideas behind it when we were torn asunder, as one is torn from the old lady about to pour out tea and the young man about to hit the tennis ball in the back garden of the suburban villa as one rushes past in the train.
>
> (83)

This enumeration of frequent intrusions by the very movement or "rush" of the train offers a covert view of modern violence, protesting the structures of perception and thought that modernity forces upon us: It protests distraction, the narrow sensory perimeters of selfish interest that modernity induces, and the delimitation of association (in this case, through conversation) by the privileging of speed. However, it also rehearses the paradoxical conditions of modernity. As it turns rapidly from topic to significantly disparate topic, the text itself seems to be reflecting and exploiting speed: "There will be nothing but spaces of light and dark, intersected by thick stalks, and rather higher up perhaps, rose-shaped blots of an indistinct colour dim pinks and blues which will, as time goes on, become more definite, become I don't know what ..." (84). The kaleidoscopic refractions of the unconscious here dilate thought in an apparently uncontrollable wave of impressions. The wafting sentence conveys shunted conventions or presumptions about our agentive formation of thoughts and argument, as anticipated in a sentence earlier on the page, which offers a clearer, if more jarring, version of such movement:

> To show how very little control of our possessions we have—what an accidental affair this living is after all our civilisation—let me just count over a few of the things lost in one lifetime, beginning, for that seems always the most mysterious of losses—what cat would gnaw, what rat would nibble—three pale blue canisters of book-binding tools?
>
> (84)

Soon after, the narrator thinks, "Yes, that seems to express the rapidity of life, the perpetual waste and repair; all so casual, all so haphazard ..." (84). Echoing the concern with "waste and repair" in the conclusion of *The Renaissance*, Woolf's digressive syntax performs the following argument from Pater's text:

> What is the whole physical life in that moment but a combination of natural elements to which science gives their names? ... Our physical life is a perpetual motion of them—the passage of the blood, the waste

> and repairing of the lenses of the eye, the modification of the tissues of the brain under every ray of light and sound—processes which science reduces to simpler and more elementary forces.
>
> (233)

Protesting the "rapidity of life ... all so casual, all so haphazard," Woolf's narrator chafes against both time and space around this point:

> But after life. The slow pulling down of thick green stalks so that the cup of the flower, as it turns over, deluges one with purple and red light. Why, after all, should one not be born there as one is born here, helpless, speechless, unable to focus one's eyesight, groping at the roots of the grass, at the toes of the Giants? As for saying which are trees, and which are men and women, or whether there are such things, that one won't be in a condition to do for fifty years or so.
>
> (84)

This, too, is a series of suggestive protests: against the enclosure of meaning and the limitations imposed upon us by our place of birth. The informality it seeks, then, would practice both linguistic and social freedom of association.

Offering a description of free association in *On Flirtation*, Adam Phillips paraphrases Sigmund Freud: "Free association itself is the psychic act of relinquishing, as far as possible, one's slavish devotion to internal censors. It is one of the advantages of flirtation that it can protect us from idolatry" (xii). The comment suggests candour itself is a mark of strange confluences between scepticism and promiscuity, both evident in the irreverent attitudes and formal variety that modernism displays. Irreverent modernist literature (not the only kind, of course, as my chapter on Eliot makes clear) bristles against the mimetic self-capitulation demanded before models of "great men" by Thomas Carlyle in *Heroes and Hero-Worship*.[1] In her quick sketch, "Carlyle's House" (1909), Woolf records a worse formality in the Carlyle residence than she had anticipated when she visited it: "I don't know what I expected to find—something at any rate less cold, and formal" (3). Against the formality of both cold domestic décor and the limp decorum that accompanies deference to heroes, modernist works seek new models of personality, relations, and association. The modernist fascination with formal associations announces a paradoxical fecundity in secular strains of literary modernism (among them, Joyce's, Woolf's, Mansfield's, and the early Auden's): On the one hand, it is against the proper as the unquestionable, stable, and mythified. As reported by Richard Ellmann, Joyce issues perhaps the most notorious modernist riposte to hero-worship with his reminder to a star-struck student, wishing to "kiss the hand that wrote *Ulysses*," that the same hand had engaged other matters; Auden repudiates self-satisfaction through notorious revisions of his work; Woolf wonders at "how instinctively one protects the image of oneself from idolatry or any other handling that could make it ridiculous" in "The Mark on the Wall" (Ellmann, 110; Woolf, 85).

However, Woolf's remark about self-protection suggests another dimension to modernist informality: the obverse of the paradox is the importance of form (rather than formality, alone) through the need to protect, preserve, refine, and even promote the self in modernism, as evident in the many displays of self-consciousness, fastidiousness, and vanity in modernist writing and modernist writers, themselves: Any easy reading of the Bloomsbury group's famous distance from repression is severely qualified in descriptions of the uneasy self-consciousness of the group's prominent members in Angelica Garnett's *Deceived with Kindness*; Auden was, in Chester Kallman's dotingly paradoxical description, "the most dishevelled child of all *disciplinarians*"; Joyce augmented his cool on the photographic record by standing for a famous portrait with his back to Carola Giedion-Welcker's camera (Zurich, 1938) or adopting dandyish postures, such as the one flaunted by his statue in North Earl Street, Dublin (Kallman, quoted in Arendt, 528; my italics).[2] The stances are not mutually exclusive. These writers' will to shape and reshape the self cooperates with self-questioning, introspective self-demythification collaborates with self-mythification in a sustained critical exercise to stage (or veil) versions of the self with a kind of illegitimate freedom—a capacity to refine or remake an identity normatively taken to be essential or permanent. This marks the self in much modernist literature as an emblem of restlessness, an overt informality. Informal language and behaviour mark a modern response to demands for inventiveness, to new arguments for sexual expression, to global crises, to dominant figures from the past, and (almost as a direct consequence in the traumatic history of racial relations) to engagements with race. Informality's ambit includes space for the kind of humour that Sigmund Freud considers not to be "innocent"—the *hostile* joke (serving the purpose of aggressiveness, satire, or defence) or the *obscene* joke (serving the purpose of exposure)" (*Jokes*, 140). It does so by unshackling us from the phantom ownership of appropriateness, giving our interactions an elusiveness and critical elasticity, both often gained through the illegitimate freedom of jokes. In his critique of Mikhail Bakhtin's notion of the carnivalesque as a socially permitted version of boisterousness, Terry Eagleton quotes Shakespeare's *Twelfth Night:* "There is no slander in an allowed Fool" (*Walter Benjamin: Towards a Revolutionary Criticism*, 81). But the strategic deployment of, or challenges to, figures of disgust and the "disgusting" through humour or comic devices in Joyce's work keeps it from the innocuous scandals accommodated with liberal ease in a lot of contemporary fiction.

Modernist writers not only depict informality in "plot-events" or poetic images, but in specific theorizations of informal tendencies. Joyce stresses the importance of an informal aesthetics in his essay "The Day of the Rabblement" (1901), when, within a critique of Yeats, he declares that "an aesthete has a floating will" (*OCP*, 51).[3] T. S. Eliot celebrates dynamic intertextual association over formal historical linearity in "Tradition and the Individual Talent," arguing famously and counterintuitively:

> No poet, no artist of any art, has his complete meaning alone. His significance, his appreciation is the appreciation of his relation to the dead poets and artists ... I mean this as a principle of æsthetic, not merely historical, criticism ... [W]hat happens when a new work of art is created is something that happens simultaneously to all the works of art which preceded it.
>
> (38)

(Eliot increasingly represses this thought in his poetic practice, but that is a discussion I will defer till my chapter on his work.) As signal modernist arguments, Woolf's essays champion informality, overtly and implicitly. In these theorizations, informality reflects a modern attitude—ways of seeing, style, or behaviour that reflect the dynamism and agitations of modernity, precisely because they do *not* obey formal injunctions to capture and freeze such restlessness into still wholes. Such disobedience is evident in Woolf's differentiation between "spiritualists" and "materialists" in one of her most-studied essays, "Modern Fiction" (1925). The "materialists"—H. G. Wells, Arnold Bennett, and John Galsworthy—"write of unimportant things" because, in their writing, there is a dilution of life through literalism: The complexity of life "escapes" such work, in which the "enormous labour of proving the solidity, the likeness of life" constrains the writer "to provide a plot" and impeccably "embalming the whole" of life (160). Fealty to such constraints amounts to prostration before dictatorial formality: "The tyrant is obeyed; the novel is done to a turn" (160). What Wells, Bennett, and Galsworthy do not record about perception and mental processes, in Woolf's view, is that "a myriad impressions" on the mind make of life "not a series of gig lamps symmetrically arranged", but, instead, "a luminous halo, a semi-transparent envelope" (160). In her repudiation of symmetry and the edicts of a prior, external organizing agency (both implicit in the passive-voiced phrase "symmetrically arranged"), Woolf questions norms and the stability of forms—the very *formality*—that they seek to enforce, as she asks, "Is it not the task of the novelist to convey this varying, this unknown and uncircumscribed spirit, whatever aberration or complexity it may display, with as little mixture of the alien and external as possible?" (160–61). For Woolf, the "uncircumscribed spirit" that informality contrasting "those we have called materialists" makes James Joyce a "spiritualist," significantly because Joyce "disregards with complete courage whatever seems to him adventitious, whether it be probability, or coherence, or any other of these signposts which for generations have served to support the imagination of a reader when called upon to imagine what he can neither touch nor see" (161).[4] Instead of the repression of imaginative or suggestive fecundity, the challenge before "the novelist ... is to contrive means of *being set free to set down what he chooses*" (162; my italics). I will give larger attention to the importance of such *preference*, over that of norms, in my chapter on Woolf's novels.

Woolf endorses informality emphatically in the conclusion of "Modern Fiction," when she famously refutes literary propriety by declaring, The proper stuff of fiction does not exist; everything is the proper stuff of fiction (164). Alongside she collapses the boundaries of Russian literature's focus on pain and English literature's focus on humour, felling the fences between tragedy and comedy, well before Samuel Beckett gives *Waiting for Godot* the subtitle of "A Tragicomedy in Two Acts," and before she, herself, composes a sophisticated mingling of humour and pain in *Orlando*. With this negation, Woolf attempts to liberate fiction from normalization, privileging illegitimate freedom, instead.

Informality vs Intimacy

In her introduction to the special issue of *Critical Inquiry* that has spurred much scholarly interest in intimacy in the last twenty years, Berlant writes:

> To intimate is to communicate with the sparest of signs and gestures, and at its root intimacy has the quality of eloquence and brevity. But intimacy also involves an aspiration for a narrative about something shared, a story about both oneself and others that will turn out in a particular way.
>
> (281)

The intimate and the informal do, indeed, have some overlap, but they differ in crucial aspects. While informality often shares the former set of attributes that Berlant describes (spareness, eloquence, and brevity), it does not hinge aspirations for shared narratives "that will turn out in a particular way." Such shared hope for a particular outcome is neither a prerequisite nor a common feature in many forms of informality. There is not necessarily either the presumption or performance of trust in informality. Informality can affirm and negate, without propriety and an intimate, private affective charge. Irreverence, for instance, can be a form of informality that need not be privately expressed. When Joyce adds blasphemy ("You'll need to rise precious early ... if you want to diddle the Almighty God") to the "The Oxen of the Sun" chapter in *Ulysses* (1922), or when the speaker of the young T. S. Eliot's poem "The Triumph of Bullshit" (likely, 1910) answers rebuffs with a refrain of "[S]tick it up your ass," the retort in each text is, of course, informal, but not intimate—they transgress even the illusion of joined hopes in shared narratives.

At the same time, informality is not the equivalent of all transgression. Peter Stallybrass and Allon White quote the anthropologist Barbara Babcock's definition of "symbolic inversion" as an equivalent for the sense in which they use the word "transgression" in *The Politics and Poetics of Transgression*: "'Symbolic inversion' may be broadly defined as any act of expressive behavior which inverts, contradicts, abrogates, or in some fashion presents an alternative to commonly held cultural codes, values, and norms be they linguistic, literary or artistic, religious, or social and political" (Babcock, quoted in Stallybrass and White, 17). This definition covers many of the nuances of the word "informality," as I employ it here. However, after citing Babcock, Stallybrass and White acknowledge that the word "transgression" has another use "which arises in connection with extremist practices of modern art and philosophy; these designate not just the infraction of binary structures but movement into an absolutely negative space beyond the structure of significance itself" (18). Informality does not involve the absolute negation or the violence of absolutes: Murder or rape is not an informal act, though, in legal terms, each falls under the category of "transgression."[5] Instead, informal acts involve behaviour that has degrees, actions that are relative, and therefore forms of relation (affirmative or negative, but relative, nevertheless). Informality frequently marks beginnings, opening paths to the destabilization of hierarchies, gesturing to the possibility of trust, but not signalling its promise. Informal moments are moments when normative pressure eases, when interaction intensifies or lightens, when affect turns. Informality destabilizes prescriptions and hierarchies of thought, action, feeling, and expression. But it does not guarantee trust or "trustworthiness." It puts into question our assumed safety from the opposites or variants of "good" emotion. It is an unpredictable, ambivalent form of sociability, of affective reception and transmission, offering ease in its more positive forms and disappointments, if not shock outright, in its negative versions. Nor is the informal, unlike the intimate, necessarily something assumed to be restricted to personal or private experience, or strongly related with it even in publicly "intimate" settings, such as bars, speakeasys, sex-parlours, and so on.[6] Unlike transgression, informality is not only "an act of expressive behavior." It is as much a part of *attitude* as it is a matter of action that transgresses norms. It informs "structures of feeling," in Raymond Williams's famous coinage in his book *Film* (1954), where he uses the phrase briefly. Williams first addresses the phrase at length in *The Long Revolution* (1961), clarifying that it both conveys structure of cultural, political, and especially conventional attitudes that make us feel in particular ways, *and* refers to the different ways of thinking vying to emerge at any one time in history (51– 65). Of course, informal attitudes are more closely associated with the latter. They are functions of the physical, political, and gendered conditions for association within spaces: The scope of analysis in each chapter of this book will shuttle to and from the personal to the social or public dimensions that modernist literature portrays.

T. J. Clark reminds us, "Modernism is our antiquity" (2). The restlessness shaping the peculiar travel of modernist narrative—its straying, its nonlinearity, its employment of impressions and resonance—marks informal attitudes that artists continue to negotiate, today: The obsessive play with form flexes formality in its social, attitudinal, and physical manifestations. I do not read informality as a *lack* of form, but as a contrast with formal or attitudinal standardization, normativity, or compliance.

Nuances of Informality

Informality gains intellectual and ethical inflections through the philosophical investments of the writers who employ it—in modernist works, it is an index of both the irrational (in the hands of, say, Joyce or Woolf) and the "great good sense" with which Hannah Arendt credited Auden (531).

The *Oxford English Dictionary* defines the word "informality" as follows: "The quality or fact of being informal; absence of formality; (as a count noun) an instance of this; an informal act or proceeding." Suggesting the variety of inflections and nuances in the word "informality," the dictionary's definitions for the word "informal" include "1. Lacking form; formless. Obs. rare."; "2. a. Not done or made according to a recognized or prescribed form; not observing established procedures or rules; unofficial; irregular"; 2. e. "Econ. Designating unregulated commercial activity which takes place outside the official or mainstream economy, and is carried out on a small scale and on a self-employed ... or irregular basis[;] Typically used to refer to any form of economic activity which goes unreported in official statistics, including illegal activity"; "3. a. Characterized by absence of formality or ceremony; casual, relaxed. b. Designating the vocabulary, idiom, and grammatical structures suitable to everyday language and conversation rather than to official or formal contexts. c. Of dress: casual; suitable for everyday wear." Further, the *OED* defines the transitive verb "informalize" as "To render informal." It is definitions 2. a. and 3. a.–c. that I will most frequently evoke in this book, though other inflections listed above will influence my arguments, sporadically. Add to these an inference from Melissa Gregg and Gregory Seigworth's definition of "affect as potential": "a body's *capacity* to affect and to be affected" (*The Affect Theory Reader*, 2; italics Gregg and Seigworth's). If, at any given moment within the literary works I discuss here, informality conveys "a body's *capacity* to affect and to be affected," it indicates that body's ability to influence and its responsiveness. In other words, informality signals both behaviour and *sensitivity*.

Redistributions of the Sensible

In modernity, such behaviour and sensitivity are shaped by various disorientations, which Karl Marx evokes when he cracks wise on the psychological reconfigurations of rapid train-travel: "production not only creates an object for the subject but also a subject for the object" (quoted in Schivelbusch, 164). Discussing another instance of such adjustment of "reality to the masses" and the "masses to reality," Walter Benjamin writes in "The Work of Art in the Age of Mechanical Reproduction" (1936), "[U]nspectacular social changes often promote a change in the receptivity of the masses which will benefit the new art form" (250). What does this do to sensual immediacy and its disturbance of hierarchies?[7] Modernist works interrogate the hierarchies that inhere in the formalization of *where* we are allowed to sense what we are allowed to sense, and where the registration of particular experience is expressible. Woolf examines the restricted "distribution of the sensible" (to borrow Jacques Rancière's phrase) within formal domesticity in *To the Lighthouse*, where the Ramsay children have sensible freedom restricted to "their bedrooms, their fastness in a house where there was no other privacy to debate anything, everything" (8).[8] Textual indications of the distribution of the sensible are also indices of the location of rationality or reasonability in moments of communication, formal and informal, rational and irrational, spoken and unspoken. Closing "Sex and Talk," her essay in the special number of *Critical Inquiry* on intimacy, Candace Vogler writes:

> The problem Kant addresses in his popular and pragmatic work isn't really that the self has margins, nor even that we share something that could be called animal nature; it's rather that adults try to claim as or for self more territory than belongs to the business of well-tempered, rational selfhood.
>
> (365)

This is the problem that blocks dialogue for the couple that T. S. Eliot chillingly portrays in the "A Game of Chess" section of *The Waste Land*. The absence of informal ease within that scene is a function of frustrated claims to "well-tempered, rational selfhood," with the mutual frustration of the woman's repeated demands for a rational solution to their impasse—her exhortation to "Think"—and (presumably) of the man's silent, supposedly rational refuge in the mind, leading to the verdict, "I think we are in rat's alley / Where the dead men lost their bones" (ll. 115–16). The text indicates that the response is unspoken, not only through its beginning—"I think"—but also by signalling withheld speech through the *absence* of quotation marks around his thoughts (and thereby reflecting the OED's definition 2. a. for the word "informal": "Not done or made according to a recognized or prescribed form"). The informal evocation of lexical convention points to a crisis in personal communication and—if we are to read the scene as symptomatic of a culture-wide impasse—a crisis in cultural practices that gives the scene its eeriness.[9] Alongside (and, I would suggest, unwittingly), the scene evokes the absence of informality, in the sense of "easy interaction," as a cause for the crisis. As I will suggest in my chapter on Eliot, *The Waste Land*'s reluctance to see informality as a valid mode for interaction keeps it from seeing that this absence itself produces much of the cultural paralysis that occupies its attention. Among the modernist writers whose work

I examine here, T. S. Eliot is the aberration, not for an absence of experiments with informality in his work, but for the ways in which his well-documented conservatism sits with those formal experiments, repressing or (at least) obstructing their subversive capacities. Keeping this in mind, I will structure this book's arguments around what I call "parrhesiastic modernism" or "candid modernism" (as manifest in the writings of Woolf, Joyce, Mansfield, and, more particularly, the early Auden), on the one hand, and Eliotic or repressive modernism, on the other. This is not to suggest that the former renders scandalous intentions, desires, and psychology transparent or that the latter keeps them entirely opaque, but it is to signify a resistance to formality in the former that the latter debilitates.

Genealogies of Formality and Informality

Several factors encourage or dissuade artistic informality in modernism: discourse, tradition, cultural and national priorities, among them. To suggest attitudes to the informal from the century immediately before "High Modernism," let me offer a dual nineteenth-century intellectual genealogy, which I will keep very brief because many others have discussed its tensions amply and brilliantly (though not so much for those between formality and informality).[10] I will investigate, as the genealogy's first part, discursive demands for formality, propriety, and morality from Thomas Carlyle, Matthew Arnold, and John Ruskin, which spur modernist restlessness with their arguments against ornament, flourish, individualism, frivolity, fusion, and easy or unrestricted association. I will contrast this set of prohibitions with the other part of the genealogy: the legacies of Thomas Hardy, Walter Pater, Oscar Wilde, and some versions of socialism, as they shape calls for language and social attitudes to be less restrictive.

Noting the absence of attention to women in memoirs from "the last century and a half," Woolf writes in *Three Guineas* (1938) that, though in

> page after page, volume after volume[,] you will find their brothers and husbands—Sheridan at Devonshire House, Macaulay at Holland House, Matthew Arnold at Lansdowne House, Carlyle even at Bath House, the names of Jane Austen, Charlotte Brontë, and George Eliot do not occur...
>
> (17–8)

The dominant Victorian men whom Woolf names in the list provoke diverse responses from modernist writers. The chasm between Carlyle's views on hero worship and those of several modernists that we have already noted widens with his exegeses on morality, its production, and its guidance. Expositing on the role of language in democratic morality, Carlyle writes in *Past and Present*, "Speech is the gaseous element out of which most kinds of Practice and Performance, especially all kinds of moral Performance, condense themselves, and take shape; as the one is, so will the other be" (417; Vol. VI). To lead such moral performance in speech, first, a culture needs, in the logic of Carlyle's commentary on "captains of industry," "a noble Master" who employs moral thought as basis for self-control and resistance to raw profit-seeking (334; Vol. XIII). For Carlyle, such a "noble Master" would lead England out of crises of both labour relations and morality through the specification of a right moral trajectory:

> Liberty? The true liberty of a man, you would say, consisted in his finding out, or being forced to find out the right path, and to walk thereon. To learn, or to be taught, what work he actually was able for; and then by permission, persuasion, and even compulsion, to set about doing of the same.
>
> (264; Vol. XIII)

Emphasis on adherence to a "right" moral path recurs, though with a larger emphasis on aesthetics, in John Ruskin's *The Two Paths*.[11] Seeing perfect art as an expression of an artist's self as a whole, Ruskin maps out the course for perfect art to follow: "Thoroughly perfect art is that which proceeds from the heart, involves all the noble emotions;--associates with these the head, yet as inferior to the heart; and the hand, yet as inferior to the heart and head, and thus brings out the whole man" (54). The emphasis on "wholeness" propels Ruskin to declare unity the goal of art—"for true art is always and always will be one ... *There is but one right way of doing any given thing required of an artist* ... only one complete and right way"—the one specified above (56, italics Ruskin's). Further, "not only is there but one way of doing things rightly, but there is only one way of *seeing* them, and that is seeing the whole of them, without any choice, or more intense perception of one point than another, owing to our special idiosyncrasies" (57, italics Ruskin's). Invoking the Aristotelian principles of the Beautiful (Order, Symmetry, and the Definite) as foundations for his views, Ruskin tries to demonstrate the failings of too literal a view of these principles as expressed in an eighth-century icon representing an angel (29–31). Ruskin claims that the angel's lack of a mouth, its excessively rounded eyes, and stylized, sharpened hands reveal "the wilful closing of [the artist's] eyes to natural facts," adding censoriously that "whenever people don't look at Nature, they always think that they can improve her" (31). Clearly, while stating an opposition to a literal application of Order, Symmetry, and the Definite, Ruskin produces an endorsement of it—his objections to the stylization of the icon found themselves on these very categories.

For a few pages after his examination of the icon, Ruskin advocates the importance of interpretation—"the great collateral necessity"—for the presentation of the truth, but his restriction of interpretation and his priorities are clear when he stresses repeatedly the formula, "Truth first—plan, or design, founded thereon" (43, 46). Ruskin does not present any means of accessing the truth, apart from a recognition of the "natural." *The Two Paths* has already warned that, if the artist departs from what Ruskin calls "the stem of life" found in "natural form," and prefers

> the designing of ornamentation, either in the ignorant play of your own fancy, as the Indian does, or according to received application of heartless laws, as the modern European does ... there is but one word for you—Death—death of every healthy faculty, and of every noble intelligence.
>
> (46, 47)

Playful ornamentation translates to "pleasure first and truth afterwards, (or not at all,) as with the Arabians and the Indians," and is offset by "truth first and pleasure afterwards, as with Angelico and all other great European painters" (66). The text adds that the perception of nature "is never given but under certain moral conditions" (70). These moral conditions are reflected in contrasting forms of ornament. Ruskin identifies the contrast to offer the artist two crucial choices, the "two paths" of his title: "[I]t is required of you to produce conventional ornament, and you may approach the task as the Hindoo does, and as the Arab did, without nature at all," or "as Sir Joshua [Reynolds] and Velasquez did, with, not the chance, but the certainty, of approximating your disposition ... to the disposition of ... great and good men" (70). While the former displays promiscuous changes and a combination of forms, the latter redeems ornament from such frivolous association. Insisting on the alignment of one's "disposition ... to the disposition of ... great and good men," Ruskin's arguments extend the Carlylesque goal of mimetic obedience to virtuous, heroic character.

Pointing to difference from such mimesis as a threat to culture, Matthew Arnold's main anxiety in his essay "Democracy" is one about modernity itself as a force of individuality and change that operates at the expense of the state. Arnold warns:

> A ... difficult change—to reduce the all-effacing prominence of the State, to give a more prominent part to the individual—is imperiously presenting itself [as] one irresistible force, which is gradually making its way everywhere, removing old conditions and imposing new, altering long-fixed habits, undermining venerable institutions, even modifying national character: *the modern spirit.*
>
> (25; italics Arnold's)

Arnold's later work makes clear his belief that the variety and transformative energy that the modern spirit emblematizes diverge from the best aspects of our selves. Underscoring this belief as it states its "faith in the progress of humanity toward perfection," the conclusion of *Culture and Anarchy* espouses a goal "to make the State more and more the expression ... of our best self, which is not manifold and vulgar, and unstable, and contentious, and ever-varying, but one and noble, and secure, and peaceful, and the same for all mankind" (181).[12] Arnold's view of the homogenized formality in "our best self" not only refuses change, but also circumscribes aesthetics: Vulgarity is to be rejected not merely as a matter of aesthetics, but (here and always) as a sign of inferior character.

Offering a potentially scandalous alternative to the models that Carlyle, Ruskin, and Arnold seek, Walter Pater describes intense registration of experience in a protean, ever-changing self as an aim in his most celebrated statement from *The Renaissance*: "To burn always with this hard, gem-like flame, to maintain this ecstasy, is success in life" (236). The quantum of experience for such ecstasy is not only evanescent but elusive, "gone while we try to apprehend it[,] constantly re-forming itself on the stream, to a single sharp impression, with a sense in it," and it is to this phenomenological dwindling that "what is real in our life fines itself down. It is with this movement, with the passage and dissolution of impressions, images, sensations, that analysis leaves off—that continual vanishing away, that strange, perpetual weaving and unweaving of ourselves" (236). This metaphor of identity's textile manufacture in relation with the world—this continual weaving and unweaving of personhood—asserts a radically *informal* view of the self. In his preface to the book, Pater asserts that what is important for a critical temperament "is not that the critic should possess a correct abstract definition of beauty for the intellect, but a certain kind of temperament, the power of being deeply moved" (x). Dispensing with unwavering absolutes as a goal for inquiry, he replaces it with the "power of being deeply moved." Movement is as much an emotional or sensorial matter as a physical one, here—and in modernism. This requires not merely responsiveness, but an active seeking of difference. Instead of aspiring to a Ruskinian-Carlylesque-Arnoldian mimetic fidelity or stabilization of the self, Pater writes in the conclusion to *The Renaissance*, "What we have to do is to be for ever curiously testing new opinions and courting new impressions, never acquiescing in a facile orthodoxy of Comte, or of Hegel, or of our own" (237). In other words, the ecstatic, gemlike burning of the self is not only a response to the sensations of the world—it is not a passive matter, but a process of curious "testing." It requires both a welcome to difference and critical consideration of it. The power of moving to the new and testing it mutually intensifies the "power of being deeply moved." At the same time, this motile power is not an exercise in experiential exits or "moving on": Pater makes clear in his essay on Coleridge in *Appreciations* that "[s]earching and irresistible as are the changes of the human spirit on its way to perfection, there is yet so much elasticity of temper that what must pass away sooner or later is not disengaged all at once" (65). Rather, in the incessant engagements of the self and the world, our elastic relations with the past gift us experiential storage, "the reserve of the elder generation exquisitely refined by the antagonism of the new" (65).

The injunction to "*court* new impressions" has, at least, three major implications for modernist informality: a social or behavioural dimension, which blurs lines of ethical considerations and decadent relations (rendering decadence itself an ethics); a political dimension, which shapes and intensifies cosmopolitanism; and an aesthetic dimension, which marks the experimental, partial, and multiple compositional styles of modernism. Concomitant to these, there are epistemological, as well as erotic, nuances in courting new impressions, which I will discuss at length in my chapter on Woolf's fiction.

As Jed Rasula reminds us, "the question of modern forms of life grew increasingly pressing throughout the nineteenth century" (248). He asks us to imagine, as a sign of this question, a dialogue or,

> better yet, a musical duet—involving two of that moment's most frequently cited dicta on cultural value. Matthew Arnold's pledge of faith in "the best that is known and thought" has its conversational partner in Walter Pater's exhortation to burn with a gem-like flame, packing as much intensity into the passing moment as you can.
>
> (248)

Commenting on Pater's conclusion to *The Renaissance*, Rasula glosses what he calls "its epicurean pledge of faith" that "art comes to you proposing frankly to give nothing but the highest quality to your moments as they pass, and simply for those moments' sake." It's accurate to call it epicurean because Pater, like Lucretius before him, defines life strictly in terms of mortality: quoting Victor Hugo, Pater says "we are all under sentence of death but with a sort of indefinite reprieve—*les hommes sont tous condamnés à mort avec des sursis indéfinis*: we have an interval, and then our place knows us no more" (*History of a Shiver*, 249). The determining criteria, then, are finitude and intensity: a biological reckoning with mortality

Finitude and intensity are important Paterian criteria, indeed, but so is postlapsarianism, an embrace of being damned or condemned (*les hommes sont tous condamnés*). This is a willingness to fall that strongly marks Joycean modernism: Declining ecclesiastical office in *A Portrait of the Artist as a Young Man*, Stephen Dedalus reaches the resonant decision that he "was destined to learn his own wisdom apart from others or to learn the wisdom of others himself wandering among the snares of the world[,] its ways of sin. He would fall" (174). Enlarging informality's role in his novel, Joyce puts even such moments of *non-normative* decision in doubt with his prior emphasis on Stephen's lack of self-mastery. Stephen's conscious agency is destabilized, and his "fall" prefigured, in the enduring contest between his mind and body. Describing Stephen in the throes of lust, Joyce underscores consciousness's lack of control in this destabilizing contest, by writing, "His blood was in revolt" (106).

Depending on the actions of the lapsed, her or his *fall* implies degrees or expanses of separation from the normative and the "proper" as not only an ethical condition, but also a spatial one. Informality works at and as a distance, or a kind of freedom, from norms and propriety. This would be a conscious or unconscious display of attitudes, ethics, and language that contrasts prescribed form, convention, morality, law, grammar, aesthetic standards, and euphemism. In this sense, informality is circumstantial, social, and demystifying, making it (in Edward Said's sense of the terms) "secular" or "worldly."[13] Thus situated, it is at any point in time, modern. Oscar Wilde, Pater's most celebrated student and precursor for Joyce's postlapsarian modernism, sets critical recognition and reconsideration against social and ethical prohibitions in *De Profundis* (1905). As an ethical dictum, Wilde punctuates his book with variations of his repeated claim, "Whatever is realised is right," no matter how dangerous it may be, as he insists, "All great ideas *are* dangerous" (4, 62, 85). With his insistence on the re-evaluation of even ideas pre-judged as "dangerous," he makes self-enhancement through self-recognition as crucial a part of his ethics as responsibility: "To reject one's own experiences is to arrest one's own development" (62). If the Paterian aspiration is to be forever courting new impressions, it comes with the aim to be "curiously testing new opinions," alongside: Sceptical reconsideration is crucial for the questioning of norms that shapes modernist informality. Wilde's resistance is not to ethical or moral actions, but to the arrogation of morality. Anticipating an analogous attitude in W. H. Auden's work (that I discuss in the fifth chapter, here), Wilde has Basil Hallward deliver the following rebuke to Henry Wotton in *The Picture of Dorian Gray* (1891): "You never say a moral thing, and you never do a wrong thing" (61). Such ethical practice demands a sophisticated self-veiling: It is ethical in its *lightness*, in its reluctance to awe, overwhelm, or oppress with morality.

Seeing, Showing, and Speaking Freely: *Parrhesia* and Form

While not all informal expression displays sophistication, the psychological concomitants of it are a lightness of behaviour and freedom (or, at least, the performance of freedom) from fear or hostility towards transgression. Informality is a kind of frankness or honesty. A normative measure of honesty is potential damage or risk to the person expressing an honest statement. In the case of the informal, such a statement, consciously or unconsciously, disavows or transforms normative ethical currency or sociocultural prestige. To whatever degree, it also disavows safety. Informality offers candour. But, in its accommodation of breezy simulations of candour, its disingenuous performances can bring hypocrisy, deception, and, perhaps with them, emotional catastrophe. Describing Thomas Hardy's influence on literature as "incalculable," Virginia Woolf declares, "His only demand upon us, and there is none more exacting, was that we should speak the truth" (507, *Essays IV*). Woolf refines this demand in her repudiation of propriety in "Modern

Fiction," when she argues that, in modern fiction, "nothing—no 'method', no experiment, even of the wildest—is forbidden, but only *falsity and pretence*" (164, my italics). To speak the truth, even when it is forbidden, is to break hallowed norms for the sake of candour and to recognize that, for "the moderns," "the point of interest lies very likely in the dark places of psychology" (162). Going by Woolf's location of the matter that modernism needs to articulate and describe, speaking the truth is to violate psychological veiling, to express thoughts that formality silences in "the dark places of psychology," and to do so without concern about saying what may be forbidden.

In other words, informality as candour involves the "free-spokenness" (*parrhesia* or *franc-parler*) that Michel Foucault theorizes in various works, but with special focus in his lectures at Berkeley in the fall of 1983 (his auditors' notes for which are collected in *Fearless Speech*) and in *The Courage of Truth*, where he explains "*parrhesia* as modality of truth-telling" (2). In the former text, after noting that the word *parrhesia* appears for the first time around 484–407 BCE in the writings of Euripides, Foucault explains that the parrhesiast (*parrhēsiastēs*) "is the one who uses parrhesia, i.e., the one who speaks the truth" (11).

> Etymologically, *parrhesiazesthai* means "to say everything"—from *pan* [nav] (everything) and *rhema* [pilj.ta] (that which is said). The one who uses *parrhesia*, the *parrhesiastes*, is someone who says everything he has in mind: he does not hide anything, but opens his heart and mind completely to other people through his discourse. In *parrhesia*, the speaker is supposed to give a complete and exact account of what he has in mind so that the audience is able to comprehend exactly what the speaker thinks (12).

There are clear instructions in this etymology: that, as a parrhesiast, you do not repress truth, there is no veiling of the heart and mind; that you attempt to include as much detail in your candid speech as you can; that you risk censure, hostility, and *comprehension*. This is a huge risk for the parrhesiastic speaker. The argument seems close to demanding simple transparency of the self. However, Foucault qualifies simple transparency for the parrhesiast in *The Courage of Truth*, when he addresses "the form of the subject telling the truth" (3). He stresses "the conditions and forms of the type of act by which the subject manifests himself when speaking the truth"—that is, *how* this subject "thinks of himself and is recognized by others as speaking the truth" (2–3). This requires analysis of

> the form in which, in his act of telling the truth, the individual constitutes himself and is constituted by others as a subject of a discourse of truth, the form in which he presents himself to himself and to others as someone who tells the truth, the form of the subject telling the truth. (3)

The truth-teller should fulfil this formal requirement under the joint signs of two principles: *gnōthi seauton* ("know thyself") and *epimeleia heauto* ("care of the self, application to oneself"), the latter with an eye to *epimelē seautō* ("take care of yourself") (4). How does the candour in informality relate with such truth-telling? How does it relate with such *form*?

Both the principles that Foucault lists ("know thyself" and "take care of yourself") point to self-consciousness as the *considered* mode in self-presentation for the *candid utterance of truth*. Discussing Cynic philosophy as a "preparation for life" later in *The Courage of Truth*, Foucault lists several Cynic statements on the importance of the dictum "take care of yourself" (238–9). The final rule in this list is that "one must make one's life conform to the precepts one formulates" (239). In explanation of the rule Foucault writes, "There can only be true care of self if the principles one formulates as true principles are at the same time guaranteed and authenticated by the way one lives" (239). Such consideration in the face of normative pressures and social risks is one that protects the parrhesiast's truth. It is embodied parrhesia—truth-telling *through the form in which it is presented.* This very form is a persuasive function for the making of a world where the self is freer from hostility—a world whose very freedoms mean that the self is better protected. The parrhesiast's candid utterances, therefore, tend towards a world where self-expression and self-protection are symbiotic. To encourage the production of conditions for the better protection of the self, the parrhesiast risks endangering the self.

Modernist parrhesia, in its ethical manifestations, adopts and adapts such risk. In "The Narrow Bridge of Art" (1927), Woolf praises Elizabethan dramatists for their "attitude toward life which made them able to express themselves freely and fully" (15). In *A Portrait of the Artist as a Young Man*, Stephen Dedalus overtly relativizes the absolutes in Woolf's praise when he declares his desire "to express myself in some mode of life or art as freely as I can and as wholly as I can" (268–9). Woolf herself already qualifies the full and free expression that "The Narrow Bridge of Art" seems to endorse with a riskier, but more nuanced, option in the "illegitimate freedom" she seeks in "The Mark on the Wall" (1921). Modernist writers are aware that words themselves are not transparent; that their interpretation takes unpredictable, uncontrollable turns; and, at the same time, that language is pliable, open to insinuation and multiple readings, especially when it is ironic. In the case of Anglophone modernism, of course, it is more precisely (or, at least, more commonly) the *text* than the writer that is the parrhesiast—the text is censored, rather than the writer banished. This recognition that draws ironic but passionate opposition to the censorship of Joyce's writing from Robert Graves, as he writes in *Lars Porsena* (1927):

> It is quite right that *Ulysses* should be censored, since its chief public in England could at the best of times be only an obscene one: and it is not

> an obscene book, but on the contrary perhaps the least obscene book ever published: that is why it is censored.
>
> (91)

The pointed anger in Graves's argument is directed at the fact the censored text conveys statements for public consumption that might disrupt the veiling or amnesia that social norms seek to preserve, and it is precisely the veiling or amnesia, rather than its acknowledgment, that is obscene.

The exuberance of Molly Bloom's erotic thoughts in *Ulysses* (that I quote in my chapter on Joyce's work) has further provocations of mischievous irony. With its embrace of irony and suggestiveness, modernist candour complicates "*plain*-speaking" and transparency. When Woolf's Orlando and her lover Shelmerdine declare that each of them is of the opposite gender than that they currently inhabit, the *text* itself playfully displays a pregnant irony in light of its own ambivalence about gender, complicating the plain-speaking of *parrhesia* (184). However, it employs its irony as an ethical lightness to assert truths about gender and, more subtly, about preferable forms and modes for persuasion through the very playfulness that it adopts. There is a combinative practice involved here: Firstly, there are risks involved in the non-normative sociability of Woolf's "illegitimate freedom"; the resistance to univocity in Auden's self-revision, as well as his scepticism; and Joyce's willingness to narrate the forbidden. Alongside, are their various forms of self-protection, as discussed above, informal *parrhesia* (that is, *parrhesia* "Not done or made according to a recognized or prescribed form"). The combination is a signature of their candid modernism. It is in this sense, then, that the conditions they evidently seek in such parrhesiastic practice are those where necessity and freedom cooperate.

Surrealization: Informality in Marx's "Realm of Freedom"

As Marx delineates the bounds of the "realm of necessity" versus those of "the realm of freedom" in the third volume of *Capital*, he argues:

> The realm of freedom really begins only where labour determined by necessity and external expediency ends; it lies by its very nature beyond the sphere of material production proper ... Freedom, in this sphere, can consist only in this, that socialized man, the associated producers, govern the human metabolism with nature in a rational way, bringing it under their collective control instead of being dominated by it as a blind power; accomplishing it with the least expenditure of energy and in conditions most worthy and appropriate for their human nature. But this always remains a realm of necessity. The true realm of freedom, the development of human powers as an end in itself, begins beyond it, though it can only flourish with this realm of necessity as its basis. The reduction of the working day is the basic prerequisite.
>
> (958–9)

Here, Marx explicitly links freedom with metabolism (as a process of appetites, needs, and their digestion), first, and then with leisure at the end of daily cycles of production. However, this view gains strong implications for aesthetic and social freedom in a longer Marxist genealogy, which overtly shapes the views of modernists such as Katherine Mansfield (with her close early ties to guild socialism) and W. H. Auden (who is emphatic about his Marxist commitments before his turn to religion).

Describing a shift in Marx's early humanist phase in his book *For Marx*, Louis Althusser writes that seeing the liberal promises of prince Friedrich Wilhelm's vanish with the prince's turn to despotism when he became the German monarch, Marx drew the following conclusion: "*The political State … encapsulates the demands of reason precisely in its modern forms. But it does not stop there. Everywhere it presupposes realized reason. But everywhere it also slides into the contradiction between its theoretical definition and its real hypotheses*" (225, italics Marx's). A decisive step had been taken: The State's abuses were no longer conceived as misappropriations of the State *vis-à-vis* its essence, but as a real contradiction between its essence (reason) and its existence (unreason).

Althusser then links this contradiction to a critique of Rousseauan liberalism: "This is the Rousseauan myth of the origins of inequality: the rich holding forth to the poor in 'the most deliberate discourse' ever conceived, so as to persuade them to live their slavery as their freedom" (234). The ideological blinkering this practice maintains is ironic in reality, as Friedrich Engels notes in *The Origin of the Family, Private Property, and the State*:

> Since civilization is founded on the exploitation of one class by another class, its whole development proceeds in a constant contradiction. Every step forward in production is at the same time a step backwards in the position of the oppressed class, that is, of the great majority.
>
> (215–6)

Civilization makes the difference and antagonism between rights and duties clear, in Engels's words, "by giving one class practically all the rights and the other class practically all the duties" (216). This division keeps them in conditions which are, for Engels, the precise opposite of the hopes of socialist materialism: As he declares near the beginning of this book, "According to the materialistic conception, the determining factor in history is, in the final instance, the production and reproduction of immediate life" (35). By "immediate life" here, Engels, of course, signifies a life where privileges and rights would merge.

Herbert Marcuse sees both social and aesthetic implications in precisely such immediacy. Dismissing various prevailing social models for their reliance on "powers of containment," Marcuse argues in *An Essay on Liberation* for "a realm of freedom which is not that of the present:

liberation also from the liberties of exploitative order—a liberation which must precede the construction of a free society" (vii). Marcuse notes that the "early Marxian example of the free individuals alternating between hunting, fishing, criticizing, and so on, had a joking-ironical sound from the beginning," which needs to be replaced with the "later Marxian concept that implies the continued separation between the realm of necessity and the realm of freedom, between labor and leisure" (20). In the latter conception, the realm of necessity would continue, and "real human freedom would prevail only outside the entire sphere of socially necessary labor. Marx rejects the idea that work can ever become play"—the working day would stay the working day, "rational but free" (21). Nevertheless, within the transfer of productive forces beyond their capitalist organization, Marcuse sees "the possibility of freedom within the realm of necessity. The quantitative reduction of necessary labor could turn into quality (freedom), not in proportion to the reduction but rather to the transformation of the working day," one in which "the stupefying, enervating, pseudo-automatic jobs of capitalist progress would be abolished" (21). This, according to Marcuse, would require "the construction of such a society that presupposes a type of man with a different sensitivity as well as consciousness: men who would speak a different language, have different gestures, follow different impulses; men who have developed an instinctual barrier against cruelty, brutality, ugliness" (21). But this transformation would be practicable "as a factor of social change only if it enters the social division of labor, the production relations themselves"—because these relations

> would be shaped by men and women who have the good conscience of being human, tender, sensuous, who are no longer ashamed of themselves—"for the token of freedom attained, that is, no longer being ashamed of ourselves" (Nietzsche, *Die Frohliche Wissenschaft*, Book III, 275).
>
> (21)

In such circumstances, social organization will be subject to imaginative (though critical) informality: "The imagination of such men and women would fashion their reason and tend to make the process of production a process of creation" (21).

For Marcuse, such unshackled imagination is a precondition for "the ingression of freedom into the realm of necessity, and the union between causality by necessity and causality by freedom. The first would mean passing from Marx to Fourier; the second from realism to surrealism" (21–2). The "surrealism" that Marcuse has in mind is not one without a referent in reality or in material conditions, but one that that is *sur-real*—one that builds *on reality*. With a Paterian elasticity, it is the function of an aesthetic imagination that augments and alters given reality: a Joycean form of illegitimate freedom. In the literature of modernism, such freedom, whether endorsed or repudiated, lies in the illegitimate, as in that which is currently available as a legitimate social or aesthetic practice. Marcuse's quotation of Nietzsche's stress on freedom as an absence of shame is crucial here: It envisages a society where freedom of social and sexual association (as suggested in the evocation of Charles Fourier's arguments on sexual freedom) is inextricable from imaginative practice. In Nietzschean terms, its adoption dispenses jointly with the uniformity of the "herd-instinct in the individual," as Nietzsche calls morality in *The Gay Science*, and the *vis inertiae*, the "force of inertia," that Nietzsche (like Pater) links with the formation of habits in *On the Genealogy of Morals* (*The Gay Science*, 115; *Genealogy*, 11).[14]

Informality as *Attitude*

Marcuse's enthusiasm for freedom from shame underscores the importance of illegitimate freedom not only as a social and aesthetic practice, but as an attitude.

Informality displays such an attitude either through candour about the self, through liberated association (which includes unrestricted possibilities for erotic invitation, if not sexual contact, itself), and through more elusive and ironic ways. Each of these, however, also demands, within the prevalent conditions that modernism addresses, an excavation or suggestive tracing of attitudes and tendencies that individuals or groups try to conceal. Willa Cather notes in her essay on Mansfield (1936) that Mansfield interrogates what Cather calls a "double life" in domesticity:

> [E]ven in harmonious families there is this double life: the group life, which is the one we can observe in our neighbour's household, and, underneath, another–secret and passionate and intense–which is the real life that stamps the faces and gives character to the voices of our friends.
>
> (109)

Mansfield extends this "real life" through her critical exploration of the validity of property, marriage, and the boundaries of community. Every work of modernist literature that I discuss here produces some version of Mansfield's bifocal reading.

Mansfield's trenchant affective archaeology, nonetheless, retains a restraint larger than the untrammelled informality in Joyce's work: The disgust at German consumption in Mansfield's first short story collection, *In a German Pension* (1911), has a vivid contrast in Leopold Bloom's gusto at breakfast in *Ulysses*. As signs of attitude rather than those of immediate historical impact, these reflect informal moments, as well as the complex intertwining of freedom and constriction in them. It is such smaller, informal matters—attitudes, perspective, emotions, behaviour, and fleeting or non-normative moments, rather than large historical and political events—and their presentation that I examine here. I organize the sequence of this book's chapters according to literary negotiations of these feelings, in relation with informality: I will explore different attitudes to and structures of freedom in the work of two stalwart modernist women, Virginia Woolf and Katherine Mansfield. Then I engage works by a pair of male modernist luminaries, T. S. Eliot and James Joyce, for their relations with constriction, particularly, in response to the challenging sensation of disgust, with its disorienting informality (as in jointly confusing sensations of intense personal proximity and formal instability). I then consider an informal pedagogy in the works of W. H. Auden as they defy received opinion and socially sanctioned behaviour.

As that summary suggests, I will trace the varieties and compromises of such defiance in verse through an examination of canonical modernist works. (Instead of tokenizing non-canonical modernist works—often shunted into the category of "global modernism" or "alternative modernities"—in a single chapter or two here, I will engage global modernist works substantially in my next book project.) This book will explore how informality marks modernism's responses to the absence of perceptual wholes, to demands for inventive poetics (such as Ezra Pound's demands for the "new"), to repeatedly revised expressions of the self (as in Virginia Woolf's *Orlando*), and to dominant figures from the past (as in the critical and ironic sympathies of W. H. Auden). Such responses span nostalgic and melancholic classicism—as in the work of T. S. Eliot—as well as exuberant and scandalous play, as manifest in the work of James Joyce. Examining particular nuances of the word "informality" in each chapter, I will read the informal as pertaining to sensory experience, aesthetic presentation, ethical deliberation or action, and attitudes within modernist works. Facing the hegemony of male Victorian legacies, modernist women writers are particularly well-equipped diagnosticians of cultural attitudes. I will investigate these works, roughly according to their dates of publication, in the following sequence: informality that offers promiscuity and humour as counters to self-absorption in works by Virginia Woolf; rebuttals to male priorities in liberalism through what I term the "feminine informal" in several short stories by Katherine Mansfield; colloquialism and contemporary intimacy as class-markers, tinged with voyeurism and contempt in *The Waste Land*; ostensibly perverse playfulness and resistance to disgust in Joyce's novels; and the fusion of protest, praise, and irreverence in W. H. Auden's elegiac poetry.

In this book's first chapter, I show that promiscuity is a main resource for the "illegitimate freedom" that Woolf evokes in "The Mark on the Wall." Here, I employ two senses of the word "promiscuous" (the first, sexual; the second, to do with composition and form) to explore humour and overtly deferred, partial narration in Woolf's *To the Lighthouse*, reading both as signs for an ethics of informality. I will then trace such an ethics in Woolf's novel *Orlando*, examining the text's complication of its main characters' often-distracted perception and wayward cosmopolitanism. This chapter will argue that Woolf's novels exercise a liberatory profanation through promiscuity in both the abovementioned senses of the word.

My second chapter reads figures of absence as functions of license for both colonial and gendered oppression. After a reading of Mansfield's "Bliss" as an exposition of domestic sublimity with which its main character, Bertha Young, struggles, I will explore the ripostes that such oppression receives through Mansfield's deployment of form. I will then broaden the scope of my reading to consider how the dynamics in "Bliss" resonate with many of Mansfield's other stories as counters to conventions of bourgeois domesticity, as shaped by John Locke's version of liberalism. Mansfield frequently protests the violence exercised in Lockean priorities through her depictions of circumscribed, formal, and heavily choreographed sites of behaviour. Within such locations, feminine experience, topography, and foliage operate with semiotic density, as emblems, symptoms, and contrasts for pain linked to the physical elisions and restrictions that formality and normalization enforce.

My discussion then concentrates on uneasy insertions of informality in T. S. Eliot's work. Analyzing the evolution of Eliot's attitudes to formality by tracing contempt and the use of slang in Eliot's early poems "The Triumph of Bullshit," "Mandarins" (1910), and "Paysage Triste" (c. 1914) through poetry from his middle career, including *The Waste Land*, I argue that Eliot's hermeticism has its signature in a withholding of self-consciousness from various figures and in disgust at modern informality. Especially in *The Waste Land*, these dynamics reflect an anxious contempt that produces a strange deadlock between form and attitude in Eliot's poetry. His arguments against vulgarity and his attitudes to colloquialism lead his works to an aesthetic, emotional, and political impasse that (as I will argue next in this project) James Joyce's work solves.

My chapter on Joyce's writings opens by interpreting implicit but strong support for mobility within the admiration for "a floating will" and an "unclean spirit" in Joyce's early essays. I connect these essays' arguments with Stephen Dedalus's disgust and its intricate links with informal or hyperformalized action in *A Portrait of the Artist as a Young Man*. I draw upon recent theorizations of disgust by Sara Ahmed, Winfried Menninghaus, and William Miller to comment on disgust as a spatial challenge, and then examine actions normatively deemed disgusting, as well as disgusted reactions, in Joyce's later novels. Linking this commentary to Immanuel Kant's claim that the disgusting obtrudes on our sense in an invitation of unsought enjoyment, I examine Joyce's deployment of a scandalous informality to counter both a sense of obtrusion and a sense of condemnation in *Finnegans Wake* and *Ulysses*. These novels nonetheless challenge dogmatic evaluation of their ethical processes through formal strategies and sceptical play even within their most flagrant moments.

Turning from modernist treatments of disgust to W. H. Auden's attempted evasions of pedantry, the book's closing chapter will engage Auden's elegiac poetry till his formal taking of the Anglican Communion in 1940. As I explore the weaving of performative irreverence and ethical arguments, I will that the critique of W. B. Yeats's vanity in Auden's elegy for Yeats complicates Auden's early critiques of ideology, and nuances the arguments against forgetting in both Auden's elegy for Freud and his poem memorializing Ernst Toller. Further, I claim that a call for making visible the unseen—dismantling the politicized hierarchies of what can and cannot be put on display—in these poems drives a questioning of socially surrendered agency and a protest against the formalization of love in Auden's poems. Their simultaneous scepticism and openness to unfamiliar relations thus work antidotally against the Eliotic attempt to seal art in a pure aesthetic realm.

This study will conclude with a section on the ethical risks of informality. Drawing upon my discussion of modernist works here, I will theorize modernist informality not as familiarity or unqualified intimacy, but as respect for the unfamiliar. Moreover, with its capacity for self-critique and agile irony, such informality eludes, and refuses to make, rigid moral demands for unqualified sincerity and self-exposure. In this sense, such modernist informality aids resistance to surveillance of others, while not evading criticism or even condemnation of itself. It, thus, opens interpretive space for reading and revision as ethical grounds.

Notes

1 As Carlyle begins his lectures on heroes and hero worship with the ballyhooed claim that "the history of what man has accomplished in this world, is at bottom the History of the Great Men who have worked here," he sees in their labour the formalization of the very soul of the world, announcing that

> all things that we see standing accomplished in the world are properly the outer material result, the practical realization and embodiment, of Thoughts that dwelt in the Great Men sent into the world: the soul of the whole world's history, it may justly be considered, were the history of these.
>
> (1)

Virginia Woolf's *Orlando* (1928) will undo such presumptions about the cryogenics for a global soul in architecture, not only through Woolf's reminders of the transience of physical form, but also of informal attitudes, which this book's first chapter will discuss.

2 For an extensive discussion of modernist self-fashioning for literary glamour, see Jonathan Goldman's *Modernism Is the Literature of Celebrity* (Austin: University of Texas Press, 2011).

3 Where necessary, I have shortened the titles of Joyce's works as follows within this book: "*OCP*" for *Occasional, Critical and Political Writing*; "*P*" for *A Portrait of the Artist as a Young Man*; "*U*" for *Ulysses*; "*FW*" for *Finnegans Wake*; and "*JJP*" for *James Joyce in Padua*.

4 Of course, Woolf herself disregards probability or coherence across her writing career, perhaps most blatantly in *Orlando* (1928).

5 Providing a list of corroborative references about such violent topics feels both perfunctory and callous. However, if references are necessary here: Sabine Hildebrandt discusses genocidal murder as a transgression in *The Anatomy of Murder*. For a poignant, insightful discussion of rape as transgression under international law, see Holly Porter's "Moral Spaces and Sexual Transgression: Understanding Rape in War and Post Conflict."

6 As Berlant notes in her introduction:

There is a history to the advent of intimacy as a public mode of identification and self-development ... [T]he bourgeois idea of a public sphere relied on the emergence of a mode of critical public discourse that formulated and represented a public's interests within civil society ... The development of critical publicness depended on the expansion of class-mixed semiformal institutions like the salon and the café, circulating print media, and industrial capitalism; the notion of the democratic public sphere thus made collective intimacy a public and social ideal, one of fundamental political interest. (283)

In yet another difference with intimacy, informality within the public sphere need not be "a mode of identification and self-development," but might well signal their opposites: sexual harassment in the street, loud racist jokes in the pub, a middle finger raised at a hostile crowd are instances of informality as anything *but* a mode of identification and self-development.

7 For a wide-ranging discussion of such effects in popular culture, see Robert Warshow's *The Immediate Experience* (Harvard University Press, 2002).

8 As Gabriel Rockhill puts it in his "Translator's Introduction" for Rancière's *The Politics of Aesthetics*, "the distribution of the sensible [is] the system of divisions and boundaries that define, among other things, what is visible and audible within a particular aesthetico-political regime" (xii). For himself, the restriction that Woolf implicitly criticizes in the excerpt from *To the Lighthouse* would mean the concerted production of a "factory of the sensible": "the formation of a shared sensible world, a common habitat, by the weaving together of a plurality of human activities" (*The Politics of Aesthetics*, 39). Woolf's criticism applies, of course, to both the formation and the maintenance of such shared domesticity in *To the Lighthouse*.

9 Pericles Lewis has suggested that the words might have a supernatural source: See Lewis's *Cambridge Introduction to Modernism*, pp. 129–51.

10 For excellent readings on the tensions that I explore in the genealogy here (especially those between Arnold and Pater), see Perry Meisel's *The Myth of the Modern*; Kenneth Daley's *The Rescue of Romanticism*; Kate Hext's *Walter Pater: Individualism and Aesthetic Philosophy*; and pp. 248–58 in Jed Rasula's *History of a Shiver*.

11 My comments on Ruskin and Arnold's arguments here are condensed excerpts of analyses that I offer in my book, *Migrant Form*. For my larger readings of their arguments, see especially pp. 2–23 and 43–50 in that book.

12 In his celebrated essay, "The Metropolis and Mental Life" (1903), Georg Simmel contrasts Arnold's concern about the modern pervasiveness of individuality, identifying the challenge of maintaining individuality against society as the source of the "deepest problems in modern life" (324). Simmel links the historical manufacture of this challenge with a complex elaboration of freedom into nineteenth-century capitalist economic principles in "Freedom and the Individual" (posthumously published, 1957). In the latter, he argues, "For clearly the doctrine of freedom and equality is the basis for free competition; and the doctrine of differentiated personality is the basis for the division of labor" (225). He, nonetheless, sees individuality as constrained in the service of capitalist teleology, and hopes that the "unforeseeable work of mankind will produce ever more numerous and varied forms with which the human personality will affirm itself

[through] new creations" (226). Simmel's appreciation for the unfamiliar and the inventive is what I see reflected in modernist practices of parrhesiastic informality.

13 Defining these terms in *The World, the Text, and the Critic*, Said argues that the tensions and contests within culture and society show "the individual consciousness at a sensitive nodal point, and it is this consciousness at that critical point which this book attempts to explore in the form of what I call *criticism*" (15). This criticism is bifocal:

> On the one hand, the individual mind ... is very much aware of the ... context, or situation in which it finds itself. On the other hand, [it is] precisely because of this awareness—a worldly self-situating, a sensitive response to the dominant culture—that the individual consciousness is not ... a mere child of the culture, but a historical and social actor in it.
>
> (15)

Given this latter activity and critical dissatisfaction, "secular criticism deals with local and worldly situations, and ... is constitutively opposed to the production of massive, hermetic systems" (26).

14 The psychological link between the embarrassment of being ashamed and customization to habit is an important one. The sociologist Norbert Elias, who sees embarrassment as "an inseparable counterpart of shame," argues that shame "arises when someone infringes the prohibitions of his own self and of society," while its concomitant, embarrassment, occurs when another person or something outside the individual "impinges on ... forms of behaviour, objects, inclinations which have early on been invested with fear by his surroundings until this fear—in the manner of a conditioned reflex—is reproduced *automatically* in him on certain occasions" (495, my italics). To put it differently, we are trained into forms of accustomation or cultural habit that, when breached or threatened with breach, produce shame or embarrassment automatically.

1 "Intoxicated Sense"

Humour and Promiscuity in *To the Lighthouse* and *Orlando*

In one of the many interruptions of her reverie, the narrator of Woolf's "The Mark on the Wall" thinks, "And yet that mark on the wall is not a hole at all" (84). Who in the text has said that it was? No one identifies the mark as a hole, earlier in the text. In the face of that missing information, the narrative structure around this moment and the inferences that it invites violate linearity—this moment is responding to (and insinuating) a thought that the text transmits as fore-written, *avant la lettre*. To be legible within Woolf's narrative, it requires an interpretive freedom and a freedom of engagement with the text, a kind of interpretive promiscuity: an analytical freedom of association.

Nevertheless, given its narrator's specifically stated or clearly implied arguments, the text suspects whimsical free-association, at the same time. The mark on the wall *interrupts* fancy, as when it curtails the narrator's projections of red knights and a red flag on a castle tower (83). In other words, within such a moment, the narrator's shifting views of the mark produce flexible—but not indiscriminate—elaborations of the stated or clear arguments in the essayistic story. This flexibility produces and ironically depends upon incongruity, a sense of disjointedness that Woolf provides as *a way out* of moments of ethical impasse, emotional confusion, or interpretive frustration, taking "the mould of [a] queer conglomeration of incongruous things," as Woolf puts it in "The Narrow Bridge of Art" (19–20). The staging of this solution provides a formal argument—an argument through form—in "The Mark on the Wall" that anticipates the subtle collaboration of incongruity with informality in *To the Lighthouse* and *Orlando*.

Promiscuities

Combining the informal with the incongruous in Woolf's novels, promiscuity is a main resource for the "illegitimate freedom" that Woolf evokes in "The Mark on the Wall." *To the Lighthouse* and *Orlando* echo such combination to assert arguments on various topics: a persistence of the past in later or current actions; incongruity as sign and resource for temporal, spatial, and psychological relations; informality as an engine of freedom; and

DOI: 10.4324/9781003009894-2

the informal self as various iterations of the influences and actions of the past—as forms of difference that suggest the latter novel's cosmopolitanism.

The *Oxford English Dictionary* offers the following definitions for the word "promiscuous":

A. 1. a. Done or applied with no regard for method, order, etc.; random, indiscriminate, unsystematic.
  b. Of an agent or agency: making no distinctions; undiscriminating.
  c. spec. Of a person or animal: undiscriminating in sexual relations. Also (of sexual intercourse, relationships, etc.): casual, characterized by frequent changes of sexual partner.
 2. Consisting of assorted parts or elements grouped or massed together without order; mixed and disorderly in composition or character; (with plural noun) of various kinds mixed together. Now *arch.* and *rare.*
 3. Chiefly Grammar. Of common gender; of either sex, of both sexes. Cf. epicene adj. 1. rare. [Example:] 1878 L. Villari tr. P. Villari *Life & Times Machiavelli* (1898) I. iii. vii. 130[: "]There were three sexes, male, female and promiscuous.["]
 4. Chiefly slang (depreciative). That forms part of a mixed or undifferentiated company.
  Obs.
 5. colloq. Casual, careless (cf. sense B. 2). Obs.

B. *adv.* 1. = promiscuously adv. 1; indiscriminately; at random. Now rare (colloq. in later use).
 2. colloq. = promiscuously adv. 2; without ceremony; casually. Now rare.

The third sense given above is obviously germane to a discussion of gender and sexuality in *Orlando*—I will gesture to it, later. Here, instead, I will emphasize my ensuing complication of the fifth nuance of the word: I will argue that Woolf's novels do indeed employ promiscuous effects, but often as the deliberate effects of a deceptive, *ostensible* casualness, rather than as unconsidered or negligent textual choices. These choices reflect Woolf's critical ambivalence with casualness to signal her disagreements with hierarchization and formality. To discuss promiscuity in Woolf's deployment of informality, I will mainly employ the senses of the word "promiscuous" in definitions A.I.c and 2 from the *OED*; the first, sexual: "Of a person or animal: undiscriminating in sexual relations. Also (of sexual intercourse, relationships, etc.): casual, characterized by frequent changes of sexual partner"; and the second, to do with composition and form: "Consisting of assorted parts or elements grouped or massed together without order; mixed and disorderly in composition or character; (with plural noun) of various kinds mixed together."

Humour and Liberated Affective Expenditure in *To the Lighthouse*

The latter sense is evident in the third part of *To the Lighthouse*, when the artist Lily Briscoe's sudden praise for Mr. Ramsay's boots relieves their interaction of the oppressive, but unspoken, gambits for attention that the widower Ramsay directs towards Lily (153–4). Seeing Ramsay "bearing down on her" for attention and emotional succour, Lily wonders:

> Surely, she could imitate ... the self-surrender, she had seen on so many women's faces[,] when on some occasion like this they blazed up—she could remember the look on Mrs. Ramsay's face—into a rapture of sympathy[,] which, though the reason of it escaped her, evidently conferred on them the most supreme bliss.
>
> (150)

Soon after that thought, however, the narrative hints at her internalization of normative gendered expectations, as it presents her shame and panic through free indirect discourse:

> A woman, she had provoked this horror; a woman, she should have known how to deal with it. It was immensely to her discredit, sexually, to stand there dumb. One said—what did one say?—Oh, Mr. Ramsay! Dear Mr. Ramsay! That was what that kind old lady who sketched, Mrs. Beckwith, would have said instantly, and rightly. But, no. They stood there, isolated from the rest of the world. His immense self-pity, his demand for sympathy poured and spread itself in pools at her feet, and all she did, miserable sinner that she was, was to draw her skirts a little closer round her ankles, lest she should get wet.
>
> (152)

Experiencing her reluctance as a sin here, Lily initially seeks an appropriately gendered response to Ramsay ("what did one say?"), but she casts off the burden. Instead of giving Ramsay the gushing concern that he desires, she offers him a banal compliment about a part of his clothing: "What beautiful boots!" (153). Marked by an almost-involuntary informality through a diversion of this psychic pressure, Lily's blurted praise lays bare and transforms Ramsay's emotional parasitism. She expects "complete annihilation" from "one of his sudden roars of ill-temper," but Ramsay smiles, instead (153). Her praise for Ramsay's boots jolts him out of the intense, self-pitying, but unspoken, calls for sympathy into gently ironic, humorous interaction with Lily. The informality implicitly compacted into this pivotal moment offers Lily relief from the pious emotional charity that Ramsay, in his invocation of such piety, initially expects as a feminine duty from her. The small, absurd, informal moment is an upheaval: It is the point where discursive pressure for propriety collapses.

This moment expands and refines analyses of the superego role as liberatory observer at humorous moments, as advanced in Sigmund Freud's writings on humour, as well as Simon Critchley's commentary on the economic structure of humour in *Infinitely Demanding*. In *Jokes and Their Relation to the Unconscious* (1905), Freud describes the relief that humour provides from "the cost of an economy of the feelings of piety" (286). Humour is, thus, a release of freed emotions or, in Freud's phrase, "liberated expenditure" (*Jokes*, 292). According to Freud, it performs another important function: It is "a means of obtaining pleasure in spite of the distressing affects that interfere with it; it acts as a substitute for the generation of these affects, it puts itself in their place" (284). Lily's reference to Ramsay's boots deflates the demands on her to provide appropriately feminine substitutes for the sympathy that he formerly received from his wife. She eludes Ramsay's call for the proper or normative response through a further substitution: Exchanging an expected, nourishing response for a banal compliment about Ramsay's shoes, Lily's focus on the shoes lightens the pious pressures of sorrow that Ramsay exerts in his call for care and, implicitly but liberatingly, profanes the almost-sacralized memory of Mrs. Ramsay that Ramsay evokes in service of his current need. This profanation is not voluntary: Lily does not plan to divert Ramsay jocularly, but she does make an incongruous substitution as per Freud's mapping of the humorous process. While Lily does not intend humour in her perplexed search for a proper reply to Ramsay, the apparent absurdity of her response produces a humorous effect. The novel, rather than Lily, clearly recognizes an aspect of the production of humour that, in his recent book on humour, Terry Eagleton appreciatively locates in the following line from Mark Akenside's "The Pleasures of the Imagination": "Some *stubborn* dissonance of things combin'd" (68, my italics). *Humour recognizes the persistence of the unwanted, but substitutes it with a dissonant response.* Lily's substitution of hyperbolic affirmation with a manifestly incongruous response relieves her of the emotional toll that the expected affirmation would take.

Freud suggests that the substitution in such situations is a gift of the superego. In his short essay "Humour" (1927), he observes that, in humour, the humorist withdraws "the psychical accent" or larger psychological attachment from the ego and transposes it onto the super-ego, giving the super-ego expanded psychological control (430–1). Consequently, to "the super-ego, thus inflated, the ego can appear tiny and all its interests trivial," so that "it may become an easy matter for the super-ego to suppress the ego's possibilities of reacting" (431). Once "the subject suddenly hypercathects his super-ego and then, proceeding from it, alters the reactions of the ego[,]" the super-ego can perform its production of pleasure, despite circumstantial strains on the subject (432). As Freud explains it, this is as if the super-ego comforts the intimidated ego by saying, "Look! here is the world, which seems so dangerous! It is nothing but a game for children—just worth making a jest about!" (432–3). Humour, then, is the super-ego's explanatory dismissal of vitiating facts. Pointing to humour's antidotal capacities in *Infinitely Demanding*, Simon Critchley contends:

> Humour has the same formal structure as depression, but it is an anti-depressant that works by the ego finding itself ridiculous. The subject looks at itself like an abject object and instead of weeping bitter tears, it laughs at itself and finds consolation therein.
>
> (81)

Critchley establishes this claim by pointing to the crucial argument in Freud's "On Humour" on humour's self-critical function, a product of super-ego's view of the ego's anxieties as trivial: "[I]n humour I find myself ridiculous and I acknowledge this in laughter or simply in a smile. Humour is essentially self-mocking ridicule" (*Infinitely Demanding,* 79). In the scene of "the blessed boots," Lily Briscoe's implicit self-mockery in her comment about the boots suggests both an appeal to, and defiance of, Mr. Ramsay's demand. Lily's self-ridiculing, nonsensical reply suggests her helpless confusion, but also, within it, her volition to disobey or even refuse Ramsay's imposition of desire and power. As Freud admiringly warns in his essay, "Humour is not resigned; it is rebellious. It signifies not only the triumph of the ego but also of the pleasure principle" (429). The scene replies richly to Critchley's question: "[M]ight there not be other ways of sublimating ethical experience than tragedy?" (78). Producing such sublimation after Ramsay turns to her for his emotional sustenance, Lily generously does not mention his need.

Freud clarifies the interpretive mechanics of joke-making when he says, "A joke is a playful judgment" (*Jokes*, 7). I mention this here to highlight that Woolf's jokes and informal play in *To the Lighthouse* and *Orlando* assert judgments, often acerbic ones. However, in the humorous, apparently absurd exchange between Lily and Mr. Ramsay, these judgments are kind, and the kindness not reserved for one character. Lily's choice prevents her own false and agonized deference to Ramsay, even as it keeps Ramsay from another's dishonest affirmation.

The scene encapsulates Adam Phillips's arguments in *Going Sane*, which imply that sanity is a form of kindness that prevents the humiliation of the self and the other.[1]

The "Random Moment": Ecstasy, Informality, and Interpretive Freedom

Evoking the sacred ironically through the word "blessed," Lily Briscoe's phrase "blessed island of good boots" could be read, further, as a light-hearted outlet for her relief in the form of an ironic, ambiguous curse: a milder version of "damn," "bloody," or "fucking" as adjectives, if you will. This underscores not only the already-ample gender politics in the scene, but other political tensions that it constellates in its improprieties. As Caroline

Levine writes, drawing on Jacques Rancière's theories of aesthetic politics, "Political struggles include ongoing contests over the proper places for bodies, goods, and capacities" (3). Of course, within classical narrative conventions, these "proper places" have also have a temporal dimension: "bodies, goods, and capacities" must appear in persuasive, sound sequence. Gesturing to the temporal in *The Edges of Fiction*, Rancière himself identifies classical philosophy's "major principle of fiction" to be the Aristotelian *peripeteia* "that inverts the expected effects of the causal chain" (115). This is because, for Rancière, the *peripeteia* cancels all prior events for the sake of a resolution and, in this sense, the "model driving it is that of construction bound for destruction" (115). He contends that modern fiction, in contrast, can be "most succinctly defined by the abolition of the peripeteia" (115). Borrowing a formulation from Erich Auerbach's *Mimesis* to specify an instance of such abolition, Rancière declares the "random occurrence" or "random moment" to be "the principle of Virginia Woolf's fiction" (115). The random occurrence, in Rancière's reading, "dilates endlessly, and includes, virtually, every other time and place," thus forming "a time of coexistence, overcome by the liberalness of space" (115). Randomness suggests thoughtless construction: The first definition of "informality" that I quote above from the *OED* is "Done or applied with no regard for method, order, etc.; random, indiscriminate, unsystematic." However, in Woolf's hands, it is the *effect* of randomness or informality in her portrayal of a moment that "dilates endlessly." It is a complex mesh of sensation, memory, emotion, and time that produces a *sense* of the permeability or even collapse of formal or normative temporal boundaries at such moments.[2] As Rancière helpfully adds:

> The random moment, in reality, is not random. Most certainly it can be produced at any instant for any insignificant occasion. But it is also the decisive moment, the moment of turning that stands on the exact boundary between the nothing and the all.
>
> (136)

A clarification of this dense insight: Woolf includes a poignant instance of such a moment in the "Time Passes" section of *To the Lighthouse* when, describing the silent scene in the Ramsays' empty living room, she writes:

> light turned on the wall its shape clearly there seemed to drop into this silence, this indifference, this integrity, the thud of something falling.
>
> [A shell exploded. Twenty or thirty young men were blown up in France, among them Andrew Ramsay, whose death, mercifully, was instantaneous.]
>
> (133)

The thud described before the bracketed narration has a sympathetic resonance: It echoes in the Ramsays' home the sound of the bomb on the French warfront that kills Andrew, but Woolf does not specify its provenance or trajectory. The thud in the Ramsays' house could mark the sound of something banal, such as a household object falling in the uninhabited space; the sound of every projectile falling in the history of global violence; merely a synaesthetic sonic effect, mingling with the light; or—given the uncertainty evoked by the qualifying word "seemed"—no sound at all. The sound gains its complex semiotic scope, precisely because, in Rancière's terms, it stands on the "boundary between the nothing and the all."

Such bold use of time and space violates a linear unfolding of events, but for Rancière and Auerbach it provides a social model, as well: Rancière reminds us that Auerbach praises *To the Lighthouse* as "a book in which he sees not only the supreme crowning of western literature but the promise of a 'common life of mankind on earth'" (126). Recalling that, two chapters earlier in *Mimesis*, Auerbach argued that "the heart of modern novelistic realism ... can represent humans only as inserted in a rapidly changing global political, economic and social reality," Rancière declares that what seems to have changed alongside—indeed, disappeared—is "that chain of actions forming a whole that comprised the very core of fiction" (126–7, 127). Consequently, the "supreme achievement" of western realist fiction now is "the destruction of that 'concerted chain of actions' that appears to be the minimal condition of all fiction" (128). Rancière stresses that what such later fiction offers as common or shared in "the random moment" is not a matter of time's content but of its form:

> If there is a politics of fiction, it ... arises from the same thing that renders it fiction[:] a way of identifying events and linking them with one another. The treatment of time is the core of the politics of fiction.
>
> (128–9)

This is so because, whether or not we subscribe to a "core," such politics is an exercise in de-hierarchization: It puts into unstratified relations things that might be deemed as discrete, disparate, incompatible, distant, or even separate. It is a matter of the mutual intensification of affect and relations, as is clear in the following passage where Lily considers her response to the Ramsay family:

> Directly one looked up and saw them, what she called "being in love" flooded them. They became part of that unreal but penetrating and exciting universe which is the world seen through the eyes of love. The sky stuck to them; the birds sang through them. And, what was even more exciting, she felt, too, as she saw Mr. Ramsay bearing down and retreating, and Mrs. Ramsay sitting with James in the window and the cloud moving and the tree bending, how life, from being made up of little separate incidents which one lived one by one, became curled and

> whole like a wave which bore one up and threw one down with it, there, with a dash on the beach.
>
> (46–7)

As the surging narrative form of the random occurrence reflects her feelings here, Lily responds to the intensity of love for the Ramsays that she feels within herself and the love that she feels in their being ("'being in love' flooded them") with an affective informality or unboundedness that verges on mysticism. As she does so, she also feels this sense of love radiate into universality, which is, on the one hand, "unreal," and, on the other, a more intense, sharper, and "penetrating, sense of the world's condition. This sense of the world expands Lily's sense of endlessly expanded relations with all of life—"how life, from being made up of little separate incidents which one lived one by one, became curled and whole like a wave"—but this is a sense of life heaving incessantly between infinity and finitude, even as it is also a wave that "bore one up and threw one down with it, there, with a dash on the beach"—a simultaneous condition of strength that feels "whole like a wave" and vulnerability that can be thrown down and dashed on its own shores. It is this latter awareness of the fragility of sympathies and their fatal susceptibility that reroutes the passage's initial trajectory from the mystical to material violence. It is this, an awareness of these joint and contrasting possibilities, that shapes the politics of sympathy in the novel.

The politics of "linking" or connection is mirrored in Woolf's smaller constructions of "random occurrences" in *To the Lighthouse*. The novel's narrative strangeness leaves implied relations within minute details and several minute moments suspended, suggestive, and unexplained. Near the beginning of the book, we read that, clearly audible within the attics of the Ramsays' house, is "a Swiss girl sobbing for her father who was dying of cancer in a valley of the Grisons" (8). The novel leaves any explanation of who this girl is, and any mention of her altogether for another nineteen pages, when we find that she is Marie, a maid whom the Ramsays employ (27). It is possible, and easy, to read the lack of explanation at the first mention of the Swiss girl as compositional negligence—a sign of Woolf's being careless. However, we can also read the absent explanation as an intended trick of Woolf's craft: a sign of her being careful under the guise of appearing carefree or even casual, here. In other words, the deferral of explanation for the weeping and status of the Swiss maid in the Ramsay household can be read plausibly as novelistic sedimentation that provides an instance for the novel's poetics of informality and politics of mobile relations. By leaving the first reference to the Swiss girl unexplained, the novel seems to be staging its informal, impressionistic poetics; asking the reader to read backwards as well as forwards; encouraging reading itself as a process of promiscuous relations through its *violation* of narrative conventions for introducing and "fully" identifying characters when they are first mentioned.

A striking variant of such violation appears in a passage that follows the narrative's traversal of several characters' perspectives and subsequent adoption of third-person narration proceeds thus:

> They all had to join in and sing the chorus, and shout out together:
> Damn your eyes, damn your eyes,
> but it would be fatal to let the tide come in and cover up all the good hunting-grounds before they got on to the beach.
> "Fatal," Paul agreed...
>
> (74–5)

The passage seems to begin with Nancy's and Andrew's impressions of Minta Doyle and turns to quote a line communally sung, before it merges with the ostensibly impersonal narrative, the thoughts expressed in which get a reply from another character. The sheer peculiarity of this exchange undoes the conventional separation between characters and narrator, not only signalling their mutual sympathies, but putting them in conversation, turning narrative into dialogue. This transforms the novel's narrative voice into something like a choric personage, employing an obviously *engaged* voice that links multiple voices, unlike detached narration that adopts, in Rancière's phrase, "the Flaubertian stupidity of the impersonal voice," and, as conveyor of its objective distance, is unresponsive, bereft of emotional intelligence and inflection—and, consequently, numb (147). Often veering from impersonality, the narrative of *To the Lighthouse* suspends grammar and syntactical formality to perform the *conditions and qualities* of characters' personal thought, as when it shows Mrs. Ramsay's thoughts here: "For Charles Tansley *had been saying* (she looked up as if she expected to hear the crash of books on the floor above), *had been saying* that people don't read Scott any more" (118; italics mine). The weird repetition of "had been saying" stages the interruption of Mrs. Ramsay's initial thought by her concern about the "crash of books," and so produces a deferral of narration, itself. As such, it strays from narrative efficiency and formal grammatical sense, but its informality conveys the intervention to underscore the sympathies and mutual influence—if not confluence—of the narrative and its characters' thoughts, which are combined even more subtly and radically in this instance than in the almost immediately following few pages of free indirect discourse that convey Mrs. Ramsay's ecstatic, non-linear, zigzagging reading of "The Siren Song" by William Brown of Tavistock and Shakespeare's ninety-eighth sonnet (119–21). As she reads, less informal, though also interrupted, syntax shows Mrs. Ramsay's mind moving from text to text, and cross-connects texts and emotions; in the earlier passage, however, performative informality is built into the fusion of her wavering thoughts and the narrative quirk that conveys them. There, by means of informal (in the sense of suggested, but not explicit) instruction, the novel's syntax clarifies the kinds of reading practices that it demands of its reader.

Such practices depend on the reader's memory and recognition of the narrative's and its characters' mutual influence—it self-consciously connects their actions, correspondence, and eccentric signs of sympathy. In doing so, it emphasizes the importance of informal contact and correspondence in the non-literal, non-linear, and non-empirical literary possibilities that comprise what Rancière offers as a politics of "linking." The open range of such possibilities lets the non-linear, non-hierarchical potential for linking function textually, as informality does in a social sense.

In such circumstances, Rancière notes, "Digression is obligatory, it is even the rule": Digression serves as the narrative and epistemological hinge in Woolf's "The Mark on the Wall" and, often, in *Orlando* (116). Ostensibly cosmetic phrases and references woven into one part of the novel anticipate, reappear, explain prior or latter parts of the text. In their suggestiveness, incompleteness, and mobility, they appear as promiscuous signs, but they assert a textual sociability—they are, obviously, not isolated, unrelated, or merely singular. They engage in a politics of relation, even as (or precisely because) they disrupt linear textual space and time.

Thawing Perfection: Freedom, Choice, and Character

The strategy of spatio-temporal disruption or (to put it another way) political ornamentation augments the interpretive elasticity that Woolf threads into her novels. Nearing a call for such elastic interpretation, Martin Hägglund differentiates between "natural freedom" and "spiritual freedom" in *This Life*: "Natural freedom provides a freedom of self-movement, but only in light of imperatives that are treated as given and ends that cannot be called into question by the agent itself[,]" whereas "*spiritual freedom* requires the ability to ask which imperatives to follow in light of our ends, as well as the ability to call into question, challenge, and transform our ends themselves" (175; italics Hägglund's). For Hägglund,

> the norms in light of which we lead our lives can be called into question, contested, and revised. Far from being an impediment to 'genuine community,' the recognition that we are responsible for the form of our shared life is at the heart of the modern, secular commitment to *democracy*.
>
> (16)

Even as he concedes that social normativity can be challenged and revised, Hägglund remains in favour of norms, however provisional. The same is true for his subscription to "democratic progress" (19). As he has it, "Being free is not a matter of being unconstrained but of being confronted with the question of what you ought to do and what you ought to believe." (352). Why the refusal of considered choice—without absolute imperatives—here? Why "ought," rather than "prefer"? Hägglund's investment in norms elides the critical consideration of preference as a preliminary condition, even a prerequisite, for freedom. Woolf, however, sustains that consideration. In formal and structural terms, the suggested, rather than literalized, argument offers Woolf illegitimate freedom. As with the hole in "The Mark on the Wall," she does not specify an exact reason for Lily Briscoe's choice to comment on Ramsay's boots in *To the Lighthouse*. In diagetic terms, of course, the moment gives Lily illegitimate freedom. When Lily's involuntarily compliment about boots overturns Mr. Ramsay's expectations, humour transforms the scene into one that permits her the "liberated expenditure" of the pressures that she initially experiences. With this crucial effect in the scene, humour functions as both manufacturer and conduit of freedom: Choice is crucial here not as obedience to or adoption of a norm, but as a preference that escapes the norm, without necessarily or wholly defeating and transforming the norm. At radically ethical junctures, modernist works such as Woolf's (and—as I will discuss later—Joyce's and Auden's) exercise and liberate *preference* as an aspect of choice, unconstrained by the normative *ought*.[3]

Rather than steer their freedom and ethics according to norms and imperatives (as Hägglund might have them do), Woolf's texts frequently and manifestly embrace *abnormality* and preferences as routes to freedom, unproscribed by bounds of normalcy or decency—as Rebecca Walkowitz has noted, Woolf "risks indecency" (80). Theorizing a form of strategic informality that breaks self-silencing decency in "The Narrow Bridge of Art," her essay published in 1927, the year in which she also published *To the Lighthouse*, Woolf argues that the modern novel is concerned with freedom and marked by the qualified considerations that freedom brings. As she lauds Elizabethan dramatists for their "attitude toward life which made them able to express themselves freely and fully," she sees their modern counterparts display a tendentious difference:

> They want not a veil that heightens but a curtain that conceals; they lay their scene in the past because they are afraid of the present. They are aware that if they tried to express the thoughts, the visions, the sympathies and antipathies which are actually turning and tumbling in their brains in this year of grace 1927 the poetic decencies would be violated

and so they "take refuge" in affected classicism "or only what blank verse with decency can say" (15). In Woolf's censure for self-concealment here, the modern playwright's anxious grasping for decency is, at least, tinged with timidity and furtiveness. She sees this, as I will discuss below, not only as a matter of hypocrisy, but as a dilution of modern psychology, the transformation of which she signals in perhaps her most-quoted statement about the change in human character "on or about December 1910" in "Character in Fiction," a claim better known through the revised version of Woolf's "Mr. Bennett and Mrs. Brown" (421, *Essays*, Vol. 3). The statement has been quoted with renewed frequency in literary studies, given the recent surge of scholarly commentary on character (such as in Jean-Michel Rabaté's *The Pathos of Distance*, Rasula's *History of a Shiver*, Wolfe's *Bloomsbury, Modernism, and the Reinvention of Intimacy*, and Amanda Anderson's in her contribution to the trio of essays in *Character*, each evoking Woolf's proclamation). In his lectures on abnormal character during 1974–75, Michel Foucault cites commentary from C. Champeaux's *Reflections on the Hermaphrodites* on the trial of Anne Grandjean, who was banned from "spending her time with women" (72). Foucault writes that, according to Champeaux:

> it is not the fact of being a hermaphrodite that should arouse or provoke our condemnation of the woman Grandjean. Rather, it is the simple fact that for a woman who has perverse tastes, that she loves women, and it is this monstrosity, which is not a monstrosity of nature but a monstrosity of behavior, that calls for condemnation. Monstrosity, therefore, is no longer the undue mixture of what should be separated from nature. It is simply an irregularity, a slight deviation, but one that makes possible something that really will be a monstrosity, that is to say, the monstrosity of character.
>
> (73)

Woolf's ambition for the modern novel in "The Narrow Bridge of Art" strongly recommends the exploration of such "irregularity." Dissatisfied that the "psychological novelist has been too prone to limit psychology to the psychology of personal intercourse," she avers that the novel to come, in contrast, will "take the mould of that queer conglomeration of incongruous things—the modern mind" (19–20). Declaring that the novel "will clasp to its breast the precious prerogatives of the democratic art of prose; its freedom, its fearlessness, its flexibility," she encourages the novelist to explore and validate even (and, perhaps, especially) irregularity and "the slight deviation" of character that Foucault mentions. As she puts it: "For prose is so humble that it can go anywhere; no place is too low, too sordid, or too mean for it to enter" (20). The modern mind's "queer conglomeration" involves unfamiliar combinations, unpredictable, deviant, unprecedented, or unacknowledged coalescences that render appropriateness and normalcy questionable, at minimum, if they do not cast normal or appropriate behaviour altogether into analytical desuetude. It is telling that, following the incongruous comment that relieves her of extending sympathy to Ramsay, Lily registers a further incongruity. Having felt that, in their mutual relief, she and Ramsay had escaped fraught norms and reached "the blessed island of good boots" as her "heart warmed to him," she wonders:

> Why, at this *completely inappropriate* moment[,] should she be so tormented with sympathy for him that ... the blood rushed to her face,

> and, thinking of her callousness (she had called him a play actor) she felt her eyes swell and tingle with tears?
>
> (154; italics mine)

The scene highlights that, frequently for Woolf, the *inappropriate*, rather than the appropriate or normal, moment works as the one most conducive to sympathy.

As she extols Greek in her essay "The Perfect Language" (1917), Woolf acknowledges that "perfection has a chill sound" (116). Even at this early point in her writing career, Woolf finds "unlikeness" as the foremost quality of its perfection—*difference* is her primary criterion for beauty, closely allied with "maturity" in the Greek works (by Simonedes and Theodoridas, among others) that she quotes in the essay (116). Her enthusiasm for mobile, elastic interpretation—of a kind of hermeneutic stretching—and fearless candour thaws the chill of forms frozen in the decency of perfection and normalcy. Describing the mature attributes of the Greek writers she admires, Woolf writes, "There is no prettiness as there is no mysticism in them. We hear the voices of men whose outlook on life was perfectly direct and unclouded" (116–7). Soon after, she relates this outlook with "absolute candour" (117). The forthrightness that she admires is accompanied by a considered reserve: "[I]t is most of all a virtue when ... there is much to restrain" (117). Maturity, therefore, reflects frankness and clear-sightedness that are organized with aesthetic fineness, affective economy, and passion, as, in Woolf's words, "it is evident that this people had everything to restrain, a love of man or woman, a love of earth, a love of life itself more passionate, it seems, than ours" (117). The latter clause indicates the importance of passion in Woolf's notion of illegitimate freedom, where her optimistic fervour foreruns the significance of candid, passionate reimagining that she clarifies in the first two essays in *Granite and Rainbow*: "Impassioned Prose" (1926) and "The Narrow Bridge of Art" (1927). In these essays, passion and "queer conglomerations" of the mind are as much psychological matters as they are of form. Jean-Michel Rabaté reminds us that the "etymology of 'character' harks back to the original sense of 'sharpening, engraving, leaving distinctive signs.' Character is a form of writing that takes into account human temperaments and historicized ethical evaluations" (86). In this sense, then, style is not only character, but also a simultaneous awareness—a "taking into account"—of it. Such awareness is, in part, what Woolf admires about the writing of Max Beerbohm, of whom she writes in "The Modern Essay," "What Mr. Beerbohm gave was, of course, himself ... He has brought personality into literature" (220). She sees Beerbohm's delivery of his own character as a personal and formal success: "The triumph is the triumph of style" (221). She gestures prominently to personality as a premier area of inquiry for modern literature, when she confidently speculates in "Modern Fiction" that "the point of interest" for the modern writers "lies very likely in the dark places of psychology"

(162). As her investment in the dark places of the mind indicates, she is intensely invested in fearless reading: the exploration of the concealed, forbidden, "indecent" aspects of psychology. She carries out such exploration with verve through the ecstatic formal, cultural, and sexual promiscuity in *Orlando*.

Orlando's Intoxicated Sense: Ecstasy and Cosmopolitan Imagination

As Orlando crosses geographical, temporal, and sexual boundaries, her promiscuous, informal (as in "casual") attention forms a distracted cosmopolitanism that flits among sights, topics, feelings, and cultures.[4] Reading the character Orlando's own distracted cosmopolitanism as an ironic instance of informality, a casual and promiscuous condition that the novel *Orlando* frequently undercuts, I will use the word "cosmopolitanism" here to convey two senses of the term, at the same time: the first, a strong interest in cultural practices across national boundaries, and the viewing of the world without national attachments or prejudices; and the second, a critical alertness towards—and awareness of—multiple affiliations. The word "cosmopolitan" comes from the Greek *kosmopolites*, from *kosmos* ("ornament," "order," "world") and *polites* ("citizens" or "the body politic")—so it originally suggested "ornament" or "ordering" of the world or its citizens, and gradually after theorizations of the world-citizen by Diogenes, Zeno, and Kant, it came to suggest perhaps its most common meaning: "citizen of the world."[5] However, as Bruce Robbins has noted, the priority of "adornment" (in the sense of "ornament") within the term's etymology is significant (253). Let me expand this nuance to stress that, in its etymological sense, cosmopolitanism ornaments the world or "world-citizenship." It offers an alternative to existent, nationally or territorially bound allegiances with unbound or deterritorialized forms of affiliation and interest, with new combinative possibilities and unfamiliar metaphors for solidarity.

Such metaphors gain a peculiar tension in Woolf's *Orlando*. As various selves and moments reflect each other in the text, metaphoricity is crucial for Orlando's changes and redirections of herself through several centuries. Her temporal and geographical wandering strongly echoes René Wellek and Austin Warren's much-cited discussion of metaphor's mobility: In the second half of this paper, I will try to show that, in Woolf's novel, the imagination, chaotic and unrestricted, shapes the transgressions of wandering through a collaboration with metaphor. Orlando's *Wanderlust* is itself spurred by imagining a series of metaphors for difference. Wellek and Warren observe in their *Theory of Literature* that "metaphor and metonymy may be the two characterizing structures of two poetic types—poetry of association by contiguity [metonymy], of movement within a single discourse, and poetry of association by comparison [metaphor], joining a plurality of worlds" (195). These definitions bring the relative fixity of metonymy (especially of its nationalistic versions) and the *Wanderlust* of metaphor into sharp relief. Woolf's uses of the metaphorical and the serial undo the self-induced sterility of the metonymic, insular modes of the national and the parochial.[6] I will argue that the emphasis on metaphor in *Orlando* is intimately related to its problematic cosmopolitanism. Metaphor provides the text not only a mode with which to enact Orlando's gender-changes and transcentennial existence, but also a means for the elaboration of an eclecticism that underscores its cosmopolitanism. The geography that Orlando traverses—diverse, morphing, vulnerable, and echo of historical conditions—functions as the theatre for the text's staging of its poetics and its ironic, unsettled (and occasionally unsettling) politics. Further, Orlando's recognition of a pervasive metaphorical charge (in gender, perception, history, narration, and in form) undoes divisions of surface and depth. This subversion plays with the idea of a consistent politics in the text, displaying a political impulse that is affected by various fluctuations of scene and tone. As *Orlando* stages these fluctuations, its earlier and later theses (like Orlando's earlier and later identities) are involved in an unceasing, mutual augmentation and renewal: As Orlando and Shelmerdine flirt with each other, Orlando exclaims, "I'm dead, Sir!" (183). Soon after, to remove any doubt that her ostensibly nonsensical exclamation signals the dual sense of "death" as "end of life" and the older connotation of "orgasm," a new paragraph begins: "After several hours of death ..." in an obvious, almost explicatory way suggesting the phrase "After several hours of making love ..." This dynamic reveals the collaboration between the cosmetic and the cosmopolitan in the novel. In this sense, tones and identities are involved in mutual ornamentation here. The story of one Orlando ornaments that of the others, working as a vital accessory to stories that could just as easily have been unrelated.

This dynamic underscores the collaboration between the cosmetic and the cosmopolitan in the novel. I would like to underscore that the word "cosmetic" is etymologically resonant with "cosmopolitan." The former derives from *kosmos* and *metic* (a "foreigner" resident in the Athenian city-state). The metics were an active part of the daily workings of the city-state, but not recognized as full citizens, and, therefore, never officially afforded a sufficient sense of inclusion.[7] The word "cosmetic," then, initially signified a literal condition of "almost-belonging"—evoking an ornamental form of citizenship, a form of civic embroidery; being in, but not of. The etymological suggestion that cosmopolitanism—like cosmetics—ornaments, embroiders, or augments surfaces also suggests that, like *metics*, the cosmopolitan never fully belongs to a single social, national, or cultural fabric: Embroidery is both *of* the surface and *offset from* it. Woolf's novel not only depicts Orlando in that condition variously, it suggests the strong connection of such a condition with the novel's arguments, techniques, and forms. While the adolescent Orlando is trying to describe a shade of green precisely in his poem, he wants to capture "the thing itself," but cannot do so because the precise description would spoil his rhyme and metre. The narrator of the text points out an additional problem: "Green in nature is one thing, green in literature another" (16). Through a privileging of cosmetic interaction, the novel's closing section rebuts both views—the teenage Orlando's and the biographer's. Echoing the "Conclusion" of Pater's *The Renaissance*, Orlando muses in a much-discussed passage, late in the novel's British (Oxford World's Classics) edition:

> [E]verything was, in fact, something else, as if her mind had become a forest, with glades branching here and there; things came nearer and further, mingled and separated and made the strangest alliances and combinations in an incessant chequer of light and shade.
>
> (308)

The younger and older Orlando's—as well as the biographer's—observations follow a trajectory that moves from literalism to an alertness about flux and metaphor: Orlando acknowledges being-in-the-world as a play of resemblance and difference—in short, of metaphoricity. Forms combine and withdraw not in a finite way that separates one thing from another, but in a medley of relations that is unceasing—"an incessant chequer of light and shade" (308). It is also significant that Orlando feels her mind transform into a landscape: "her mind had become a forest": psychology, vision, and geography share their shape-shifting cosmopolitanism overtly here. In other words, the later Orlando's perception itself reinforces the novel's poetics of transfer. The very modes that sustain such a poetics are those that sustain more alert, inclusive versions of cosmopolitanism: celebration of alliances and multiple combinations, without the demand for permanence or strict definition. The privileging of impermanence in Woolf's work displaces regularity, repetitions of the expected, and routine. Revelling in such displacement, and heeding the Paterian warning about habit formation as "failure," *Orlando* thwarts habituation.[8]

Rebecca Walkowitz suggests this practice, noting that Woolf's disruptions of first-person perspective and "tones of comfort or confidence," as well as her willingness to risk indecency, help her to "imagine models of social critique that would resist social codification" (80). As Woolf ambivalently observes in "The Narrow Bridge of Art," the contemporary mind is "full of monstrous, hybrid, unmanageable emotions" and "[f]eelings which used to come single and separate do so no longer. Beauty is part ugliness; amusement part disgust; pleasure part pain. Emotions which used to enter the mind whole are now broken up on the threshold" (12, 16). Walkowitz has argued that Woolf's cosmopolitan narrative strategy in *Mrs. Dalloway* is "evasion," utilizing the vacillations of which "Virginia Woolf suggests that autonomous thinking sometimes involves the refusal to think purposefully" (4–5). Woolf's mode of formal suggestiveness in *Orlando* is not merely evasion: It is interruption and promiscuous accretion. (Consider the irruption of multiple interpretation *as an interruption of narrative* through the novel's interspersed images of Orlando, which include photographs of Vita Sackville-West. This scatter of images slyly and simultaneously defines Orlando as an individual, as an intertext for the biographer's narrative in the novel, and as a national or even international cluster of personae.) Woolf's strategic uses of interruption add an important aspect of informality to her narrative: It transforms the narrative from the formalized monopoly of a single narrating voice into a dialogue—or even a multilogue—among the biographer's perspective, different media, Orlando's various selves, and conversations with an imagined reader, which I will indicate, below. This mode is not an avoidance, but an unruly assertion that does not come "single and separate"; it gathers more weight with the combinations and diffusions of complex feelings that Woolf sees in the contemporary mind.

Moreover, *Orlando* occasionally deviates from these modes, producing a political and interpretive *impasse* that I will read as a function of wider tensions within modernism. Of course, several modernists—Conrad, Joyce, and Woolf herself—are uneasy with contemporary practices of empire and produce scathing critiques of oppression. However, they also sustain the cultural impulses within the machinery of empire (Joyce less than others, but even so). In *Orlando*, as in Joyce's later novels, cultural biases both suggest and undo themselves.[9] To illustrate this dynamic, I will focus mainly on Orlando's experiences in Turkey, but will link them with other parts of the text. Soon after arriving in Turkey, Orlando smells "sour odours [that] rose even to the heights of Pera itself and seemed the very breath of the strident multicoloured and barbaric population" (116). The obvious Orientalism here is almost immediately succeeded by the following passage:

> That he, who was English root and fibre, should yet exult to the depths of the heart in this wild panorama[,] should feel a passion of affection for the bright, unseasonable flowers, love the unkempt, pariah dogs beyond even his elk-hounds at home, and snuff the acrid ... smell of the street eagerly into his nostrils, surprised him. He wondered if, in the season of the Crusades, one of his ancestors had taken up with a Circassian peasant woman; thought it possible; fancied a certain darkness in his complexion; and, going indoors again, withdrew to his bath. (117)

Later, in other instances of the text's—but not Orlando's—ironic ambivalence, Orlando decides that gypsy embraces are almost surely insincere, but two Malay bears referenced earlier have "trusty hearts" (146, 107). Irony, then, offsets *and* sustains several moments in the text that are overtly xenophobic. However, as Paul de Man notes, "irony enforces the repetition of its aberration"—the irony of *Orlando* cannot be arrested (de Man, *Allegories of Reading*, 301). *Orlando* shows that we cannot read an ironic statement as merely one statement, and that it is necessarily multiple. The text's statements have an aberrant quality built into themselves, because they have their opposite or obverse built into themselves. Thus, the novel's irony has no decided, stable zone: It cannot be bound into a single interpretation or hermeneutic region. It has no abiding, singular narrative adherence or allegiance. In short, irony mirrors, and colludes with, *Orlando*'s cosmopolitanism, tracing several eccentric—and even self-contradictory—paths, and thus revealing what James Clifford and (after him) Bruce Robbins have called "discrepant cosmopolitanisms" (Clifford, 96–116; Robbins, 259).

Woolf structures her novel and her main character as a series of (sexual, aesthetic, conceptual, political, and ethical) revisions—Orlando and *Orlando* display major changes in the second half of the text. The latter half of the text is dominated by Orlando's perspective, rather than by the biographer's academic commentary and asides. However, it is, presumably, the biographer who is still narrating the text: In likely confirmation, the biographer has rejected (or strayed from) his or her earlier stated intention to "follow in the indelible footsteps of truth" and to report facts (49). While Orlando broods about being "alone" and moans about everything ending in death, these bleak views are transformed as Orlando herself/himself is transformed (34, 46). Discrepancies in Orlando's character are determined as much by external signs as by her/his psychological changes. Resonating with Foucault's insight on monstrosity as "a slight deviation," above, the novel shows that irregularity is as much a matter of character as of form: When the biographer interrupts his description of Orlando's coach-ride to London, the narrative turns to contemplate "a vacillation from one sex to another" in human character, as is also true of Orlando:

> For it was this mixture in her of man and woman, one being uppermost and then the other, that often gave her conduct an unexpected turn. The curious of her own sex would argue, for example, if Orlando was a woman, how did she never take more than ten minutes to dress? And were not her clothes chosen rather at random, and sometimes worn rather shabby? And then they would say, still, she has none of the formality of a man, or a man's love of power.
>
> (189)

Here, Orlando's psychological and sartorial inconsistencies are further signs of her femininity and informality.

For the cosmopolitan to be a cosmopolitan, her love of the local needs a sense of at least the limitations of her immediate surroundings. In *Orlando*, there is a complicated manifestation of this awareness. Orlando experiences a strong "scopic drive" (to borrow a concept from Jacques Lacan's "The Split between the Eye and the Gaze").[10] The drive to see propels—almost impels—Orlando to seek sights beyond the borders of the immediate and, frequently, the literal. For Orlando, this need to see is related to her art, to sexuality, and to geography. After she spots the Parthenon and the Acropolis while she is still in Turkey, the text stresses this need as an important appetite: "How good to eat!" exclaims Orlando while admiring the Turkish landscape (137).[11] Orlando is speaking the gypsy's language (presumably, Romany) and the narrator notes that the gypsies have no word for "beautiful," so Orlando's declaration of pleasure at the gratification of her scopic appetite has several simultaneous functions: At least, it makes a claim to its own linguistic sufficiency or superiority (in its insistence on the deficiency of the gypsy's language); it stresses Orlando's admiration of unfamiliar terrain; and it suggests a hungry sensuality bound up in that admiration. Woolf wryly notes that the powers of Orlando's "eyes were admirable" (138). Woolf also makes it clear through her irony that Orlando's vision cannot traverse the world as Orlando imagines it does during her time in Turkey. Woolf, therefore, questions the arrogant assumptions Orlando makes about the power of her vision. The text is aware of the constraints of Orlando's assumptions/vision, even as it plays with the fixity of places itself: At times, physical locations work as *literally* floating signifiers in the novel's cosmopolitan illogic. When Orlando arrives in Turkey, "domes seem to be afloat" (116). Punctuated with reminders of flaws in its main character's sight, the novel amplifies and complicates Orlando's rash cultural assumptions, and therefore reveals *its own awareness* to be more carefully cosmopolitan than Orlando's.

Such complication of Orlando's (and, more often, its narrator's) assumptions is merely one of the ways in which the novel relies on redirection or narrative fluctuation. In *The Myth of the Modern*, Perry Meisel notes that Woolf's career has three phases: the psychoanalytic, which ends with *To the Lighthouse*; the magic realist, which has its major iteration in *Orlando* (but I would contend that *Flush* is a part of it, too); and a more normative postmodern phase, which peaks in *Between the Acts*. If we agree with Meisel and call *Orlando* a magical realist text, we recognize the importance of redirection in the novel. Magical realism depends on an unexpected redirection of logical sequences and, in *Orlando*, even of sequential logic. As Orlando continues her traversal of centuries, the scene for the novel's actions is, of course, only an external, material geography where physical acts take place, but also time and the self as phenomenological and psychological locations. As Orlando enumerates and rehearses her selves mentally in the novel's second half, we find a rare inclusion of the pungent informality afforded by slang in Woolf's works. Orlando questions her own snobbery (echoing one of Woolf's repeated questions about her own snobbery) in an exchange that unfolds through a dialogue in her own mind and, supplementing that dialogue, can even be read as a multilogue with an imagined reader, as follows:

> A snob am I? ... My ancestors? Proud of them? Yes! Greedy, luxurious, vicious? Am I? (here a new self came in). Don't care a damn if I am. Truthful? I think so. Generous? Oh, but that don't count (here a new self came in).
>
> (227)

Tinges of vulgar speech offset Orlando's defensive view of her snobbery during this consideration, pointing ironically to tendencies of language, thought, and behaviour that snobs might want to conceal. The absence of Orlando's recognition of these tendencies here shows, by its very lack, the novel's awareness of unregistered, fugitive relations—even of the self with its own past. After listing Orlando's several assertions about Victorian literature, the biographer declares, "[A]nd so at last she reached her final conclusion, which was of the highest importance, but which, as we have already passed ... six lines, we must omit" (278). The rapid listing of months and selves to suggest casually the passage of time furthers the novel's practice of deflections and redirections—which themselves form relations of fluctuating strength and duration. These include the multiplication of signs (even presumably unwanted ones, as in the quickly passed-over colloquial phrase) in a process of rapid, recognized or unrecognized the world's influence on thought and identity.

Supplementing this procession of relations with philosophical subtlety near *Orlando*'s ending, the text's use of promiscuous metaphor—of carrying objects beyond their boundaries—is clearly an act of relation. For Jacques Derrida and for Gayatri Spivak, the acknowledgement of the relatedness of the world is expressed through the process of what Derrida calls *mondialization* or "worlding."[12] In her *Critique of Postcolonial Reason*, Spivak defines "worlding" as "the reinscription of a cartography that must (re)present itself as impeccable" (228). If it is a reinscription, it is a revision, and a corruption, in a sense. Corruption and contamination become forms of "worlding." In an informally gleeful and ironic instance of this, Orlando craves Rustum's pipe, "filled though it was with cow-dung" (136). Cosmopolitan relation is, by definition, a form of mingling and, therefore, impure, vulnerable, and open—informality makes it more so. In the final paragraph of "The Leaning Tower" (a paper that she read to the Workers' Educational Association of Brighton in May 1940), Woolf urges her audience to subvert exclusive impulses through the means of art, in general, and literature, in particular:

> Let us trespass at once. Literature is no one's private ground; *literature is common ground. It is not cut up into nations; there are no wars there.* Let us trespass freely and fearlessly and find our own way for ourselves. It is thus that English literature will survive this war and cross the gulf—*if commoners and outsiders like ourselves make that country our own country*, if we teach ourselves how to read and to write, how to preserve, and how to create.
>
> (181; emphases mine)

This non-fictional assertion is anticipated in the "fictional" assertions of *Orlando*. The novel's deflections and exuberant support for the corruptions of "worlding" signal the longing for ecstasy that Orlando repeatedly announces. This is a Utopian ecstasy: As it highlights the "intoxicated sense" that Woolf's narrator craves in "The Mark on the Wall," this is a mobility produced by the unshackling of institutionalized, orthodox pressures. Making a claim for such liberation, Woolf's novel performs an aleatory gesture—the simultaneously self-affirming and identity-dissolving gambit of the cosmopolitan.

In a discussion of Woolf's attendance at the legal trial of Radcliffe Hall's *Well of Loneliness* as a potential witness on the book's behalf, Christine Froula writes that Woolf found herself impressed by the reason of the law, its astuteness, its formality:

> Here have we evolved a very remarkable fence between us & barbarity; something commonly recognised; half humbug & ceremony therefore—when they pulled out calf bound books & read old phrases I thought this; & the bowing & scraping made me think it; but in these banks runs a live stream. What is obscenity? What is literature? What is the difference between the subject & the treatment? In what cases is evidence allow-able?
>
> (Woolf, quoted in Froula, 10)

Here, Woolf's appreciation of *formality* as a "fence" keeping out "barbarity" is very different from the formality she repeatedly deplores in domestic occasions and sexual relations. As Froula argues, "It is 'the reason of the law'—as institution, abstract rule, deliberative procedure—and not the 'rational individual' that she finds 'a remarkable fence' against barbarity" (10). The reaction that Froula quotes nonetheless clarifies Woolf's ambivalent attitudes on race, which complicate the informal cosmopolitanism in her novels. As brief evidence of this, recall Orlando's farewell to the gypsies (146). Their embraces, the narrative suggests, were truly insincere or could be taken as such.

Ambivalences, as well as affective and emotional fluctuations, inflect the exuberance that critics have projected on *Orlando*, citing Woolf's own description of it as a "lark." Clearly, the novel indulges its restless will through informal means to aesthetic freedom: insinuations, ellipses, irony, and play that liberate it from the strictures of classical aesthetics. Into this textual romp, Woolf weaves gestures to death, not with customary gloom, formal solemnity, ceremonious rhetoric, or even an extended focus on its spectral effects (as in the "Time Passes" section of *To the Lighthouse*). She shows death in Orlando not with bitterly mordant humour, but, mirroring her views on the hybridity of modern emotions in "The Narrow Bridge of Art, with humour that is playful and sympathetic, at the same time. The novel takes several postmodern turns as it exhibits what Jean-François Lyotard saw as a signature of the postmodern: a refusal of "the solace of good forms" (81). In its refusal of such solace, Woolf's novel does not express simple mourning, even in its depictions of death during the Great

Frost (33–4) and the freezing of the old "bumboat woman, who was carrying her fruit to market" (36). In her portrayal of the latter, Woolf adds social criticism, again not in open rage, but with trenchant irony:

> The old bumboat woman, who was carrying her fruit to market on the Surrey side, sat there in her plaids and farthingales with her lap full of apples, for all the world as if she were about to serve a customer, though a certain blueness about the lips hinted the truth. 'Twas a sight King James specially liked to look upon, and he would bring a troupe of courtiers to gaze with him. In short, nothing could exceed the brilliancy and gaiety of the scene by day. But it was at night that ... to the fine music of flute and trumpet the courtiers danced.
>
> (36)

The sequence in this casual digression from the uncannily vibrant image of the dead woman to that of the oblivious festivities of the elite here is crucial to convey Woolf's use of interruptive informality for her critique of social neglect and forgetting. The flitting, veiled qualities of grief in the passage intensify its mourning and anger by promiscuous means.[13] Here, the text drifts rapidly into tones that could be read as frivolous or delighted, giving its anger a gravity through the informal devices of misleading registers.

Through such strategies, the novel's peculiarities include a combination of mourning (both a reflection and complication of Orlando's own spasmodic morbidity) and play, which transmits an uncanny melancholy that has received substantial scholarly attention in recent decades. Woolf's sophisticated twining of these contrasts complicates her earlier, less qualified—though still formally daring—treatments of death, mourning, and many of the epistemological problems they entail. Studying such treatment in her essay "Virginia Woolf and the Death of Modernism," Jacqueline Rose argues, "Loss of belief may represent a new freedom, but Woolf shares with Freud the conviction that it is also a danger and a threat" (75). She then asks, "[W]hat is Freud doing when he makes ambivalence a peculiarity of the melancholic?" (76). Rose reminds us that "Freud himself was the one who most convincingly argued that the object which has been murdered is precisely the one which is most mourned, that murdering an object is the start of identification and not the end" (77). She follows this note, however, with another pungent question: "What limits is Freud packing around the idea of mourning?" (77). In reply, Rose asserts that "to side with [Woolf's] reason is to sidestep the thread of her writing which unwinds, unbearably and at the risk of what she herself more than once called her own 'madness,' from the place of the dead" (77). Rose's main contention is this: "Virginia Woolf's life and writing can be read as the creative response to Freud's anxious imperative—only in so far as there can be no end to it, only if the end is pre-given, let mourning begin" (78–9). Through a reading of Rachel Vinrace's death in *The Voyage Out*, Rose demonstrates how Woolf liberates mourning in her novel through an audaciously incisive proposition. Observing that "madness might … be the unacknowledged codeword for death" in debates about Woolf's sanity, Rose sees Woolf's art and modernism itself as suggesting analogous conditions of epistemological, psychological, physical, and spatial derangement: "[m]odernism … as a way of refusing appropriate relations of presence and absence which should hold between the living and the dead" (82, 84).

Extending the analogy, Rose offers a beautiful definition of the unconscious as a theatre for such play of learning and lack: "Knowledge with a foretaste of its own ignorance, or knowledge brushing at its limits, would be one way of defining the unconscious" (87). Orlando the character and the novel display such knowledge in the absurdly joint appearance or apparitions of Shelmerdine and a wild goose (respectively, promiscuous symbols for absolute love and the pursuit of absolute meaning as a "wild goose chase") at the novel's ending. In a claim that could be transposed to explain Orlando's transcentennial existence as the endurance of literary influence that continues to mark a modern, Rose proposes that haunting, "or being haunted, might indeed be another word for writing" (87). With its astringent dual recognitions of mortality and the endurance of written works, Woolf's later work does not sever its sympathy for mourning. However, its informality couching its sympathies while sparing them overt morbidity and didacticism, *Orlando* unsettles the grimness and manifest anguish in Woolf's earlier treatment of death.

The agility of metaphors in the novel recalls the etymology of the word, "metaphor": *meta* + *pherein*: "borne across" or "carried beyond" reflects such passage. Mingling with the novel's variegated kinds of metaphorical transport, as discussed here, Orlando's literal transfers of sexual preference extend the novel's textual promiscuity: his lovers include Clorinda, Favilla, and Euphrosyne, quickly listed in the novel's early pages; Sasha; Shelmerdine; and the Archduke Harry/Archduchess Harriet. Woolf compacts many of the novel's own processes into the processes of Orlando's various erotic flirtations. Elaborating on sexual promiscuity's functions in his book *On Flirtation*, Adam Phillips paraphrases Freud to offer a description of free association: "Free association itself is the psychic act of relinquishing, as far is possible, one's slavish devotion to internal censors. It is one of the advantages of flirtation that it can protect us from idolatry" (xii). Considering the uncertainties that flirtation activates and sustains (there is no guarantee of sexual consummation in flirtation, itself), Phillips offers a provocative insight when he claims that flirtation is "an early version of the experimental life, of irreverence as curiosity" (xiv). He asks (and the question applies well to the ambiguities in Orlando's cosmopolitanism): "[D] oes flirtation merely enforce the rules it claims to disavow?" (xxiv). Phillips argues that it does not because of flirtation's open-ended uncertainties and its overt distance from morality. He concludes that "it is one of the virtues of flirtation that it avoids making a necessity of virtue. By unsettling preferences and priorities flirtation can add other stories to the repertoire by making room for them" (xxv). Phillips's insights have an uncanny resonance with the formal strategies and sophisticated attitudinal informality in *To the Lighthouse* and *Orlando*, despite the two novels' marked differences. Their narrative logic is built by means of brief suggestions and repetitions or permutations of words and conditions—in short, by promiscuous association.[14]

How does modernism interrogate barriers to such association? How does it criticize formality in domestic or social interactions? How does it see freedom restricted within domestic and social realms? How does modernist informality trace social hypocrisies? How does it expose ironies and barriers to association within conditions, arguments, and concepts that apparently welcome freedom—breezy performances of gender-inclusivity, statements of putative sympathy, and canonical notions of freedom, themselves?

Notes

1 See esp. pp. 175–99 in *Going Sane*.

2 Woolf herself struggles to explain such complexity, but provides hints of explanation in the sequence of her thoughts, as she contemplates her memories of her family's experience of their stays at St Ives in *Moments of Being*:

Figuratively I could snapshot what I mean by some image; I am a porous vessel afloat on sensation; a sensitive plate exposed to invisible rays; and so on. Or I fumble with some vague idea about a third voice; I speak to Leonard; Leonard speaks to me; we both hear a third voice. Instead of labouring all the morning to analyse what I mean, to discover whether I mean anything real, whether I make up or tell the truth when I see myself taking the breath of these voices in my sails and tacking this way and that through daily life as I yield to them, I note only the existence of this influence; suspect it to be of great importance; cannot find how to check its power on other people ... Which of the people watching the incendiary bomb extinguished on the hill last night would understand what I mean if they read this? – I erect a finger post here, to mark a vein I will some time try to work out; and return to the surface; that is St Ives. (133)

Echoing the moments of recognition of her narrator in "The Mark on the Wall," Woolf's return to consciousness of her present—her immediate circumstances—seems to follow a chain of temporal proximity and impressions. Memories of St Ives lead her thoughts about idiosyncratic notions of "great importance," which, in turn, make her consider an event from the past day, apparently drawing her closer to—and, eventually, into—a consideration of the present that still addresses a recollection, and seems still haunted by the past. The resulting use of the present tense in reference to a place in memory and so in the past ("that *is* St Ives") *after* her "return to the surface" of the present is significant for a reading of the unstable geometry of what Auerbach and Rancière might call a "random moment."

3 Woolf's writing sustains such resistance to imposed desires and norms. She writes famously in her journal entry for March 19, 1919, "And more & more I come to loathe any dominion of one over another; any leadership, any imposition of the will" (256).

4 Aware of the coalescence of sexualities and genders in Orlando, I will mostly refer to this character here with the pronouns "she"/"her"/"hers," both for the sake of space and to employ words in which the pronoun "he" uneasily and improperly sits. For similar reasons, in discussions of moments when the charac-

ter appears as a boy or young man in the novel, I mostly employ male pronouns to refer to him.

5 For a succinct history of political theories on cosmopolitanism, see Robert Fine and Robin Cohen's essay, "Four Cosmopolitan Moments" (Vertovec and Cohen, pp. 136–62).

6 Blending force with evocation, slogans of nationalism ("Long Live the Queen!," "Go, Stars and Stripes!," "The Indian Tiger will crush the Limey!") employ metonyms precisely for the expression of aggressive insularity.

7 In his classic *The Ideology of the Athenian Metic*, David Whitehead contests Johannes Hasebroek's "primitivist manifestos," which, according to Whitehead, enumerate the different rights and privileges of Athenian citizens and metics in a dichotomy that is "demonstrably overdrawn" (117). Whitehead scrupulously shows the complexity and varying degrees of the metics' belonging in the Athenian city-state, in a rich analogy for historical variations in cosmopolitan intensity and engagements. See Whitehead's book for a brilliant study of the metics' conditions in classical Athens, and Fine and Cohen's essay for a concise summary on the role of the metics in the city-state.

8 Christine Froula glosses Woolf's investment in civilization as one asserting Kantian morality, Wolfe sees Woolf's as restoring an essence to feminism. However, *Orlando* disrupts the stability of those concepts with its reminders of flux: everything is partly something else.

9 See Derek Attridge and Marjorie Howes's arguments about Joyce's colonial ambivalence in *Semicolonial Joyce*, and Joyce's own ironic and anxious use of a mysterious sexuality in figures of Oriental male otherness (for instance, "Turko the Terrible" in *Ulysses* and his reappearance, alongside Alibaba and the forty thieves, in *Finnegans Wake*).

10 In his essay, Lacan adds this third drive—the drive to see—to the sex drive and death drive that Freud views as psychological impellers.

11 The mingling of *wanderlust* and whim in this scene strongly echoes the following thoughts, from Nancy's perspective, in *To the Lighthouse*:

> There was something, of course, that people wanted; for when Minta took her hand and held it, Nancy, reluctantly, saw the whole world spread out beneath her, as if it were Constantinople seen through a mist, and then, however heavy-eyed one might be, one must needs ask, "Is that Santa Sofia?" "Is that the Golden Horn?" So Nancy asked, when Minta took her hand. "What is it that she wants? Is it that?" And what was that? Here and there emerged from the mist (as Nancy looked down upon life spread beneath her) a pinnacle, a dome; prominent things, without names.
>
> (74)

The open-ended desire for relations, and investment in the persuasiveness of phenomenological (rather than empirical) experience, in these scenes recall the informal potential of the "random occurrence" that both Rancière and Auerbach see as the "principle" of Woolf's work.

12 In a 1999 speech to UNESCO, Derrida offered the French word *mondialisation* as one that should resist its translation and its supposed English and German equivalents: "globalization" and *Globalisierung*. *Mondialisation* is a term that has gained bloated and blunted significance through casual use, which necessitates a reconsideration of it and a *contract* (Derrida's italics) for a new education about it. It conceals a paradox that is both against the vilification and beatification of the term *mondialisation*: Certain unprecedented, unchallengeable factors justify the concept of globalization and are marked by massive techno-scientific changes—the circulation of people, commodities, modes of production, and

sociopolitical models; the more-or-less regulated opening up of the world economy—but the opening of borders, the progress of legislation, esp. the practice of international law, and the displacements of sovereignty that globalization "calls forth" depend less than ever on techno-scientific knowledge or power as such (373). That is, *mondialization* is a preferable term because, as is widely recognized, under the triumphalist heading of "globalization," the homogenization, or supposedly equal spread of opportunity worldwide, hides historic and new inequalities and hegemonies (what Derrida calls *homo-hegemonizations*).

13 In *Dying for Time*, Hägglund reads mourning itself as a promiscuous act, fusing fidelity and infidelity. It is an act of fidelity:

> since it stems from the attachment to a mortal other and from the desire to hold on to this mortal other. On the other hand, mourning is an act of infidelity, since one can only mourn if one has decided to live on without the other and thus leave him or her or it behind. This betrayal is certainly unavoidable—the only alternative to surviving the other is to kill oneself and thereby kill the memory of the other as well—but the violence of living on is nonetheless real.
>
> (117)

14 As Deborah Parsons glosses Woolf's essay "Street Haunting" in a chapter on the creative engagement of the flaneuse with urban public spaces, she suggests precisely such promiscuous association, noting that Woolf's narrator in the essay functions as "an enormous eye" that "put[s] on briefly for a few minutes the bodies and minds of others" (27).

2 Marking Absence

Mansfield's Feminine Informality vs. Lockean Liberalism

Katherine Mansfield's "Bliss" keeps indeterminate the precise relations between past experience and current sensations or thoughts. Especially when the story presents Bertha Young's negotiation of intense experience (ecstasy in the case of this discussion), the correlation between ecstatic pleasure and plot-based pain, if you like, remains evocative, rather than specific. These relations are not literalized by a simple causality, but linked to a sense of overwhelming, a sense linked to the grandeur or largeness, coupled with terror or pain, that classical and Enlightenment theories emphasize as a signature of the sublime. While there is no grand heroic gesture or encounter with an immense natural force in "Bliss," Mansfield's story, nevertheless, deftly engages the sublime by frequently fusing evocations of the sublime with a scalar departure from the grandeur associated with sublimity: It convolutes the direct proportion or implicit equivalency of, on the one hand, the size of sources displaying sublimity, and, on the other, the intensity of the ecstatic pleasure or bliss that they provoke.[1] This chapter will focus on the complex workings of this convolution in "Bliss."

Feeling "a little shower of sparks" radiate from her ecstasy at the beginning of "Bliss," Bertha Young traces the source of the shower to a sensation of having "suddenly swallowed a bright piece of the late afternoon sun" (145). In this strange mapping of sensation, Bertha feels not as if she has swallowed the sun itself, but a part of the sun that remains active within her: the "bright piece ... burned your bosom, sending out a little shower of sparks," which recurs in images of fire and burning across the story (145).[2] The sense of derangement and natural displacement here reflects the confusion that Bertha senses has no adequate expression in standardized language and formal sobriety: Immediately after feeling the sparks of bliss, she wonders, "Is there no way you can express it without being 'drunk and disorderly'?" (145). Considering intoxication as the only condition of expressive adequacy to describe the sublime, the question evokes the confused imagination that the ecstatic experience catalyzes. Bliss produces not only a sense of inadequate representation, but also disorientating inversions of scale (as is further evident in Bertha's ensuing contemplation of a table that seems to "melt" into dusky light and a glass dish) (146). As she processes this sense

DOI: 10.4324/9781003009894-3

through a series of inconsistent images, Bertha is overcome by this strong, ineluctable sensation of bliss, but she also feels as if she herself has "swallowed" its source. Thus, she thinks of herself as being the container of the source, but under its power and unable to contain its overwhelming force, at the same time. Jean-François Lyotard reminds us in his appendix to *The Postmodern Condition* (1979) that, for Immanuel Kant, the sublime sentiment is "a strong and equivocal emotion: it carries with it both pleasure and pain" (77). Lyotard adds, "Better still, in it, pleasure derives from pain [and] this contradiction, which some would call neurosis or masochism, develops as a conflict between the faculties of a subject, the faculty to conceive of something and the faculty to 'present' something" (77). However, while we can indeed conceive of sublime immensity or infinity our imagination cannot present such vastness to us, producing an epistemological crisis that resembles Bertha Young's own failures to find correspondence for her dizzying internal "crises" in the facts of her "external" life.

Classical literary criticism on the sublime confirms this sense of disorientation in encountering the sublime. According to Longinus, the sublime ecstasy that grandeur produces in us overwhelms—rather than persuades—us, drawing from us "amazement and wonder" that "get the better of [us]" (143; 2008).[3] There is a manifest violence to such overwhelming: As Longinus puts it, "Sublimity tears up everything like a whirlwind ... at a single blow" (144; 2008). In other translations, "thunderbolt" or "bolt of lightning" replace the word 'whirlwind" (1965, 1995). The violent effect is, nonetheless, linked with grandeur in the sublime. The sublime oration or poetic moment can convey itself or heroic action as embodied, physical action and further, as Stephen Halliwell (2012) suggests, as "an intrinsic 'greatness of mind/spirit' [that] requires an intuition of eternity to function in this context as a symbolic correlate of the unlimited powers of the human mind, the infinite (extra-cosmic) reach of thought itself" (357).

In the *Critique of Judgment* (1790), Kant divides this possibly-joint signification of infinity and physical grandeur from sublime objects into two kinds: the "mathematical sublime"—related to vastness or profusion, producing a feeling of infinitude in quantity—and the "dynamic sublime," related jointly with a feeling of vulnerability in terror before overwhelming force and pleasure because such terror is experienced from a safe vantage.[4] In "Bliss," Bertha struggles with variants of these two categories for sublimity: bourgeois prosperity as the mathematical sublime, which works through serial accumulation, and sexual or sensuous freedom as the dynamic sublime. Her concomitant sense of inadequacy partly reflects that of the viewer's or listener's sense of inadequacy before the sublime (as noted by Longinus, Kant, and Edmund Burke), as well as an awareness of wholes unavailable to human imagination and representation (as noted more recently by Lyotard and Neil Hertz).

Such unavailability aggravates Bertha's perplexity not only through gestures to dizzy exultation or overwhelming vastness: Mansfield questions the latter through an inversion of scale, repeatedly evoking the removal of *small* details, both through Bertha's responses to others and through the gaps in her evaluation of her own experience. "Bliss" shows how such elision abets both the production of grandeur and the confusion in presumed ecstasy and bourgeois bliss. As Bertha tries to reconcile these, she lacks what Hertz calls "a compensatory positive movement" in the Kantian encounter with the sublime—"the mind's exultation in its own rational faculties, in its ability to think a totality that cannot be taken in through the senses" (40). Bertha's exultation founders *en route* to thinking a totality: The obliviousness in her bliss brings her to repeated interpretive exhaustion, which she then reads unidirectionally, either as a problem in her own character or as an appreciable sign (see my discussions of her self-descriptions as "absurd" and "too happy," and of her responses to Harry's buoyancy, below). However, "Bliss" itself is insistently aware of the paradox in claiming bliss or ecstatic pleasure in the face of the disorientations that Bertha's sense of domestic sublimity provokes.

Burke's theorizations of the sublime implicitly display this paradox in *A Philosophical Enquiry into the Order of Our Ideas of the Sublime and the Beautiful* (1757).[5] Even in this work from an early stage in his career, magnitude signals greatness for Burke. Evoking science, Burke argues in the *Enquiry* that, if the rays a retina receives

> vary their nature, now to blue, now to red, and so on, or their manner of termination as to a number of petty squares, triangles, or the like, at every change, whether of colour or shape, the organ has a sort of … rest, but this relaxation and labour, so often interrupted, is by no means productive of ease; neither has it the effect of vigorous and uniform labour.
>
> (125)

It is, instead,

> a teasing [sic] fretful employment, which at once wearies and weakens the body … by continually altering [its] tenor and direction [to] prevent that species of uniform labour which is allied to strong pain, and causes the sublime. The sum total of things of various kinds … should equal the number of uniform parts composing some *one* entire object.
>
> (125–26)

Importantly, Burke's accommodation of variety comes with a demand for the uniformity of parts to compose a greater whole. Size matters here, not only because a work ethic that stretches itself has its reward in sublimity, but because Burke sees a lack of magnitude as equivalent with a lack of effect and worth:

> The mind in reality hardly ever can attend diligently to more than one thing at a time: if this thing be little, the effect is little … the mind

> is bounded by the bounds of the object; and what is not attended to, and what does not exist, are much the same in effect; but the eye or the mind (for in this case there is no difference) in great uniform objects does not readily arrive at their bounds; it has no rest, whilst it contemplates them; the image is much the same every where [*sic*]. So that every thing great by its quantity must necessarily be one, simple and entire.
>
> (126)

There is a literalism driving Burke's theses, one that prefers size and wants greatness externalized, seeking merit manifest in size. The effect of the little is little, within the logic here. This is overwhelmingly the case, even when Burke notes that:

> as the great extreme of dimension is sublime, so the last extreme of littleness is in some measure sublime likewise ... we become amazed and confounded at the wonders of minuteness; nor can we distinguish in its effect this extreme of littleness from the vast itself.
>
> (66)

Burke's gesture to the possible sublimity of "littleness" is lost with that final clause: "we distinguish in its effect this extreme of littleness from the vast itself." The absence (or difficulty) of the effort to maintain an awareness of this difference allows Burke to reinstate the predominance of the large in his valuation of greatness by quantity. This greatness is not only immense, but it is "necessarily one, simple and entire." The ironic coexistence of uniformity and a lack of perceptual rest justifies Burke's equation of size, simplicity, and greatness. Bertha's own thoughts reflect this "uniformizing" view of plenitude when, eliding the very possibility of alternatives or exceptions to the satisfactions of her bourgeois life, she thinks, "Really—really—she had everything" (148).

Hypnos and Hypnosis

Let me comment briefly on the role of smallness or "littleness" in Burke's and Kant's arguments. For Kant, "*the sublime is that in comparison with which everything else is small*" (88; italics Kant's). According to this logic, sublime feeling dominates our experience, overwhelming registration as a Longinian "whirlwind" or "thunderbolt." Overwhelmed, we do not register the small: We suspend nuanced reading and ignore details, as is evident in "Bliss," when Bertha verges on recognizing or even expressing helpful details, but is unable to reach such insights as she faces the versions of sublimity that agonize her. Rather, she seems to intuit her inability when contemplating the mathematical sublimity to which she has access and thinks, "I'm absurd. Absurd!" (148–9). Such indication of aporiae equips "Bliss" to subtly trace—rather than explicitly state—what is unavailable in Bertha's experience. Mansfield, thus, reveals the *lack* in sublimity that classical depictions see as semiotic plenitude that exceeds or renders superfluous the registration of the small in the aggressive flood of sublimity. Affect, rather than conscious thought, is Mansfield's critical aid in such mapping of absence. Longinus discourses on the spoken sublime—that is, sublimity in spoken or narrated forms; Mansfield attends to the unspoken, the unconscious, and the *felt*, rather than the seen. Lacking the exteriority of performative display, Bertha's sense of the sublime gains a psychological urgency in "Bliss."

The story makes clear that, within Bertha's circumscribed world, the sublime functions as the misread; it is not so much a source for pleasure as a sign of what is unavailable to Bertha. Mirroring the experience of the sublime that imposes a sense of our representational limits, Bertha experiences sublime ecstasy when both sensing and more self-consciously considering norms of bourgeois domestic success as the sublime. *The Oxford English Dictionary* gives the etymology for "ecstasy" as follows: "to put out of place—the classical senses of ἔκστασις [*ekstasis*] are 'insanity' and 'bewilderment'; but in late Greek the etymological meaning received another application, viz., 'withdrawal of the soul from the body, mystic or prophetic trance.'" If the very etymology and classical connotations of ecstasy suggest that an ecstatic mind is "put out of place," then Bertha's ecstatic experience in her home—in her proper "place," if you will—offers a plangent irony. Combining opposed emotions, its supposed transportive power serves only to make Bertha feel more constrained and astonished by pain. Aggravating the problem, there is no single or clearly identified source or force that is responsible for the sublime pain and panic acting upon Bertha in "Bliss": The fluctuating and conjoined pressures of marriage, domesticity, property, maternity, repressed sexuality, bourgeois social interactions, and consumer culture obviate a simple transfer of correspondences between causes and effects.

Sublimity's unbrookable surfeit of signs (which Burke and Kant rationalize into uniformity) does not permit its audience temporal or intellectual sufficiency to trace such correspondence, making the audience's "knowledge" inadequate and partial, at best. Such a view effects the reduction of the subject experiencing the sublime and the hyper-formalization of the sublime itself into largeness and even grandeur, as it is for Longinus. The asymmetry produces the restlessness and desperation that, as I will show later here, the formal sophistication of Mansfield's story reflects an ethical argument to unpack the grandeur of privileged form in classical and bourgeois models of happiness. Intense sensation agitates Bertha into an evaluation of her emotions: she reads such sensation against the standards of a received index of happiness, as emblematized in her inventory of bourgeois satisfaction. A strenuous happiness in her conscious thoughts loses repeatedly to her bewilderment about her life. The Greek word for the sublime, *hypnos*, shares an etymological node with the words "hypnosis" and "hypnotized": the combining form of the Greek ὕπνος or "sleep." This etymological genealogy hints that the strong sensation of sublimity is the result of something like stilled curiosity, curiosity that the vacuity and evacuations of strong feeling in bourgeois domesticity deny to Bertha. After she considers the intense smell of jonquils in her living room, she enters a simultaneously aesthetic and introspective evaluation of sensation: "How strong the jonquils smelled in the warm room. Too strong? Oh, no. And yet, as though overcome, she flung down on a couch and pressed her hands to her eyes" and, immediately, she murmurs, "I'm too happy–too happy!" (148). At this juncture of confused emotions and overwhelming sensation, the story tellingly links Bertha's sense of inadequacy to a sense of excess: the "too strong" jonquils are a marker that she has violated some border of optimal happiness and is, therefore, undeserving or unable to bear the happiness she feels. Through the leaps and gaps in Bertha's self-implicating interpretation, Mansfield makes clear that Bertha's "excessive" happiness is defined by hasty reading.

The "Hertzian Sublime": "Un-insulating" Dissatisfaction

In short, Mansfield conveys psychological and semiotic mobility by exploring the immobilization and separation of smaller nuances in Bertha's evaluation of her circumstances. The story shows such immobilization of signs within the local or the domestic when it suggests Bertha's neglect of Harry's fondness for ostensibly candid crudeness (with his offhand references to "pure flatulence" or "kidney disease") and of a cannibalistic aspect to his appetites (for "the white flesh of the lobster" or "pistachio ices" that remind him of "the eyelids of Egyptian dancers") (148, 152). Such scenes turn habitual response stasis into figural explorations of what is unspeakable and inescapable, at the same time. Bertha reads her own affective intensity through figures: "a little shower of sparks" and a "bright piece" of the sun, emerging from a "bright glowing place" in her bosom (145). As her helpless focus on *parts* suggests, interpreting or narrating sublime experience is an attempt to link metonymically aspects of the overwhelming semiotic rush that sublimity unleashes. This is overt in her list of metonyms for bourgeois satisfaction (which peaks with her cook who makes "the most superb omelettes"), each metonym becoming a figure for the larger sublime force acting upon her.

Reading the relation between sublime and figurative language in Neil Hertz's redefinition of sublimity, Jonathan Culler explains in his essay "The Hertzian Sublime":

> The indefinite plurality, threatening to the integrity of the self, is tropologically reduced to a single opposing force which can be recognized in a one-to-one confrontation and give rise to the dialectical recuperation ... But Hertz shows that this is a specular rather than a dialectical process. The reduction is sought by consciousness to master an epistemological

> threat to the status and integrity of the subject by misrecognizing it as a structured conflict *between* subjects. The compensatory positive movement of the mind that has been checked is not just a *result* of the confrontation of the sublime but its telos, what the mind was seeking in the first place.
>
> (977)

Culler proceeds to identify this "brilliant conversion of the Longinian and Kantian sublime to an economy of the sublime that pervades the most trivial scenarios of the self" as "the Hertzian sublime" (977). Noting Hertz's interest in Longinus's "transfers of power" from the sublime actions of gods and heroes to the sublime articulations of the texts or poets that describe them, Culler writes that, within instances of sublimity in Longinus's text, "the subtle metonymic echoes between one citation and another ... work to build up a pattern of linkage between the actions of gods and heroes ... and the sublime speech acts of poets" (973). Given the objects in her list of things worth having (a marriage between "pals"; money; "modern" friendships, garnished with books and music; house and garden; and a new, skilled cook), Bertha Young has the metonyms for bourgeois mathematical sublimity to transfer to herself in "Bliss." However, instead of directly conveying the sublime into her life, when Mansfield puts Bertha in the position of a reader interpreting the accumulated material of bourgeois "sublimity," Bertha is trying to gauge why she feels the burning pain of her assumed ecstasy—in one of the story's prominent ironies, she tries to interpret what such bourgeois bliss *lacks* at the same time as she thinks, "Really—really—she had everything" (148). The moment points to the contradictory temporal dimension of material ownership that Sara Ahmed has analyzed as follows:

> If objects provide a means for making us happy, then in directing ourselves toward [an] object, we are aiming somewhere else: toward a happiness that is presumed to follow. The temporality of this does matter. Happiness is what would come after. Given this, happiness is directed toward certain objects, which point toward that which is not yet present.
>
> (26)

This is the view of happiness that "Bliss" asserts. Mansfield's deft relation of parts gives her story an enthymemic form—a form that asserts its arguments evocatively, rather than explicitly. This stands in subversive contrast to the violence of the sublime, a violence that guarantees the sundering of our interpretive capacities from sublime thunderbolts, *a priori*. For the text itself, Bertha's unease and confusion provide ways of implying, rather than explicitly stating, an ethics of dissatisfaction.[6] Dissatisfaction appears as Bertha's yearning for change, but not as an *acknowledged* appetite for surprise, in the story. From the beginning of "Bliss," Bertha craves unfamiliar experience: She has an "air of anticipation, waiting for something ... divine to happen ... that must happen ... infallibly" (145). Surrendering her agency to formulaic domesticity, she faces her burning agitations through nervous maternity, presumed marital bliss, and its devastating rupture, amid an anxious yearning for the certainty of unimaginable change. Her checklist for successful bourgeois life and her own estrangement from her baby provide metaphors for the confusion in these priorities, as well as a negative inventory for the intensity of experience unavailable to her—an intensity that might indeed produce sublime pleasures, were it not pre-empted by Bertha's oscillations between ecstatic vagueness and painful, though always-incipient, analysis.[7]

"Subjective Correlatives": Sedation and Strong Feeling

Against such vague happiness or painful frustration, Mansfield pits small detail and nuance, fleeting moments and expressions as sources of the metaphysical and semiotic excess that Longinus, as well as Kant and Burke, attribute to the large. This is anything but to say that the smallness to which Mansfield gives such importance lacks *semiotic* immensity: Rather, it is to say that Mansfield's version of the small compacts what Stephen Halliwell describes as the "interlocking elements" of the Longinian sublime—intuition, emotion, and metaphysics (366). In light of this inversion of scale, Mansfield's version of sublimity operates on a kind of geometrical paradox: minutiae function as triggers for intuitive, emotional, and metaphysical immensity in "Bliss." This counterintuitive immensity alone, although alongside other factors (cultural diagnoses, gender relations, national and international histories, among them), rebuts T. S. Eliot's patronizing compliment that it is Mansfield's skilful use of "minimal" material that renders her work "feminine" (343, "[The Feminine Voice]").

For Eliot:

> The only way of expressing emotion in the form of art is by finding an 'objective correlative'; in other words, a set of objects, a situation, a chain of events which shall be the formula of that *particular* emotion; such that when the external facts, which must terminate in sensory experience, are given, the emotion is immediately evoked.
>
> (48, "Hamlet")

In giving the location of emotion such emphasis and such restriction simultaneously, Eliot both stresses the importance of psychology and simplifies it. His stress on correlatives as *objective* delimits their semiotic possibilities within his interpretive system, which Mansfield pries open with her symbolist shifts, associative subjectivity, and uncertainties. In Mansfield's work, however, these "external facts" or forms of "surplus" (dissatisfactions or unease as oblique signs of social pressure, for instance) are ethical assets, suggestive artistic engines that propel stories such as "Bliss."

In the story, the pear tree operates as an emblem of stasis and devastation in Bertha Young's life, with an unattributed speaker (presumably, but not necessarily, Bertha's consciously speaking self) echoing Pearl's murmured phrase:

> "Your lovely pear tree–pear tree–pear tree!"
> Bertha simply ran over to the long windows.
> "Oh, what is going to happen now?" she cried.
> But the pear tree was as lovely as ever and as full of flower and as still. (155)

The tree, which Pearl explicitly mentions to Bertha, has a vertiginous series of associations in the story: The story's formal associativity and mobility are emphatic analogues for the conditions that Bertha lacks. Sharply contrasting the restrictions of the Eliotic "objective correlative," Mansfield employs sublime ecstasy as a fertile "subjective correlative" in "Bliss," relating through impressionistic but figurative details and vivid "correlatives" that do not follow the one-to-one correspondence that Eliot orders, but, nevertheless, clarify and nuance the relations of Bertha's ecstasy or bliss with her anxiety and misconstrued reasons for disappointment at herself. For Eliot, such excess is, paradoxically, a deficiency, an artistic shortcoming; for Mansfield, it is an asset, an artistic engine that propels stories such as "Bliss." In a scene rich with metaphorical potential and nuance, to Bertha, the pear tree seems immune to both immaturity and decay: "Bertha couldn't help feeling … that it had not a single bud or a faded petal" (148). Alongside this figure of the "natural" or the unmediated or the undamaged:

> [d]own below, in the garden beds, the red and yellow tulips, heavy with flowers, seemed to lean upon the dusk. A grey cat, dragging its belly, crept across the lawn, and a black one, its shadow, trailed after. The sight of them, so intent and so quick, gave Bertha a curious shiver. (148)

That the cats have both intention and quickness seems to provoke Bertha into stammering, "What creepy things cats are!" (148). Soon after this paragraph, Bertha thinks her white and green outfit for the party "wasn't 'intentional'" (149). At these moments, Mansfield signals the absence or lack of intention as the absence of a will to action. Such absence functions as a pivot for Mansfield's exploration of normalized behaviour and entrenchment in the familiar versus proscribed, but liberating, choices that signal decisive, quick erotic intention, mobility, and desires that might be deemed animalistic or even feral.[8]

"Bliss" implies that the antidote for Bertha's pain lies in risking the strange or the unfamiliar, and erotic, alternatives to Bertha's established life: The cold of Pearl Fulton's arm signals the erotic pull of the unfamiliar, offsetting the painful heat that persists in Bertha. This is a pull that, Bertha recalls, she "always" feels from "beautiful women who had something *strange* about them" (149; italics mine). Mansfield leaves ambiguous the precise connotations of the word "strange," but the sentence obviously employs the word to underscore Bertha's unspoken erotic investment in the non-normative or the unaccustomed.

Bertha's potential relationship with each of these women is stifled by presumably heteronormative prohibitions on homosexual "inclination," to borrow Adriana Cavarero's term. Evoking Hannah Arendt's 1965 lectures on Kant (entitled "Some Questions of Moral Philosophy") at the New School, Cavarero stresses Arendt's note that "every inclination turns outward, it leans out of the self in the direction of whatever may affect me from the outside world" (5–6). Arendt's point not only reminds us that "the meaning of the word inclination points to a geometrical imaginary; it also, above all, clarifies that, in the theater of modern philosophy, center stage is occupied by an I whose position is straight and vertical" (6). In a description that would render Bertha's homoerotic fascination with "strange" women altogether "horizontal," Cavarero observes, "The 'upright man' of which the tradition speaks, more than an abused metaphor, is literally a subject who conforms to a vertical axis, which in turn functions as a principle and norm for its ethical posture" (6). Establishing norms as functions of his posture, the upright man admits to no deviation from probity in thought or action. In "Bliss," Harry's buoyant candour and zest are mimetically "modern" performances of such probity that his furtive affair with Pearl Fulton reveals not only to be false, but also the negative of Bertha's nervous but unrealized extramarital sexual interest in women. The inertia silencing this interest partly fuels Bertha's anxieties—she does not *express* such interest nor her suspicion that Pearl Fulton's frankness was limited—and, as corollaries, her disappointments and uncertainties, as well as her deflections of her own desire (148). We get the first sign of such deflection near the story's beginning when she asks (in free indirect discourse), "Why be given a body if you have to keep it shut up in a case like a rare, rare fiddle?" and answers herself with "No, that about the fiddle is not quite what I mean" (148). Bertha's self undergoes an unsettling that further explains the absent attribution for some pieces of speech in "Bliss"—the absence of attribution reflects a non-attributable self, as Bertha faces, in Cavarero's words, a "thrust of inclination [that] knocks the I from its internal center of gravity and, by making it lean to the outside[,] undermines its stability" (6).

In a sense, Bertha herself considers her own experiences as external to her, as reflected in yet another of her thoughts about the pear tree: "And she seemed to see on her eyelids the lovely pear tree with its wide open blossoms as a symbol of her own life" (148). The tree appears here as afterimage and rationalized analogue, which the story gradually seems to offer as an emblem (with its "wide open blossoms") of what Bertha's life lacks, as well as the sedated quality of her life, if we note the story's closing description of the tree ("lovely as ever and as full of flower and as still") and if we (following Bertha) read the tree as "becalmed" (148, 155, 148). As such, it offsets Bertha's own emotional upheavals while seeming to be forcibly calmed.

Submitting to sedation—agreeing to a process that renders one "becalmed"—is submitting to the action of allaying and assuaging, of another force *making* the agitated subject calm or quiet. This is a condition of mediated, sometimes enforced, calm that might offer itself as a route to ecstasy—but only with the numbing of the senses. The false offer produces the interpretive impasse in which Bertha finds herself at story's beginning and ending. Bertha considers the process of sedation itself—a sedate life—the source of sublimity while intuiting the lacunae and unavailability of alternatives in her life of putative bliss. The story clarifies the alternatives before her through a kind of negative logic: She could indeed experience not the Kantian dynamic sublime, but a dynamic pleasure, were she to engage details more closely, and—in the logic of the story—to consider, appreciate, and risk a break from the metonyms for her dissatisfaction: the marriage between "pals"; money; friendships marked by sniping gossip, self-absorption, and pretensions to cultural refinement; property; and the domestic sequestration of her priorities. The apparent absence of alternatives for Bertha in her paralysis reflects the impasse in her life of insulated interpretations, neglect of "littleness" or detail, and imagination, leaving an intuitive excess in the subjective correlatives of Bertha's ecstatic experience.[9] This ecstasy produces an effect that recalls the Late Greek etymological nuance for the word "ecstasy": "withdrawal of the soul from the body, mystic or prophetic trance." As the ending of "Bliss" repeats Pearl Fulton's comment on the pear tree from earlier in the story, Bertha's paralysis seems prophetic. The canonical theorizations of Longinus, Kant, and Burke do indeed associate the sublime with immensity, pleasure, and pain, but not with anguish—a sense verging on bereavement or terminal sorrow—as Mansfield does in "Bliss": In the absence of detailed recognitions, Bertha is at an imaginative loss by the story's ending. If the sublime agitates feeling, Mansfield, in contrast, leaves her story suspended amid subjective correlatives that evoke the loss (the pear tree, Bertha's unattributed penultimate comment, and the ending's resonance with Bertha's obliviousness, earlier in the story), with a foreboding that verges on decidedness. The story's last word, of course, is "still" (155).

What cultural priorities maintain this stillness? What kind of philosophical precursor lays the grounds for the domestic habits and priorities stifling Bertha Young? Mansfield's stories provide us evocative answers to these questions.

Absent Forms

In a well-known passage from Mansfield's "In the Botanical Gardens" (1907), the narrator walks out of the neatly arranged gardens into an unmediated landscape, senses hostile emanations emerging from it, and then thinks, "Shall I, looking intently, see vague forms lurking in the shadow staring at me malevolently, wildly, the thief of their birthright?" (10). Presumably, the birthright is freedom or a prior claim to the land, the exact location of which the narrative does not name. The "vague forms" that the passage evokes also lack precise identification in the narrative. Through the lack of facial or other detail for the human body in many of her stories, Mansfield suggests the transformation of women into disembodied psychologies and colonized people into shadows, projections, or even emanations—diminished, erased, or invalidated selves. Here I will read these transformations as functions of male colonial and liberal (more precisely, Lockean) priorities.

Exalted in the liberal philosophical canon, John Locke produces notions of male freedom and license for conquest that exercise both colonial and gendered oppression. Travelling from the seventeenth century to the twentieth through the vast influence of figures such as John Locke, Jean-Jacques Rousseau, and John Stuart Mill, liberal concepts are important to an understanding of Mansfield's work because, as dominant shapers of capitalist bourgeois modernity, they are crucial and influential sources for the bourgeois social and personal pressures that Mansfield's stories resist. Through a focus on the collaboration of overt statements and form in Mansfield's stories, I discuss here the liberal priorities that Mansfield unravels: the self supposedly liberated by the social contract; the idea of "natural freedoms" and rights—especially the right to happiness through the putative security, pleasures, and protections of property; the candour that the institution of modern marriage catalyzes; and the putative expansions of opportunity, social and sexual, for women within the liberal state.

Such concepts produce an often-unacknowledged and enduring violence in the name of liberal-colonial dominance, as well as liberal-bourgeois domestic obstructions, which Mansfield shows to be formalizations of male desires. Her stories evoke the rhetoric of liberalism to critique several liberal concepts and values variously, providing ripostes for their oppression through Mansfield's deployment of form. I will first examine Mansfield's uses of textual, somatic, and behavioural form as a critique of liberal links with colonialism; next, I will explore her formal moves to unpack liberalism's oppressive effects upon women; and then I will close this chapter with comments on Mansfield's endorsement of informality. What I call "liberal" here refers specifically to a Lockean version of liberalism, but, of course, its influence endures in various strains of later liberal thought: Duncan Bell has recently clarified the wide range of attitudes to empire expressed by liberal philosophers, while nevertheless recognizing that "few rejected all its forms, and most […] endorsed the formation of settler colonies" (6). Mansfield's work formally resists such endorsements by marking their consequent damage through absent bodies, speech, personhood, freedom of association, interpretation, and memory.

Contesting Locke and Colonization

The above-quoted moment from "In the Botanical Gardens"—with its evocation of rights and property through the notions of "birthright" and "theft"—and several other moments in Mansfield's stories (on which I focus, below) resonate strongly with Lisa Lowe's arguments on the paradoxes coded into liberal notions of freedom. In *The Intimacies of Four Continents*, Lowe reads the conjoined, collaborative effects of colonial and liberal classification thus:

> *Race* as a mark of colonial difference is an enduring remainder of the processes through which the human is universalized and freed by liberal forms, while the peoples who created the conditions of possibility for that freedom are assimilated or forgotten. [R]acial ... distinctions designate the boundaries of the human and endure as remainders attesting to the violence of liberal universality.
>
> (7; italics Lowe's)

Lowe stresses what she terms "the economy of affirmation and forgetting that structures ... liberal ways of understanding" and "civilizes and develops freedoms for 'man' in modern Europe and North America, while relegating others to ... spaces that are constituted as backward" while defining these "others" as "unfit for liberty" or "incapable of civilization" (3, 3, 7, 7).

In contrast, Locke's *Two Treatises of Government* (1689) reserves property for those who are "capable" of civilization, which, for him, has Christian faith and reason as its hallmarks. Locke declares in his first treatise, "Man has a *Natural Freedom*" and "all that share in the same common Nature, Faculties and Powers, are in Nature equal, and ought to partake in the common Rights and Privileges" (190; italics Locke's). However, his second treatise makes it clear that title to property is itself a function of right religious belief: "He that in Obedience to this Command of God, subdued, tilled and sowed any part of it, thereby annexed to it something that was his property, which another had no title to, nor could without injury take from him" (291). Lowe notes that, in classic liberal political narratives, the turn to political society from the state of nature is justified against the threat to human life and property in the natural condition of war, against which "[l]iberal government secures the 'peaceful' conditions of individual and collective security by transferring the violence of the state of nature to the political state" (8).

Encouraging this transfer, Locke includes a provision for rightful conquest as "an Absolute Power over the Lives of those, who by an Unjust War have forfeited them" (387). Leaving the state of nature for political society, the liberal citizen retains the right, in Locke's words, "to destroy a Man who makes War upon him" on the grounds that "such Men are not under the ties of the Common Law of Reason, have no other Rule, but that of Force and Violence, and so may be treated as Beasts of Prey[,] dangerous and noxious Creatures" (279). This repeal of others' humanity not only rationalizes conquest, but, for Locke, also cancels their claims to "natural freedom" and property. Lowe demonstrates at length how the liberal-colonial state drew on Locke's arguments for three main uses: to produce arguments about rightful conquest, to claim the right to (appropriated/"settled") property, and to justify the slave trade as an extension of the acquisition of property.[10]

Paradoxically, an acceptable life in Lockean liberal society *after* the acquisition of property entails further dissolutions of the self. According to Locke,

> Man is *naturally free* from subjection to any Government, tho' he be born in a place under its Jurisdiction. But if he disclaim the lawful Government of the country he was born in, he must also quit the Right [to inherited property] that belonged to him by the Laws of it, and the Possessions there descending to him from his ancestors.
>
> ('*Two Treatises*', 394; italics Locke's)

Such dissent, even though it comes from an individual whose humanity Locke does *not* seek to repeal, becomes another reason to invalidate claims to possessions or property. As Lowe reminds us, "At the end of the eighteenth century, political emancipation became a new form of human freedom, in which the individual person, dissolved into the concentrated sovereignty of the collectivity, became *human* through citizenship in the unity of political society" (14; italics Lowe's). Any aberration from such unity is, then, an aberration from liberal selfhood. This unity not only forbids its members to, in Locke's words, "disclaim the lawful Government of the country" of their birth, but, in its sanction for the destruction of infidels and demand for right belief, it also delimits possibilities of association with difference. Circumscription by, and acquiescence to, the liberal system work as prerequisites for selfhood in it.

The two stories by Mansfield that perhaps most vividly (though very differently) unpack the legacies of liberal circumscription through female characters' joint experience of colonialism and patriarchy are "The Daughters of the Late Colonel" (1920) and "How Pearl Button was Kidnapped" (1912). Haunted by their father's authority lifelong, the sisters Constantia and Josephine in "The Daughters of the Late Colonel" are mired in their father's expectations that they doggedly seek to maintain rather than resist, even after his death. The racial prejudices that they display (for instance, against imagined Sri Lankan mail-runners, on whom each sister projects different deficiencies and vices) are inextricable from the patriarchal thought-systems that the sisters internalize and that shape their goal of appropriateness at several points in the story (221). The sisters' domestic confinement in London and anxieties about the non-domestic sphere hinder them from even the possibility of an actual encounter with, or even sight of, a Sri Lankan mail-runner. Tellingly, in "How Pearl Button was Kidnapped," too, it is a female character who is denied freedom of association in a colonial scene that the story depicts through associative strategies. Anticipating Mansfield's more experimental, non-mimetic later stories, "Pearl Button" works through suggestion and partial presentation: As policemen arrive to carry Pearl back to her family's "House of Boxes," the story signifies their profession with the metonymic phrase "little blue men"; earlier in the story, synecdoche, metonymy, and impressionistic details indicate men and women who are Māori, but who are not identified as such explicitly (39).

Cancelling Pearl's association with the Māori community, the "little blue men" uphold both the law and bourgeois norms of family-belonging that confine experience and sensuous freedom, which is evident when Pearl instantly asks, "Please can I eat that?' as a Māori man playfully offers her a peach (37). As the story's closing sentence repeats the phrase "House of Boxes," it implicitly decries the cancellation of pleasure in encounters with difference and its enclosure in domestic "boxes"—metaphors for containment and frequent metonyms for possessions. The story has already offset closed bourgeois domesticity with Pearl's fascination with the unpredictable form of sea-waves and delight in unfamiliar experience, openness, and conviviality of the Māori community. Doing so while repudiating property as a kind of hoarding, it subtly disavows the arrogation of relations and of form.

Mansfield links the futility of absolute containment, enclosure, and claims to dominion with an affective, historically concealed, or emotional charge in landscapes and topography. Discussing Mansfield's inclusion of a "sense of guilt at white settler intrusion" in "In the Botanical Gardens" and the "savage spirit of the land [that] roams unchecked at sundown" in "The Woman at the Store" (1912), Janet Wilson writes, "The white settler point of view is undermined in an aesthetics of narrative fracture in these earlier stories – ellipses, omissions, paradox – whereby ghostly emanations from the past [...] constitute the divided and ruptured condition of colonialism" (29). An emanation functions, of course, as an effect and residue of events. Marks of absence or incompleteness, the emanations that Wilson discusses are poignant signs of precisely the conditions that Lowe evokes. The "aesthetics of narrative fracture" in Mansfield's work deploys such signs as ripostes to the relegation or transformation of the colonized into figurative shadows, silhouettes, or even mere emanations.

In light of this, Mansfield's work is less susceptible to Edward Said's well-established charge of the absence or elision of the colonized subject in ostensibly anti-imperialist modernist works by artists as varied as Joseph Conrad, Graham Greene, Oliver Stone, and Francis Ford Coppola. For Said, the main problem in these latter works is that they retain imperialist structures of attitude and reference, even as they ostensibly critique imperialism. As Said argues in *Culture and Imperialism*, "In their view, the outlying regions of the world have no life, history, or culture to speak of, no independence or integrity worth representing without the West" (xix). This, for Said, extended a colonialist trait:

> If you were British or French in the 1860s you saw, and you felt, India and North Africa with a combination of familiarity and distance, but never with a sense of their separate sovereignty. In your narratives [...] your consciousness was represented as the principal authority.
>
> (xxi)

On many occasions, such consciousness seems to be the main filter in Mansfield's narratives (as in "Daughters of the Late Colonel"), but "How Pearl Button Was Kidnapped" offers a telling exception: Mansfield's appreciation for Māori warmth, generosity, intelligence, and humour in the story removes—if not dismisses outright—colonial authority from the primary narrative consciousness in the story. Her delineation thus refuses the dehumanization of the colonized that Lockean liberalism requires and sanctions for conquest. Further, the active and prominent (rather than absent, recessive, invisible, or furtive) roles of various Māori characters in the story and the warm respect from its narrating consciousness, as well as the indeterminate ethnicity and race of the narrator, differentiate the text from the works of the artists that Said mentions.

Locke's support for conquest over other races and places hinges, of course, on narratives where a colonial consciousness is, in Said's words, "represented as the principal authority," textually reflecting colonial erasures of others. Mansfield employs overtly peculiar means to map such violence in her sceptical depictions of circumscribed, formal, and heavily choreographed sites of behaviour. Describing the karaka trees that are to be concealed behind a marquee for the titular event in "The Garden Party" (1921), the narrator of the story, implicitly adopting its main character Laura Sheridan's perspective, says, "They were like trees you imagined growing on a desert island," their "proud" and "solitary" bountifulness displaying "a kind of quiet splendour" (288). The narrator wonders with more sympathetic urgency, "Must they be hidden?," immediately before the narration adopts an authoritative or resigned view and responds, "They must" (288). Though the story has a mobile narrative vantage, reflecting identifiable and unidentifiable perspectives because of its abundant free indirect discourse, its sympathy for the trees is overt before the latter, decisive response. Through a subtle anthropomorphization with her use of the word "proud," Mansfield evokes a silent and isolated group forced into concealed or unnoticed existence here, possibly hinting at a colonized population or even a botanical version of a Montaignian "noble savage" whose "splendour" is tamed for the normative displays at a bourgeois event. But the story neither literalizes nor substantiates a unitary analogy. Laura's sympathetic perplexity about the concealment or disregard for the karakas ambiguously anticipates her perplexity after her visit to the dead carter's home, but has no obvious or precise relation with plot-events in the text. The passage shows us that normalized concealment and disregard make even what is appreciable absent. Destabilizing interpretation through its ambiguity, yet inviting regard for the trees that is prohibited by an unspecified discursive, cultural, or familial source, the passage could be read as a gesture to both the disregard and the prohibitions that colonial and liberal-bourgeois imperatives produce. Its ambiguity expands its semiosis, inviting a range of readings that amplify its pathos.

Contesting Lockean Arguments about Women

Locke's arguments that men have no *a priori* political power over women, that women possess rationality, and that women share parental authority have had their feminist defenders.[11] However, as Teresa Brennan and Carole Pateman have shown in their celebrated essay, "Mere Auxiliaries to the Commonwealth," "Locke retains […] patriarchal claims about the 'natural' authority of fathers, but hidden beneath a gloss of 'consent'" from mothers and wives (191). Locke indeed specifies "the Wife's Share" to which she might have title through her own labour (391). Further, he concedes a woman's freedom from consensual subjection to her husband—and even the liberty to "separate from" her husband—but on condition: "if the Circumstances either of her Condition or Contract with her Husband should exempt her from it" (321, 173). Nevertheless, the "gloss of consent" that Brennan and Pateman describe cracks when, repeatedly forgetting his own distinction between "parental" and "paternal" authority, Locke declares that a man's will takes over "that of his wife in all things of their common Concernment" and that "the last Determination, *i.e.* the Rule' in family life 'falls to the Man's share, as the abler and the stronger" (174, 321). Noting the limits of the protection that a father can provide his dependents in the state of nature, Locke offers a social contract through "consent" to a liberal government as the rational choice for a society's protections. He conjecturally assumes that future generations, too, will add their consent to a father's consent in a social contract. Locke's conjectural history, in Brennan and Pateman's words, "provides the necessary basis for his … justification of the liberal, constitutional state as the only form of government appropriate to a developing capitalist society" (194). Locke's own qualifications on women's rational participation in this society are telling in *The Reasonableness of Christianity* (1695), where he manifestly delimits women's capacity for reason, as well as that of labourers:

> 'Tis well if men of that rank (to say nothing of the other Sex) can comprehend plain propositions, and a short reasoning about things familiar

> to their Minds, and nearly allied to their daily experience. Go beyond this, and you amaze the greatest part of Mankind: And may as well talk *Arabick* [*sic*] to a poor day-labourer.
>
> (209; italics Locke's)

It is possible that Locke views these limited capacities for women and labourers as, in Nancy Hirschmann's words, the results of "pragmatic realities" in preponderantly domestic duties and class differences, respectively, but, as Hirschmann writes of Locke's arguments in *Of the Conduct of the Understanding*, "The fact that most of Locke's educational recommendations are explicitly for boys and are acknowledged to be inappropriate for girls suggests that he believes girls should not be *allowed* to develop reason to the same degree as boys" (45, *The Subject of Liberty*). Even if that is so, the delimitation has severe repercussions: Not denying women's rationality but doubting the sufficiency of women's reason for lawmaking (while also giving centrality to the exercise of male power), Locke justifies the exclusion of women's participation in the liberal, constitutional state's political life. Brennan and Pateman remind us that "economic independence (especially as exemplified in property ownership) became the major criterion for citizenship" in the eighteenth century (195). However, given increasing barriers to women's entrance into professions and the public sphere, from "the end of the seventeenth century, women's economic independence and legal status began to be undermined" in England, as the numbers of businesswomen engaged in trade and crafts shrank rapidly across two centuries (195). Shaping this legacy by reserving the professional and political sphere for men, Lockean liberalism masks the diminution of women's capacities behind the concession of their share in "parental" authority, relegating them to domestic dependency upon men.

This dependency is aggravated by Lockean definitions of freedom and power emblematized in property. In *An Essay Concerning Human Understanding* (1689), Locke defines happiness as "the utmost pleasure we are capable of" and deduces that "the greatest happiness consists [in] *having those things*, which produce the greatest pleasure; and in the absence of those, which cause any disturbance, any pain" (239, 247; italics mine). Soon after that in the same text, he asserts, "Liberty, 'tis plain, consists in a power to do or not to do; to do or forbear doing as we *will*" (247; italics Locke's). As Thomas West has noted, Lockean "laws of nature are rules of convenience that are useful to human happiness" since, for Locke, "the ultimate ground of morality and political right is human well-being" (5). The combination of "having things" and acting according to one's will thus cements the Lockean alliance of morality, human well-being, and freedom with property. If property itself is an emblem for the self's freedom in liberal civilization, then Mansfield traces the aporiae of this freedom in several stories. In the throes of "burning" ecstasy but confined to domestic engagements, Bertha Young thinks of civilization as "idiotic" twice within the first two pages of "Bliss" (145). In the first instance, she follows the thought "How idiotic civilisation is!" with "Why be given a body if you have to keep it shut up in a case like a rare, rare fiddle?" (145). Next, we read:

> "No, that about the fiddle is not quite what I mean," she thought, running up the steps and feeling in her bag for the key – she'd forgotten it, as usual – and rattling the letter-box. "It's not what I mean, because – Thank you, Mary" – she went into the hall. "Is nurse back?"
>
> "Yes, M'm."
>
> "And has the fruit come?"
>
> (145)

Bourgeois distractions leave her on the verge of self-diagnosis and social diagnosis here.

Caught between intuitions of dissatisfaction and the liberal appetite for *propertied* happiness, she nevertheless lists for herself the contents of her life that should let her reproduce a model of liberal well-being, concluding the list with "new cook [who] made the most superb omelettes..." before she thinks, "I'm absurd. Absurd!," and notes that she is feeling dizzy.[12] The indices of domestic satisfaction and a sense of absurdity are followed by more distraction: she attributes her dizziness to the spring, instead of further considering herself or the civilizational dicta that provoked her initial sense of being "shut up in a case like a rare, rare fiddle" (145).

Under the weight of such dicta in "The Garden-Party," Laura Sheridan feels compelled to reproduce her mother's formal greeting when the workmen arrive at the Sheridans' house. The story counters this mimetic need in behavioural, formal, and political terms. Implying its distance from Plato's mimetic imperatives, "The Garden Party" reverses the trajectory of the male philosopher's movement in Plato's allegory of the cave: that is, from the cave towards the light and back to the cave with epistemological revisions (conscious insights and certainties). Laura, however, moves from her well-lit, privileged home to the darkness of the worker's dwellings (where Scott the dead carter lies), and then back to the world of light with contrasting epistemological revisions (*unconscious* insights and *uncertainties*). In this latter world, workers, whom Mrs. Sheridan (Laura's mother) neither invites to the garden party nor acknowledges, provide the services that make the occasion a site of unqualified joy: "Ah, what happiness it is to be with people who all are happy," notes the story's narrator while describing the event" (295). Through Laura's visit to a worker's dwellings, however, Mansfield acknowledges the pain of exclusion as the forgotten grounds of happiness at the party, evoked through absence and suggestion more than presence.[13]

Presumptions of knowledge and desire function as the obverse of such forgetting in Mansfield's work. In "The Garden Party," Mrs. Sheridan's certainty when she tells Laura to take arum lilies to the dead carter's home is obvious: "People of that class are so impressed by arum lilies," she says

(296). Such confidence about another's mind is echoed by Laura's brother Laurie when, near the story's ending, he answers Laura's agonized, incomplete question, "Isn't life – isn't life..." with "*Isn't* it, darling?" (298). As Laurie forecloses Laura's speech, Laura remains in a struggle to express what she is feeling. Such a struggle has echoes in "Bliss," as Bertha faces Harry's blustering certainties and confidence in his marital deception.

In "The Daughters of the Late Colonel," which stages the frustration of the colonel's daughters through overtly anti-mimetic means, the text's rage against fetishized, prescribed mourning for a patriarch is linked to the daughters' memories and projections about their father. As the colonel's daughters avoid an unknown, unpredictable world through sequestration in genteel formality, they desperately seek a mimetic stabilization of racial, social, and familial hierarchies in order to sustain the preferences and demands of their father. The single moment of liberation that they experience (*without* recognizing it as a moment of liberation) is when they choose to do what they consider inappropriate or, as they put it, "weak": locking up the spirit of their father in his own wardrobe, an uncharacteristically bold act that, obviously, needs them to be anything but "weak" (220). Here, Mansfield's semiotic inversions (mainly, of the common meaning of the words "strong" and "weak") underscore her non-Platonic aesthetic and behavioural preferences through the story's implicit approval of this moment. Outside this moment, the sisters feel unacknowledged dissatisfaction and unrecognized pain that supplement and exceed their understanding.

Feminine Informality

For Mansfield, these forms of semiotic "surplus" (dissatisfactions or unease as oblique signs of social pressure, for instance) are assets, suggestive artistic engines that propel stories such as "Bliss." They stage what Hélène Cixous termed *l'écriture féminine* or "feminine writing." Cixous underscores the *indefinition* of *l'écriture féminine*: "It is impossible to *define* a feminine practice of writing[,] for this practice can never be theorized, enclosed, coded – which doesn't mean that it doesn't exist. But it will always surpass the discourse that regulates the phallocentric system" (883). However, she sees in such writing some crucial specific features:

> Flying is woman's gesture – flying in language and making it fly ... [W]omen take after birds and robbers just as robbers take after women and birds. They ... go by, fly the coop, take pleasure in jumbling the order of space, in disorienting it, in changing around the furniture, dislocating things and values, breaking them all up, emptying structures, and turning propriety upside down.
>
> (887)

Such syntactical and formal disorientation and impropriety, if you will, are evident in "Bliss" when Bertha Young's curtailed self-diagnoses evaporate into dashes within the longer passage from the story discussed earlier, here. Later in that story, immediately after Harry feigns disregard for his lover Pearl Fulton (whom Bertha praises), we read a paragraph that begins with the words, "Oh, Harry, don't dislike her" and continues to address Harry pleadingly (154). The paragraph has no lead-in or lead-out—no "she thought," no "she silently protested," no "her mind cried out." Bertha's thoughts are disembodied here, as if separated from her—signalling free indirect discourse, but also, and yet again, the chasm dividing her emotions, her thoughts, and her appearance in the story amid her compromises in her marriage. The lack of attribution for the protest signals estrangement or disorientation from the self—given the importance that Locke places on possessions as a criterion for the liberal self, it signals the reduced selfhood of an economically dependent married woman. So does the text's penultimate spoken phrase, which is, again, unattributed: "Your lovely pear tree – pear tree – pear tree!" (155). Locke's logic of rationalization and repeal of alterity, to be stable, demands forgetting and linear narrative: Once invalidated within this logic, the Other remains dehumanized, capacities and possibilities cast into oblivion. The invalidation allows Lockean man to proceed without a backward glance at what he has invalidated: Locke does not so much as mention the possibility of the production or presence of variants or alternatives to forms of the civilization or law that he sees as the signature of one's humanity. Sharply different from this erasure and reliance on linearity, the very form of Mansfield stories demands remembrance.

The significance and poignancy of the unattributed comments—and several other points—in "Bliss" rely on their indication of cross-connections, which require recall and reconsideration. (Once we discover the fact of Harry's affair with Pearl Fulton near the ending of the story, and then recall that Pearl Fulton had gazed at the pear tree in the Youngs' garden with Bertha in apparent affirmation of Bertha's domestic pride, earlier in the story, we can see the link between the pear tree and Bertha's unexpected anxiety about her marriage, as well as the cruelty in Pearl's ostensible affirmation.) Each of these moments calls for retrospective, non-linear reading and for an agile interpretation that reads for textual relations through the disordering of strict sequence or syntax, thereby underscoring its *écriture féminine*.

To support *écriture féminine* is not to propose any kind of essential femininity. Such informality is "feminine" in the sense that it is denied the power of convention, reflecting the signature attribute that Cixous evokes for women in "The Laugh of the Medusa": "When I say 'woman,' I'm speaking of woman in her inevitable struggle against conventional man" (875). Having thus defined gender on the basis of action, rather than biological essence, Cixous proceeds to rebut essentialism or generalization further through an important recognition: "[F]irst it must be said that in spite of the enormity of the repression that has kept them in the 'dark' – that dark which people have been trying to make them accept as their attribute – there is, at this time, no general woman, no one typical woman" (876). Declining typification, Mansfield gestures repeatedly to the delimitation of feminine roles as functions of personal or social relations, material conditions, and their psychological effects. Instead of essential or delimited femininity, she supports the mobility in initiative, freedom of association, and sceptical criticism, each of which has a behavioural and structural analogue in her stories' underexamined aesthetic and ethical preference for a feminine informality.

The textual forms in Mansfield's work that resist, critique, subvert, or exceed conventionally sanctioned expression have their behavioural analogue in an easing and reconstitution of normative interaction. A combination of such form and behaviour is what I am calling "informality" here. If the lightening of restrictions in informal moments reflects the possibilities in the non-normative (in the ways that Cixous's views on women's "flight" suggest), then, in this sense, Mansfield's work destabilizes hierarchies of prescribed expression through the relations of form and behaviour. Early in "The Garden Party," more than the tall workman's industry or skill, it is his "easy" smile, his "easy way," and colloquial speech (especially the phrase "a bang slap in the eye") that first impress Laura.[14] Observing his sensuous relish as he "snuffed up the smell" of a sprig of lavender, Laura indignantly considers the scarcity of men that she knew who "would have done such a thing" and the absurdity of "boys" with whom she had to dance at ritualized "Sunday night supper[s]" (288). Colloquialism and unexpected physical ease return to the story at the dead workman's house, as Em's (Mrs. Scott's) sister touches Laura unselfconsciously ("she brushed past Laura over to the bed"), saying, "Don't be afraid, my lass" before she tenderly draws down the sheet covering the dead man, and says, "'e looks a picture. There's nothing to show. Come along, my dear" (297–8). Although Em's sister says that the dead man "looks a picture" but "there's nothing to show," the easy warmth of the woman's manner and Laura's sense of distance from her family's priorities at this point permit Laura strong, though incoherent, insights that are unspeakable in her liberal-bourgeois home. Such moments are signatures of the protest in Mansfield's work. Against restricted, formulized, and unquestioning behaviour, Mansfield endorses initiative and scepticism alongside easy interaction. Against numb mimetic propriety, she deploys experimental form. Against silence and repression, she places memory and imaginative expression. The signs of absence in her stories show that sanctioned forgetting is, in effect, a production of absence, whether it be of the humanity of the colonized, the capabilities of women, or the rich potential in unfamiliar experience. If liberalism asserts a willed *inattention*—especially a forgetting of its exclusions and genealogical links with colonialism—then the *écriture féminine* and informality of Mansfield's stories assert a politics of attention.

Notes

1 Mansfield's early poem, "This is my world, this room of mine" anticipates this strategy, extending the perspectival defiance of some eighteenth-century works, such as Xavier de Maistre's *Voyage Around My Room* (1794). For Mansfield's poem, see Margaret Scott, ed., *The Katherine Mansfield Notebooks* (hereafter referred to as "Notebooks," followed by volume and page number), Vol. 1, p. 28.

2 The specific recurrences of fire imagery are on pp. 147–8, 150–3, and 155. The fact of numbing repetition is crucial for Bertha's stupefaction in the story, producing in Bertha what Sianne Ngai has called "stuplimity," rather than the classically conceived pleasures of the sublime: See Ngai's *Ugly Feelings*, especially pp. 248–97.

3 Acknowledging the obscurity of Longinus's identity that makes classical scholars frequently render his name in quotes, I consciously employ his name without quotation marks here. The words quoted in this sentence are from D. A. Russell's translation in *Classical Literary Criticism* (Oxford World's Classics, 2008). To differentiate the three translations of the text that I cite here, I will specify each parenthetically by its date of publication within the body of my arguments.

4 See especially pp. 86–104.

5 My commentary here compacts, with obviously different emphases, my larger reading of the colonialist priorities that Burke's theory of sublimity houses in my book *Migrant Form* (New York: Peter Lang, 2010), esp. pp. 7–9, 21–3, and 41–2.

6 For a reading of this dissatisfaction when it manifests as boredom in Mansfield's stories, see Saikat Majumdar, *Prose of the World: Modernism and the Banality of Empire* (New York: Columbia University Press, 2013), pp. 71–99.

7 Cf. The brief commentary on Mansfield's early stories, as they display her "anger and disgust with the physical traumas and disfigurements of pregnancy," including a view of "child-bearing [as] the most ignominious of professions," in Lee Garver's "The Political Katherine Mansfield" (228).

8 Cf. The "strange beast" of *wanderlust* that "began to purr" uncannily *from* Vera's bosom in Mansfield's story "A Dill Pickle" (121).

9 Even though Bertha sometimes sees objects (such as the pear tree) intensely or imagines things in or even as fragments (e.g. the "piece" of burning sun in her chest), the story shows us, through the various details she does not register, that seeing things in pieces is, of course, not necessarily seeing them in detail.

10 Colonised labour, colonial profits, and territorial acquisition shared crucial links with the global dominance of the liberal world order. Prominent recent studies of those links include Bell's *Reordering the World: Essays on Liberalism and Empire* (Princeton, NJ: Princeton University Press, 2016); Jennifer Pitts, *A Turn to Empire: The Rise of Imperial Liberalism in Britain and France* (Princeton, NJ: Princeton University Press, 2005); Dipesh Chakrabarty, *Provincializing Europe* (Princeton, NJ: Princeton University Press, 2000); and Uday Singh Mehta, *Liberalism and Empire* (Chicago: University of Chicago Press, 1999).

11 Among such appreciations of Locke are Mary Shanley, "Marriage Contract and Social Contract in Seventeenth-Century English Political Thought," and Melissa Butler, "Early Roots of Feminism: John Locke's Attack on Patriarchy," in Nancy J. Hirschmann and Kirstie M. McClure, eds., *Feminist Interpretations of John Locke* (University Park: Pennsylvania State University Press, 2007), pp. 17–38 and 91–122.

12 Mansfield, "Bliss," pp. 148–9. For a scholarly discussion of Mansfield's antagonism towards property and her engagement with guild socialism through A. R.

Orage's magazine *The New Age*, see Lee Garver's article "The Political Katherine Mansfield," *Modernism/Modernity*, 8: 2 (April 2001), pp. 225–43.

13 I lack the space to relate Mansfield's stories with the effects of Lockean liberal capitalism upon the working classes, here. For analysis of those effects, see, as an extension of several Marxist critiques of private property, the particular focus on Locke in Richard Stivers, *The Illusion of Freedom and Equality* (Albany: State University of New York Press, 2009).

14 Mansfield, "The Garden Party," p. 287.

3 Eliotic Contempt

Mansfield's attentiveness to suspended sympathies and the unsaid within formal circumstances has a bleaker obverse in T. S. Eliot's poems. Although "The Love Song of J. Alfred Prufrock" and several other works in Eliot's first collection of poems clearly register the trauma and emotional stultification that result from pressures to "prepare a face to meet the faces that you meet," Eliot's poems nonetheless announce an increasing investment in many of those pressures as he expands his theoretical writings and poetic output. Eliot's writings are discrepant among the modernist texts I discuss in this book, because (other than "Tradition and the Individual Talent") they predominantly tend to employ informality for negative effects—to withhold, withdraw, or refuse affirmation, rather than argue for it. Taking an itinerary that begins with ostensible protests against formality, his work tends increasingly to co-opt for conservative purposes techniques that could, potentially, form informal relations. The manœuvre involves Eliot's conflation of formality with a series of disavowals through manipulations of tone, idiom, regret, despair, and sombre warnings, all of which point to personal and cultural crises. I will examine this turn from apparent helplessness, grief, and despair to rejection or even condemnation, as Eliot grafts contempt upon concern in both his poetry and his prose. Eliot's works explicitly announce, or more mutedly suggest, these crises as impasses for which Eliot seems to have oracular solutions, voluntarily or otherwise. The contempt in his work, then, functions as a sign of his bemusement at individual or cultural plunges into self-damaging, immoral, and (to employ a term that the later Eliot embraces) "pagan" choices.

In *The Anatomy of Disgust*, William I. Miller differentiates what he calls "downward contempt" (contempt from the powerful for those who they see as lacking political, social, and intellectual influence or abilities) from "upward contempt" (displayed by those with less political, social, and intellectual power than established wielders of such power). Giving his chapter on contempt and class tensions the title of "Mutual Contempt and Democracy," Miller remarks:

DOI: 10.4324/9781003009894-4

> Downward contempt becomes less complacent because it now suspects it is being paid back in kind. The high can no longer as easily maintain the Hobbesian contempt of indifference. Only the insentient fool is indifferent to threat. One can pose as indifferent, but this is a strategy designed to veneer fear and gnawing doubts about the figure one cuts in a world all of a sudden much more densely populated. The servants are no longer quite invisible.
>
> (227)

Such a veneer shapes much of the structures of reference in Eliot's work as his career evolves. In his painstaking study *T. S. Eliot and Ideology*, Kenneth Asher has charted the lifelong continuity of Eliot's conservative philosophical inheritance from the French reactionary politics of Joseph de Maistre and Charles Maurras by way of Irving Babbit during Eliot's years at Harvard. Asher argues that this provided "the *specific* framework of ideas that organized Eliot's intellectual and artistic career," but he also acknowledges that there were several turns and complexities within this inheritance (161; italics Asher's). I will stress Eliot's arguments in "Tradition and the Individual Talent" as one of those turns, but mainly to show a peculiar tension between his formal experiments and his reactionary formality. Unlike Eliot's arguments in that essay (and despite his insistence in *After Strange Gods* that tradition is not "immovable"), his analyses in *The Sacred Wood*, *After Strange Gods*, and *The Idea of a Christian Society* advocate hermetic art as a defence against the mutations of vulgarity (19). After tracing the evolution of Eliot's attitudes to formality within contempt and the use of slang in Eliot's early poems through poetry from his middle career, including *The Waste Land*, I will return to a discussion of the hermeticism that Eliot embraces openly in the latter half of his career.[1]

Informality as Disavowal: *Inventions of the March Hare*

A gleeful, defiant informality flashes through a lot of Eliot's early work, which he, significantly, hides or delays from publication. Contempt shapes the speakers' demand that snooty ladies "stick [their snobbery] up [their] ass" in "The Triumph of Bullshit"; the aristocratic airs assumed by the titular characters in "Mandarins," who practise "conversation dignified," but not "intellectual nor mean," even though the eldest mandarin has "intellectual double chins" (1910); the apparently subservient, crude, and opportunistic Lulu in "Ballade pour la grosse Lulu" (1911); and the deficient respectability of the girl boarding the omnibus ("An almost denizen of Leicester Square") in "Paysage Triste" (c. 1914). However, the idiosyncratically flippant or louche rhetoric in these texts leaves their speakers themselves open to contempt, the poems' frivolity enlarging their ambivalent distribution of sympathies among their various characters. Eliot's more solemn early works present an even denser attitudinal ambiguity. Exploring such ambiguity in

Eliot's imagery, Charles Altieri sees Eliot's "The Love Song of St. Sebastian" dramatize a "Baudelairean cult of an intensity not containable within the images used to express it" (159). Altieri sees most of the poem's affects conveyed through "fairly standard links of penitence to masochistic fantasies" (159). However,

> the last stanza proves far more strange, insisting on an affective leap that challenges all received emotional grammars, as well as established principles of good taste. In its opening sentence the poem almost coyly suspends action in order to let the speaker linger over the details of the head Sebastian holds on his lap, as if the poem were gathering energies that the position we see from a distance will not be able to contain. Then the poem in effect makes clear the radical impulses deferred and intensified by that delay. It establishes a delicious economy between the other loving the speaker "because I should have strangled you / And because of my infamy," while the speaker recognizes, "And I should love you the more because I had mangled you / And because you were no longer beautiful / To anyone but me" (159; Eliot, *Inventions of the March Hare*, 78–9).

Altieri sees the "subjunctives here derive from the psychic worlds of 'Prufrock' and 'Mandarins.' But the emotions asserted ... display a directness and absoluteness of feeling that cannot be explained ... The lines insist on causality, yet there is no available framework by which to interpret that causality" (159–60). Nevertheless, for Altieri:

> Eliot's speaker does seem to mean exactly what he says. So there remains only the option of taking the assertions quite literally by locating some world or level of the world in which the expressions seem to make cogent sense in themselves. These lines invite allegory but repudiate allegorical interpretation.
>
> (160)

Altieri sees this interpretive challenge extended through a vacillation, within the works in Eliot's collection *Poems 1920*, between "poems that try to subsume desires into forms so tight that pure statement prevails, and poems that create a scene so stretching dramatic coherence that we have to postulate some psychological space for the speaking which no practical narrative can contain" (160). This stretched coherence is a sign of a crisis between formal innovations and overt statements in Eliot's work. Altieri notes of "Sweeney Among the Nightingales": "The [poem's] concluding perspective invokes the abstractness of allegorical space, but it insists that this space can only be adequately filled by the literal image the poem stages" (160). This difficulty seems to arise because of a bifurcation between Eliot's experimental uses of form (allegorical play, disorienting syntax, fractured perspectives) and his conservative impulses (that narcissistically presume and restrict various subjectivities), a peculiar cleavage that reaches a crisis in *The Waste Land.*

Determinist Purgatories: Varieties of Despair and Their Final Causes

After an early insistence on the separation of morality and form, Eliot's theoretical arguments and social stances suggest a preference to close the gap and see aesthetic signs as signs of formal morality. He declaims in "The Function of Criticism (1923), "I do not deny that art may be affirmed to serve ends beyond itself; but art is not required to be aware of these ends, and indeed perform its function, whatever that may be ... much better by indifference to them" (69). In a significant, but not altogether opposed, shift in position within his first set of editorial notes to his journal *The Criterion*, he deems the word "life" as "more dangerous" than the word "morals," "because the term 'morals,' at worst, stands for some order or system, even if a bad one; whereas 'life,' with much vaguer meaning, and therefore much greater possibilities of unctiousness, may be merely a symbol of chaos" (421). Later in his career, he claims in his study of Dryden (1932), "The purpose of poetry ... was to amuse; but it was to amuse properly; and the larger forms of poetry should have a moral significance" (63). Reading Eliot's shift to a sterner moral formality in the latter claim, Ashley Marshall has argued in "T. S. Eliot on the Limits of Criticism" that Eliot "clearly discerns in his poet-critic predecessors an inclusion of poetry's moral and social uses ... As his understanding of Dryden and Johnson shifts, his definition of autonomous literary study changes as well"—a change signalled already in *The Waste Land* (620). *The Waste Land*'s scenes of disgust, disavowal, and alienation in moments of sexual contact are anticipated by the poems in *Prufrock and Other Observations* (1917), prominently as an anxiety that courses through Eliot's work. The anxiety is reflected in Eliot's use of form in his most famous poems: fractured and wavering, as they enact a sputtering that is horrified by its own lack of "unity." This is especially the case if you read the poems' form through the attitudes that they convey—supposedly "open" form that is insistently defined, however, by the anxieties and claustrophobia that the text reveals. Eliot offers an (I suspect) unwitting explanation for this feature of his work in the third part of his commentary on Dante, which is on the *Vita Nuova*, when he declares that the key to understanding the *Vita Nuova* is to "find meaning in final causes rather than origins" (59). Eliot's privileging of the unfolding of a reading not necessarily from its provenance, but definitely from deterministic points of causality helps us to explain why he might project a single cause or small group of causes as decisive for not only material challenges and obstacles, but also psychological traumas and pressures. The poems in *Prufrock and Other Observations*, as well as *The Waste Land*, rehearse this tendency in various ways. The experimental aspects of these poems' form—in their fragmentation, their tonal numbness in the face of anxiety, their caesurae signalling moments of collapsed or impeded communication—signal effects while *prior* incapacity, pain, claustrophobia, apathy, and emotional asphyxiation seem to be the causes for the fractures or damage signalled by the poems' form. These signals have an overdetermining engine in Eliot's work: *an attitude of formality* in the sense of *uneasy* association, repulsion, and anxiety in the face of inversions and transgression of normative moral and social codes, especially behaviour that seems "excessive" in its intense articulation or intimacy.

"Hysteria" begins with an almost-hypnotized observation of loud laughter: "As she laughed I was aware of becoming involved in her laughter and being part of it, until her teeth were only accidental stars with a talent for squad-drill." The scale and size of the laughing woman's mouth obviously cannot *literally* accommodate the poem's speaker; but, in the speaker's eyes, the mouth has become boundless and cannibalistically absorptive: "I was drawn in by short gasps, inhaled at each momentary recovery, lost finally in the dark caverns of her throat, bruised by the ripple of unseen muscles." As Elizabeth Grosz notes in her analysis of Jean-Paul Sartre's views on slime and viscosity, the "fear of being absorbed into something which has no boundaries of its own" is not proper to that "something" (194). In short, the fear is not an attribute of the thing that is seen to be threateningly absorptive. What seems to threaten the poem's speaker into nervous disorientation is an uncontrollable fascination with details of the woman's body that are not even visible: he feels "lost finally in the dark caverns of her throat, bruised by the ripple of unseen muscles" (32). The extended informal expression of laughter functions both as repulsive and threatening to the speaker: It seems unending. The fact of the unseen as the location of threat suggests that the speaker has projected threats onto invisible parts of the woman's body, imagining a corporeality for the loci of his fear. Aggravating those threats is the speaker's sense of being "lost finally in the dark caverns of [the woman's] throat"—a confused captivity, a paradoxical fascination during disorientation, a sense of being corporeally absorbed: a vertiginous sense of being stuck.

As Sara Ahmed has argued:

> [I]ncorporation can lead ... to surfaces becoming less sticky. But the stickiness of that surface *still tells us a history of the object that is not dependent on the endurance of the quality of stickiness*: ... where the object has travelled through what it has gathered onto its surface, gatherings that ... call into question its integrity as an object.
>
> (91)

Citing Grosz's work, Ahmed notes, "slimy things become disgusting only given the maintenance of an order of things, which allows such absorption to become threatening" (90). Ahmed explains the threat as a function of active relations:

> Stickiness then is about what objects do to other objects – it involves a transference of affect – but it is a relation of "doing" in which there is not a distinction between passive or active, even though the stickiness of one object might come before the stickiness of the other, such that the other seems to cling to it.
>
> (91)

In "Hysteria," Eliot's speaker's gaze clings to the space of viscosity that is the laughing mouth. The fascination seems to begin before the poem does: The poem starts *in medias res*, signifying an ongoing temporal and epistemological perturbation.

If the speakers in Eliot's poetry seem numb, helpless, anxious, or apathetic before threats, Eliot's poems frequently insinuate a traumatized past to explain their speakers' numbness or impotence. This, then, does not mean that the works have implied an emotionless past for these speakers. In *Literature, Ethics, and the Emotions*, Kenneth Asher observes, "Contributing to critics' general failure to recognize the importance of the emotions for Eliot is undoubtedly the fact that the foundations of his view are set forth in the relatively obscure and often technically daunting pages of his doctoral dissertation on F. H. Bradley" (52). As he discusses Bradley's epistemological and metaphysical arguments, and Eliot's defence of them, Asher notes:

> As is the case with any object in Bradley's metaphysics, we can only assume the existence of discrete others in the first place at the price of falsification. How can feelings that, in their more extended, ordinary sense at least, we think of as relatively subjective give us any access to the minds of these shadowy others?
>
> (57)

Eliot's "La Figlia Che Piange" (1917) suggests unqualified access to "shadowy others," as it stages its tangled recall of a disappointing scene. The poem pivots on presumptions of access to "shadowy others" and penumbral feelings, if you will, as it suggests a mutual retrospective dialogue between the artist and his model:

> So I would have had him leave,
> So I would have had her stand and grieve,
> So he would have left
> As the soul leaves the body torn and bruised,
> As the mind deserts the body it has used.
>
> (ll. 8–12)

The spoken or thought lines in the poem seem to have various possible sources: They could be read as products of a consciousness that has authority over both the model and the artist, given the first two quoted lines that hint at former control over both; the voice of the artist reconsidering his own actions and, later, seeking to undo their psychological ravaging of the model; or thoughts that occur separately to the artist and the model, which the poem presents sequentially while withholding attribution to either, other than by indications of their source through gendered pronouns that differentiate each source from the other. In this early poem, Eliot has its speaker (or speakers) regretfully recall the setting of manner—a scene of formulized posture—through the retrospective questioning of his own formality. The speaker tacitly acknowledges formality as the affective mode that produces the moment of emotional crisis, specifically through his investment in a *set* scene and a *set* self: "I should have lost a gesture and a pose" (l. 22). This could easily be read as a protest against formalized interaction, but it turns quickly into a frustrated self-absorption (enlarging and complicating the speaker's repulsion for corporeal absorption): As the poem increasingly concentrates itself around the thoughts of a male speaker, the girl evoked in the title is less the focus of his thoughts than his own actions and choices. A reflexive withdrawal from conversation or other dialogic activity characterizes several male figures in Eliot's works (think of Prufrock's preference to scuttle "across the floors of silent seas" or of the man in "The Game of Chess" section in *The Waste Land*, whose unspoken reply places him "in rat's alley / Where the dead men lost their bones"). Conscious of emotional paralysis in "Portrait of a Lady," where the poem's speaker sees that his conversation with a woman "slips / Among velleities and carefully caught regrets," Eliot himself stays stuck in velleities before the informality that his stylistic and presentational initiatives demand. The tendency also marks (or, rather, mars) the supposedly unifying effects of montage in *The Waste Land*, as I will clarify, later; for now, let me point to it as a recurrent form of desired or involuntary solipsism in Eliot's poetry.

Distinguishing metaphysical solipsism from epistemological solipsism, Asher writes:

> The former maintains that only the self is real; the latter that private experience is the only source of knowledge. Now the first of these Bradley can dismiss summarily by reminding us that in immediate experience there is no distinguishable self at all, and even later when self is sorted out, it could only be from a non-self that must exist over and against it. All this is convincing enough. It is the second, epistemological solipsism that proves more troublesome to put aside.
>
> (58)

Such epistemological vexing challenges readings of the last two poems in *Prufrock and Other Observations*, because male appropriations of, or projections on, women's subjectivity confuse these appropriative or projecting male figures, themselves. The girl who cries in "La Figlia Che Piange" and the woman who laughs in "Hysteria" represent the same threat: the threat of passion. Eliot's "Portrait of a Lady" mirrors Lily Briscoe's panic before emotional demands in *To the Lighthouse* as its own speaker's, but the poem is too invested in *deficits* of volition (that it evokes through the word "velleities") to permit any liberated emotional expenditure. This is a hallmark that standardizes Eliot's fear of ecstasy and intensity, especially in non-normative expression (sharply contrasting Woolf's stress on intensity and intensification). In Eliot's later work, it shapes a contempt and melancholy condescension that employs non-normative expression, but with various disavowals of it. While the early Eliot does show an appreciative or sympathetic view of the modern through intertextuality in his poems ("La Figlia…" urges—and, to an extent, performs—a reconsideration of the Pre-Raphaelite idealization of women, for instance). However, the connective functions of intertextuality stall or skew these poems' preferences and allegiances so dramatically to one text, that intertextuality operates as a means of simple insult, rather than one of affirming or fertilizing relations. The Pre-Raphaelite posture that the artist seems to initially order his model to reproduce and the speaker's post-Freud regret result in melancholia about his formality: "I should have lost a gesture or a pose." Other than when they exploit, mock, or intimidate others (such as in many of the poems in *Inventions of the March Hare*), Eliot's speakers prefer informality only in retrospect and unconsciously. Even so, registration of informal, deviant, or non-normative actions threaten them. Memory and the unconscious function as exposing or shaming mechanisms that dissolve authoritative selfhood, as evident when the speaker of Eliot's "Preludes" reminds either a displaced self or another interlocutor of times when he woke at night and "watched the night revealing the thousand sordid images" of his soul (images in which Joyce will critically revel). Thus, memories or other markers of the undesirable as the "improper" or illegitimate shape much of the threat of disintegration in these works.

Colloquialism and Withheld Self-Consciousness: Disgust in *The Waste Land*

As a sign of waste and wasting away, the disintegration of civilization and civilized language overtly horrifies the poem. By extension, *The Waste Land* denies the possibilities for re-assembly from these "waste-materials." This denial is evidence of contempt in Eliot's celebrated system of allusion: The poem juxtaposes all its evocations of a glorious textual and material past with those of a vulgar, numb present through a series of cruel ironies. However, Eliot depicts the present through references to its decay and allusions to prior texts, paraphrasing classical or early modern texts to suggest contemporary apathy and linguistic decay, which is particularly grotesque during the poem's use of modern urban slang. In such uses of slang, Eliot's hermeticism has its signature in an anxious withholding of self-consciousness from various figures in Eliot's poetry. This is especially true of working-class figures as they speak colloquially in these poems, perhaps most famously in the closing verse of *The Waste Land*'s "A Game of Chess" section. Such absence of both sympathy and syntactical propriety repeatedly marks the poem's scenes of contemporary informality.

In his excellent survey of modern tendencies within spatio-temporal dynamics, Peter Conrad argues, "Modern times promised … the establishment of heaven on earth. Creativity would cease to be the eccentric prerogative of individuals, with society itself revealed as a work of art" (301). Conrad lists various instances for such democratization of art, including Satie's "clacking typewriter" as a musical instrument, Antheil's sirens and fans, and Joyce's evocation of street-noise as "the voice of God" through Stephen Dedalus in *Ulysses* (301). Conrad's next instance is "Eliot's *The Waste Land* [which] anthologized shoddy popular songs and gossip overheard in bars" (301). The difference between the first set of examples and that from *The Waste Land* is one of appreciation. While Satie, Antheil, and Joyce celebrate conventionally unappreciated forms, Eliot's sprinkling of popular song and barroom gossip in *The Waste Land* amounts to a morbid catalogue. The poem's evocation of the "Shakespeherian Rag" and the colloquial callousness of the conversation at the bar hollows out any appreciation from them. These signs of the demotic remain unappreciable within their context in the poem, underscoring, rather than leavening, apathy and alienation in the waste land.

Describing alienation from the self, Marx notes in the *Economic and Philosophic Manuscripts* of 1844, "the activity of the worker is not spontaneous activity" (62). With such work belonging to another—that is, the capitalist who profits from this activity—and the consequent alienation from the worker's self, the worker "feels that he is acting freely only in his animal functions—eating, drinking, and procreating …" (62). The scene at the bar in *The Waste Land* evokes each of those three functions, of course, but with a disavowal of, or disdain for, them. Discussing the "realm of necessity" and "the realm of freedom" in the third volume of *Capital* (post. 1894), Marx makes abundantly explicit the temporal juncture at which freedom begins: "where labour determined by necessity and external expediency ends" (958–9). In *Wage-Labour and Capital* (1847), Marx clarifies that such a terminus of formalized activity marks the point where necessary and externally expedient activity is transformed into life itself, saying, "Life for [the worker] begins where this activity ceases, at the table, at the tavern seat, in bed" (19). In short, *informal* activity marks the start or (more precisely, here) resumption of life for the worker. As such, it marks the realm of freedom—as much for eased association, as for eased articulation. Engels does not address freedom of association itself in an overt way within the section where he notes, in *The Origin of the Family, Private Property, and the State*, that bourgeois civilization founds itself on class exploitation, he clarifies that such a social foundation protracts class antagonism "by giving one class practically all the rights and the other class practically all the duties"

(216). How does the distribution of rights and duties that Engels indicates translate to attitudes and forms of behaviour? In Eliot's poems, the working classes are denied self-consciousness, and, thereby, behavioural rights.

In the scene at the bar in *The Waste Land*, Eliot begrudges such freedom through an evocation of the absence of formal (in the sense of "grammatical") speech, as within this exchange:

> He said, I swear, I can't bear to look at you.
> And no more can't I, I said, and think of poor Albert,
> He's been in the army four years, he wants a good time,
> And if you don't give it him, there's others will, I said.
> Oh is there, she said. Something o' that, I said.
> Then I'll know who to thank, she said, and give me a straight look.
> (ll. 146–51)

The quip with which the exchange closes might be taken for wisecracking wit, even cause for irreverent mirth, in another context. However, in light of the physical and psychic tolls of frequent child-bearing and an urgency to maintain standards of feminine appearance ["You ought to be ashamed, I said, to look so antique. / (And her only thirty-one.)"], this discussion of Lil's predicament cancels humour and, wielding such cancellation upon every affirmative emotion, it aborts at least two possibilities in informality: It denies eased interaction the liberating emotional expenditure of humour, and it withholds complex, sensitive, intelligent affirmation from expressions of easy interaction, making intimacy itself oppressive. (Candace Vogel reads the tensions between the couple in "A Game of Chess" as the consequence of too much intimacy, rather than of informal ease.) That is, at the same time, a withholding of access to attitudes. Denied self-consciousness and humour, the colloquial speech of the working classes is denied the capacities to perform symbolic inversions of social codes persuasively. The women's conversation at the bar underscores their ethical *incapacities*, if anything. Sympathy and complexities in attitude are the province of mythic, canonical figures, who display grammatical speech and (occasionally) more refined intelligence with the privileged classes in *The Waste Land*. Eliot's setting of this scene in a tavern, one of the rare spaces that Marx credits as a locale for worker's freedom, shows us the poem's outlook to informality in negative relief. Consciously or otherwise, Eliotic determinism (manifest in Eliot's fetishization of final causes in his essay on the *Vita Nuova* and suggested by the insistence on justifying cause in his essay on *Hamlet*) forecloses emotional range and flexibility in *The Waste Land*, reducing the manifest flexions and fractures in its form signs of cultural distortion and injury. This sets the course for every emotion in *The Waste Land* to end in desensitization or despair, producing a pervasive psychological reductiveness in the poem.

Eliot's essay "Hamlet" (1919) anticipates this psychological and semiotic reduction, radically morphing the arguments of "Tradition and the Individual

Talent." Notoriously citing J. M. Robertson's study of Shakespeare's play, Eliot decrees in "Hamlet":

> The upshot of Mr. Robertson's examination is, we believe, irrefragable: that Shakespeare's *Hamlet* ... is a play dealing with the effect of a mother's guilt upon her son, and that Shakespeare was unable to impose this motive successfully upon the "intractable" material of [Thomas Kyd's *Spanish Tragedy*].
>
> (46)

Further, he notes:

> Of the intractability there can be no doubt. So far from being Shakespeare's masterpiece, the play is most certainly an artistic failure. [Shakespeare] left in it superfluous and inconsistent scenes which even hasty revision should have noticed ... Both workmanship and thought are in an unstable condition.
>
> (47)

The refusal of semiotic surplus, inconsistency, and instability—and therefore on both textual and psychological mobility—is Eliot's main act in his establishment of criteria for artistic success: The refusal extends even to Hamlet and *Hamlet.* Upon a relatively simple and brief list of reasons, he condemns the play as an artistic failure, while later conceding that the "grounds of *Hamlet's* failure are not immediately obvious" (47). The rush of prescriptions and absolutes in the essay—"for 'interpretation' the chief task is the presentation of relevant historical facts," "The upshot [is] irrefragable," "the play is most certainly an artistic failure," and "We are surely justified"—Eliot's argument forecloses and evades all the fertile relations and interpretive challenges that *Hamlet* invites. Within the circumscribed realm of such foreclosures and evasions, *Coriolanus* is, for Eliot, "Shakespeare's most assured artistic success" (45–6, 46, 47, 47, 47). Such strictures bring Eliot to his celebrated concept of the "objective correlative":

> The only way of expressing emotion in the form of art is by finding an "objective correlative"; in other words, a set of objects, a situation, a chain of events which shall be the formula of that *particular* emotion; such that when the external facts, which must terminate in sensory experience, are given, the emotion is immediately evoked.
>
> (48)

In giving the location of emotion such emphasis and such restriction simultaneously, Eliot both stresses the importance of psychology and simplifies it. He sees the external as a precise and sufficient analogue for the internal, while Mansfield sees both as veil after related veil (to evoke Nietzsche's commentary on Dionysiac reading), unlimited, shifting, and resistant to formulae.[2] Such resistance thwarts the significative fortress that Eliot seems to seek in, and for, criticism. His stress on correlatives as *objective* delimits their semiotic possibilities, which Woolf and Mansfield pry open with the strategic informality in their works' suggestive shifts in signification, associative subjectivity, and uncertainties.

True to his formula, Eliot fills his poem with vignettes that give us objective correlatives for cultural desensitization and decay. That turns the poem into a catalogue of bleak causes and effects or, more precisely, causes and effects in a self-confirming chain of despairing propriety. His reductionist insistence on formality serves Eliot's montage of the disconnected and the appalling in *The Waste Land.* The sweep of this montage shows us various forms of informal contact—that between the "nymphs" and their "friends," sardonically mentioned in "The Fire Sermon" and presumably bereft of right feeling; or that among the performer and audience for the "Shakespeherian Rag," which punctuates the night, oblivious (or, as an instance of demotic culture, perhaps injurious) to an ailing culture; or that of the women speaking in the bar in "A Game of Chess"—as *problems*, as signs of an ailing culture. For Marx, these scenes of sex, eating, and drink point to the realm of freedom that would be the precise dialectical location from alienating cultural forces. In other words, within this simple logic, *The Waste Land* would rather sustain a feature of modern social structures that it ostensibly bemoans: alienation, itself.

According to Eliot's instructions in the poem's accompanying notes, the various views offered in the poem constellate in Tiresias' point of view. Tiresias, an undeniably abject figure in mythology, has an aerial—and, thus, *elevated*—vantage in the poem. Elevated by dint of its attribution to a figure from the formal, classical past, his abjection is validated in ways that are unavailable to the abjection of figures, such as prostitutes (the "nymphs" in "The Fire Sermon"), in the informal, decaying present. The elevation of vantage and downward perspectival trajectory shape Tiresias' diagnostic pessimism for global culture, of which he has an apparently unimpeded view, like the narrator's formal panoramic access in classical epics. His descriptions presume and restrict various subjectivities, even as they seem to disavow such access in the waste land's communicative famine. His authority is implicit not only in his prophetic certainty ("I Tiresias … / Perceived the scene, and foretold the rest"), but also in the poem's celebrated use of allusion (ll. 228–9). While Tiresias has experienced the pathos and pleasure of both sexes, he isn't the most sympathetic of speakers, as reflected in Eliot's allusions. Eliot uses allusion invariably as an instrument of insult or index of lack in *The Waste Land*. The poem's allusions, when ironic, are in contemptuous negation of the present, which is rendered especially unappreciable in comparison with the glories of the past, each instance setting in motion the spectre of a humiliatingly superior textual preterite, as in the contrast with Cleopatra's grand entrance in Shakespeare's *Antony and Cleopatra* that

Eliot evokes at the beginning of "The Game of Chess" section (ll. 77–110); the poem's evocation of Goldsmith's *The Vicar of Wakefield* in the typist's apathetic response after the departure of the "young man carbuncular" (ll. 249–56); and the broken utterance in the allusion to Augustine's *Confessions* that closes "The Fire Sermon" (ll. 307–11). When manifestly serious, as when referencing places of his convalescence and cuckoldry—Moorgate and Margate, respectively—Eliot's autobiographical allusion virtually confesses his repression of the Paterian poetics in his system of allusion, at large: "I can connect / Nothing with nothing" (ll. 296–302). Rather than recognize any connection with the world as a resource for organization, this statement proclaims a repudiation of it. *The Waste Land* enlarges that repudiation by repeatedly using its allusion to establish contemptuous comparisons between a glorious and fertile, if not virile, past and a sterile present.

Such comparison gets a prominent rehearsal in Tiresias' narrative of the sexual encounter between the typist and the "young man carbuncular." Exhibiting what Miller terms "downward contempt," Tiresias' initial characterization of the "young man carbuncular" is virtually a sneer: "One of the low on whom assurance sits / As a silk hat on a Bradford millionaire" (68). If Tiresias—often taken as the poem's main speaker—operates as a figure for the sterile, the transhistorically traumatized, and the sexually neutral, the poem's speaker's inability to relate things ("I can connect nothing with nothing") reflects the text's inability to appreciate anything within current conditions. In a sense, the confession amounts to an organizational failure: Reprising his concern with order in "The Function of Criticism," Eliot acknowledges that "Tradition and the Individual Talent" "was dealing then with the artist, and the sense of tradition which, it seemed to me, the artist should have; but it was generally a problem of order; and the function of criticism seems to be essentially a problem of order too" (68). If the speaker in *The Waste Land* seeks order, but can connect "nothing with nothing," then the present has failed tradition, exhausting its ties with the past in decadence that makes *desirable* connections impossible to find in the present. Read within the matrix of this thought, the speaker's inability to connect things in the poem is an organizational failure that, through the speaker's defeated effort, renders the object of organization unworthy of engagement.

Modernity, thus, is deemed superfluous in the poem, its superfluity a synonym for that which is unnecessary or undesirable, and so: waste. It is in this sense of "waste" that we can read the second word of *The Waste Land*'s title, thereby rendering the modern not only as undesirable (a common reading of the world that the poem describes), but also as superfluous, one that we can do without. It is this latter sense that clarifies the melancholia of the poem as a dismissive gesture or reaction—a form of disgust. As Sara Ahmed observes, "To name something as disgusting – typically, in the speech act, 'That's disgusting!' – is performative. It relies on previous norms and conventions of speech, and it generates the object that it names (the disgusting object/event)" (93). Significantly, for Ahmed,

> to say something is disgusting is still to "make something"; it generates a set of effects, which *then adhere as a disgusting object* ... To name something as disgusting is to transfer the stickiness of the word "disgust" to an object, which henceforth becomes generated as the very thing that is spoken.
>
> (93–4; italics Ahmed's)

In *The Waste Land*, "stickiness" gains a temporal and iterative, rather than material, adhesion—what "sticks" as the disgusting is not a physical substance, but that which persists as a matter of behaviour, speech, and psychological tendency or effect. *The Waste Land*'s disgust at the modern as superfluous or waste underscores perception that, in turn, reflects the melancholiac who suffers a fall in self-esteem and the "paraphrenic" narcissist who finds the world entirely hostile and therefore inappreciable, according to Freud's essays "Mourning and Melancholia" and "On Narcissism: An Introduction," respectively.[3] As I suggest in my discussion of "Hysteria," above, disgust as response to a sense of being trapped, of an incapacity to effect change that is evident in the declaration of one's incapacity to connect things. This is also a sign of *The Waste Land*'s peculiar repression of relations, even as it exploits informal devices (non-linearity, incoherence, partial articulations, montage, and slang, among them) for its depictions. I will discuss this repression, a little later, after I discuss readings of Eliot's theory of impersonality in "Tradition and the Individual," which some interpretations of the essay take as an argument forbidding relations (that, in their view, explains Eliot's authoritative doomsaying in *The Waste Land*), and others see as calling for a passive reception of voices from the past.

Anxious Formality: Authoritative Selfhood and Concealment

Constructing the latter kind of argument, Tim Dean argues in his essay "T. S. Eliot, Famous Clairvoyante" that "impersonality represents a strategy of access for Eliot, rather than a strategy of evasion" (44). In Dean's view, Eliotic impersonality transforms the poet into a passive medium with "occult" access to the voices of literary precursors.

As Dean has it, "To the extent that it clears a space for otherness at the expense of the poet's self, the impersonalist aesthetic should be considered ethically exemplary rather than politically suspect" (44). In his consideration, "Tradition and the Individual" displays such exemplarity in its engagement with concealment. Dean describes two kinds of hiddenness: "one associated with the impersonalist mask, which is generally thought to conceal the poet's true self and its interests; the other associated with the occult, which involves modes of being that are thoroughly alien to the self" (44). Reading the access that Eliotic impersonality allows to be of the second kind, Dean argues:

> Sexuality in Eliot involves hiddenness not as a mode of concealment, but as an occult mode of access with erotic implications. His impersonalist theory of poetry compels Eliot—even in the face of his own conscious intentions—to embrace a passivity and openness that renders him vulnerable to what feels like bodily violation.
>
> (45)

Dean links such an "embrace" to Eliot's "propensity for embodying these qualities in women and sexually ambiguous youths such as Saint Sebastian and Narcissus" while claiming that "from [Eliot's] impersonalist practice something fundamental remains to be learned about the relation between transhistorical conceptions of poetic utterance and modern forms of sexuality" (45). No doubt, such a relation exists—Dean deftly examines many of its fertile aspects. However, Dean makes too quick a leap in extrapolating a connection between Eliotic impersonalist practice, on the one hand, and, on the other, the fertile symbiosis of transhistorical views of poetry and modern sexuality. That Eliot's own poetic practice demonstrates such fertility is open to many questions. I will explore some of them here.

In an important turn within his argument, Dean declares:

> My conception of impersonality as ethically admirable relies in part on a psychoanalytic critique of self-mastery and, in particular, on [Leo] Bersani's thesis [in "Is the Rectum a Grave?"] that a whole range of social and cultural ills are attributable to the ideal of authoritative selfhood.
>
> (50)

Opposing authoritative selfhood, Dean endorses what he terms "self-dispossession, instead" (50). For his understanding of Eliot's impersonalist practice in *The Waste Land*, Dean finds a helpful resource in "Bersani's framing the counterintuitive appeal of self-divestment in terms of homosexuality, since Eliot too has recourse to ambiguously sexualized figures in his experiments with the self-dissolution that impersonality entails" (50). This raises my first question about his argument: Is intertextual intensity/engagement/relation *self-dissolution*, precisely? To borrow Dean's own logic from an earlier part of his essay: Self-investment need not be self-fetishization. As Dean sees it (in my view, accurately), self-divestment diverges from

> Enlightenment notions of individual sovereignty and self-possession, upon which rests a fundamental idea of political liberty. Any conception of selfhood that emphasizes self-dispossession—and hence challenges the sense of freedom consequent upon subjective autonomy—is bound to be regarded with suspicion.
>
> (50)

I agree, but *not* for the reasons that Dean states, especially with regard to Eliot. Dean finds in Eliot's theories of impersonality and escape from personality

> a technique of self-dispossession that entails a structural rather than a psychological form of masochism ... [I]mpersonal masking—the speaking in a voice other than one's own—involves the poet in a suspension or diminution of self that tends to accompany the poetic medium itself, irrespective of his or her own preferences.
>
> (54)

If there is such self-diminution in Eliot's poetry, then how do we read the class contempt evident in Eliot's depiction of, for instance, the barroom conversation in *The Waste Land*? If, as Dean puts it, Eliotic "impersonation may be a way to inhabit other existences—a way to transform oneself by becoming possessed by others[,]" then how do we practise such inhabitation of "other existences" without some exercise of simulation, assumption, and possession of their views (rather than "becoming possessed by" them)? Is nothing other than self-lessening or a kind of auto-dispossession (which may even be a contradiction in terms) the aim for a poet who takes Eliot's advice on impersonality and a related expression of emotions?

Theorizing "significant emotion" in "Tradition and the Individual," Eliot claims that:

> very few know when there is expression of *significant* emotion, emotion which has its life in the poem and not in the history of the poet ... And he is not likely to know what is to be done unless he lives in what is not merely the present, but the present moment of the past, unless he is conscious, not of what is dead, but of what is already living.
>
> (689)

Dean glosses these lines as follows: "Eliot's atavistic emphasis on the dead ancestors' continuing life ... makes his conception of poetry appear shamanistic or occult. Poetry is what you get when the ancestors become undead" (55). But what is "significant emotion" in the essay's own terms? If Eliot emphasizes that our task in "locating significant emotion" is to be "conscious, not of what is dead, but of what is already living" instead, then that is not to say that these "ancestors become undead"; it is to say that literary precursors are *always-already alive* (44). They live in the sense that they are engaged textually, surviving through a discursive life in the practices and memory of their successors—in the manner that W. H. Auden identifies while describing the continued lives of poets (see the next chapter for a discussion of the latter). If we are to read the poetics of "Traditional and the Individual Talent" in this light, they emerge as dialogic, encouraging the poet towards "*surrendering himself wholly to the work* to be done" for active critical dialogue with the textual past, rather than "self-dissolution," submission, or passivity before "undead" ancestors (44; my italics).

Many years ago, Perry Meisel offered an incisive reading of Eliot's essay that helps to answer the many questions that Dean's arguments raise. Explaining a Paterian facet to Eliot's theory of poetic tradition, Meisel insightfully notes that, rather than the simple identification of man and artist, for Pater, "personality is instead something fashioned, something aesthetic from the start" (*The Myth of the Modern*, 72–3). Such a view of aesthetic personality is clear in "Tradition and the Individual Talent" when Eliot argues, "The poet's mind is in fact a receptacle for seizing and storing up numberless feelings, phrases, images, which remain there until all the particles which can unite to form a new compound are present together" (41). As Meisel notes:

> Eliot's own mind is, by implication, itself a reflexive receptacle here for what Pater has already called the "particles" of language in [his essay] "Style" ... What we mean by uniqueness or personality, then, argues Eliot, following Pater rather than rejecting him, is not the self-engendered emergence of creative originality ex nihilo, but a rearrangement of tradition in a new work that simply gives the appearance of being new. (73)

Meisel adds that, as Eliot turns more overtly religious in the years between *The Waste Land*'s publication and his conversion to the Church of England, his "poetics become in this process no longer even the functionally dialogical poetics [of] 'Traditional and the Individual Talent' and that *The Waste Land* both represses and uses" (*The Myth of the Modern*, 109). Meisel's description of the essay's poetics as "functionally dialogical" is significant. For the Eliot of "Tradition and the Individual Talent," tradition is a system of reading, revaluation, and sustained textual immersion, rather than self-abnegation to the status of a mere medium or mere self-dissolution before influence. Eliot's call for "significant emotion" is a call for informal relations, in as much as it is a call for an informal (non-biological or conventionally familial) inheritance. It is not consent to "bodily violation," but a form of self-enhancement and self-reconstitution that asserts a critical informality in the making of its inheritance. It is not, as Dean seems to suggest, a dissolution of agency, but, in Eliot's words, a "seizing and storing up numberless feelings, phrases, images" that the engaged poet's mind can then "unite to form a new compound." As an exercise in *seizing* and storing up for reconstitution, such an informal relationship with one's inheritance is an active, rather than passive, employment of tradition.

Withheld Thought, Illegibility, and Voyeurism: Despair and Hierarchies

Diverging from the dialogism and openness to relations in "Tradition and the Individual Talent," *The Waste Land* disguises its own active relations—and voyeuristic intrusions—into the lives of others as a kind of critique voiced with a pain-numbed detachment, but, as evident in moments of surrender and terminal despair, such detachment fluctuates in the text. The poem is frequently looking into intimate scenes and private spaces, both fascinated by them and implicitly censorious of them. However, its voyeuristic gaze has access to the precise feelings of the objects of its voyeurism. In light of that thought, the narrating voyeur is appalled by his own readings as analyst and diagnostician in the text. Further, after its panoramic itinerary that is nonetheless distanced from immediate considerations in the scenes that it observes, the interpretive energy of this speaking subject of *The Waste Land* seems depleted—if not exhausted—by those scenes, as evident in this subject's admission that it can "connect nothing with nothing." From careful exhortation to sustain textual relations that we "must obtain ... by great labour," Eliot's work seems to arrive at a point of defeat, where it can relate "nothing with nothing." *The Waste Land* seems both to announce, authoritatively, a world evacuated of worth and to confess, simultaneously, its incapacity to produce a coherent reading of the world. The speaker cannot connect things because, in the poem's view, things in the world do not seem worth connecting and, therefore, unworthy of relations. However, despite such melancholia, *The Waste Land*'s perverse intertextuality keeps suggesting relations (if only those of shared cultural desolation, isolation, apathy, and aridity).

This is a sign of its anxiety to maintain a classical formality that its intertextuality distresses. This apparent contradiction brings out another aspect of the poem, suggested in Meisel's insight that "*The Waste Land* both represses and uses" the functional dialogism in the poetics of "Traditional and the Individual Talent": The poem arrives at its confessions of interpretive defeat not so much out of raw anguish, as of its perverse will to merge its nostalgic classicism with the informal procedures of intertextuality. Famously glossing Joyce's utilization of myth in "*Ulysses*, Order, and Myth" (1923), Eliot reveals more about his own methods in *The Waste Land*, rather than a precise view of Joyce's. Eliot describes the latter's use of myth as "a way of controlling, of ordering, of giving a shape and a significance to the immense panorama of futility and anarchy which is contemporary history" (282–3). Of course, the will to control and order "anarchy" is rife with paradox. In contrast to Joyce's interest in permutation, Eliot's need to stabilize what he sees as anarchic modernity leads to the tension between formality and intertextual relations, which manifestly lapse into nostalgic despair in *The Waste Land*. Peter Conrad rightly informs us that "T. S. Eliot made simultaneity a defining feature of the modern mind, which is capable of entertaining incompatible ideas and sensations" (61). Eliot did so, but his mode of conveying simultaneity changes the very notion of things happening together if they are simultaneous: In the struggle between order and anarchy that Eliot finds in the world, *The Waste Land* seems to declare a surrender of relations. The simultaneity it wants to convey is, in the poem's (stated, rather than repressed) logic of relations, one that conveys the connection of nothing with nothing, and, therefore, an *absence* of simultaneity in an ineluctable, despair-driven fragmentation of temporality itself. It is telling that "What the Thunder Said," the poem's final section, announces what would, conventionally, be portents of the future—coming rain, divine injunctions, and spiritual solutions (read by various critics as signs of hope and a return to fertility and order)—in the *past* tense.

Apocalyptic Formality: The "Becoming Unreadable of the World"

What structures and trajectories of feeling produce such a balefully despairing contradiction? How do we arrive at a crisis between a self's will to order and separate, on the one hand, and its appetite for informal or suggestive association—a libidinous will to connect—on the other? Examining paranoid narcissism in his essay, "On Narcissism: An Introduction," Freud dismantles the distinctions between the ego and the libido through the concept of an "ego–libido, an energy pertaining to the ego–instincts" (59). With the paranoiac's withdrawal from the world, the cathexis that the ego would otherwise perform with objects in the world is diverted towards a libidinous energy in the paranoid mind itself. According to Freud, "paranoia is frequently caused by a wounding of the ego, by a frustration of the gratification desired within the sphere of the ego–ideal" (82). The extreme condition of narcissism is the opposite condition of love. In love, the subject offers himself (or herself) for a connection with an external object in the world, rather than declaring terminally that he or she can "connect nothing with nothing." Narcissism is marked by the paranoiac's withdrawal from the world, the connection that the ego would perform with the objects in the world is diverted towards an internal libidinous energy, impelled by what Freud describes as "the paranoiac's phantasy (or self-perception) of the 'end of the world'" (59). There is a paranoid narcissism in claims to exclusive knowledge or anticipation of a stop to history, as well as the ad hoc informality in the childish prophecy of such a stop in Eliot's "The Hollow Men" (1925): "This is the way the world ends, / This is the way the world ends, / This is the way the world ends ...." Examining an analogous moment in his essay, "'Always Present': T. S. Eliot and Re-cantation," Tony Sharpe argues:

> The same repetitive predicament[,] the horrors of merely circulating, is enacted also in the roundelay from "The Hollow Men"; in it, place, time ... and activity all cohere to point to one end, which is that of a comic-desperate unprogression (*Poems*, 1: 82):
>
> *Here we go round the prickly pear*
> *Prickly pear prickly pear*
> *Here we go round the prickly pear*
> *At five o'clock in the morning.*
>
> (374; italics in the original)

As if the title of his poem were not enough to signal what Sharpe calls "unprogression," Eliot features the repeated claims in the infantile refrain as the main instance of his poem's arguments. Simulating the informality of a mocking chant, "The Hollow Men" proclaims both captivity in formalized routine, as well as a decisive and final moment—the end of the world—and so claims certainty. In its declaration of an "apocalypse," then, Eliot's poem refuses hope and, through its gleeful mockery, seems to enjoy morbidly a sense of destruction and closure.

As Altieri sees it, most philosophers "deal with the values that emotions produce in instrumental terms: what happens within the emotional state matters much less than the consequences the particular affects produce for our practical lives" (156). This tendency contrasts that of Gilles Deleuze, who, for Altieri, necessitates an understanding of how emotions themselves "also constitute substantial sources of value ... This need makes for substantial complications. For we then have to address the fact that *dealing conceptually with value in relation to our affective lives requires our reconciling two distinct models of judgment*" (156; italics Altieri's). The first of these models involves judgment oriented towards actions; the second engages values that, for Altieri, are "embedded in the dispositional traits that the emotion brings into focus" (157). Such reconciliation is what modernist appreciations of paradox (such as those that I will discuss in the next chapter) require, well before Deleuze's theories, but it is also what the Eliotic strain of modernism tries to keep at bay. According to Altieri, Eliot's "modernist art gathers much of its energy from its critique of the still standard narrative formats that have been considered the obvious mode for contextualizing emotions within intentional contexts. Narrative formats encourage our thinking of the emotions in temporal, causal terms" (152–3). While Eliot complicates subjectivity in the mingled, unattributed desires voiced in "La Figlia Che Piange," the later Eliot implicitly traces linear causality for modern misery through repeated reminders of modernity's turns from (if not abandonment of) the priorities and practices of a classical past in *The Waste Land*. The world, for Eliot, seems excessively tended towards individualism and idiosyncratic choices.[4]

Later still, Eliot explicitly deems current conditions and tendencies of the world as the cause for its termination through the chant in "The Hollow Men." Perhaps at his most damning, Eliot adopts a negative *telos* (and so a form of linearity) for his apocalyptic mode in *The Idea of a Christian Society*, where he warns that "a wrong attitude towards nature implies, somewhere, a wrong attitude towards God, and that the consequence is an inevitable doom" (49). Such overt and covert attraction to linear logic, and an initially anxious but eventually censorious attitude towards "a wrong attitude" disrupt the putative informality and radically experimental form that have drawn enduring critical reverence for Eliot's work. The implicit censure in Eliot's remark stems in part from his anxiety about the displacement of religion from culture and, by extension, the diminished centralization of authority in a divine figure. Within this logic, the atheism and scepticism in W. H. Auden's early work (which I will discuss in the next chapter) function as democratic force. Taking the dissemination of democracy and "upward contempt" to be conjoined social facts, Miller writes in *The Anatomy of Disgust*:

> The low now have available to them the Hobbesian contempt of just not caring to attend to their superiors, and it is this which does so much to engender anxieties in the superior, for the superior cannot fathom that he or she could be so utterly disattendable.
>
> (234)

For Miller, the maintenance and disturbance of circuits of power determines the volume of contempt directed "upward" or "downward." Eliot adopted a striking combination of form that suggested the potential for a political thrust "upward" and content or philosophical bases that drove his contempt "downward." Much-debated as its legacies and arguments are, Eliot's despairing disgust and the unease in his work are functions of a will to stabilize socialization, aesthetics, and politics within hierarchies, not so much because he thinks in a clear-cut binary between order and disorder, but because his philosophical formality has to negotiate his fascination with experimental structures. His works' foreclosure of ethical potential in informality keeps them from acknowledging informal affirmations and elastic Paterian connections between cultures past and present. His arguments against vulgarity and his attitudes to other kinds of informality lead his works to a disgusted aesthetic, emotional, and political paralysis that, as I will show next, Joyce's work solves.

Notes

1 Unless *Inventions of the March Hare* is specified as the source of a poetic citation here, all citations of Eliot's poetry in this book are from *T. S. Eliot: The Complete Poems and Plays* (London: Faber and Faber, 1985).

2 In *The Birth of Tragedy*, Nietzsche contends, "Whenever truth is unveiled, the … eyes of the artist remain fixed on what still remains veiled, even after the unveiling" (72).

3 See "Mourning and Melancholia" in *General Psychological Theory* (165); "On Narcissism: An Introduction" is included in the same book on pp. 56–82.

4 Eliot decries such tendencies repeatedly, as he spots them across history. In his essay on Ben Jonson in *The Sacred Wood*, he pronounces upon the inapt location of Shakespeare's characters, writing, "The characters of Shakespeare are such as might exist in different circumstances than those in which Shakespeare sets them" (112). Deploring D. H. Lawrence's "lust for intellectual independence" in *After Strange Gods*, he declares Lawrence's "insensibility to ordinary social morality" "so alien to my mind that I am completely baffled by it as a monstrosity" (63–4).

4 Joyce's Challenges to Disgust

A disgusted response, however brief, presumes that a disgusting object deserves sensory condemnation and expulsion. Seeing that object as representative of contamination and undesirable contact, such a response quickly cancels consideration of it. Our rejection of the object announces both our perception of the object as a form of harmful dirt and our conscious or unconscious urge to be cleansed of it. It seeks to preserve the integrity of the self within selected or desired conditions, rather than permit entry to pollution from outside the bounds of the desired self. Bounded security is, thus, a prime goal in disgusted reactions during which such security feels breached. To prevent it from rupture or even shattering, an impregnable perimeter for the self and its experience is crucial—disgust insistently seeks to dismiss whatever threatens their integrity. The insistence on unchanging boundaries, aligned with our desires, makes disgust a desperate effort to stabilize form. This chapter explores how such alignment is contested by the informality in James Joyce's novels.

Winfried Menninghaus has theorized disgust in spatial terms:

> The fundamental schema of disgust is the experience of a nearness that is not wanted. An intrusive presence, a smell or taste is spontaneously assessed as contamination and forcibly distanced. The theory of disgust, to that extent, is a counterpart—although not a symmetrical one—of the theory of love, desire, and appetite as forms of intercourse with a nearness that is wanted.
>
> (1)[1]

Disgust, by this logic, is a sensation that seeks simultaneously to repel and regulate the conditions of experience for the disgusted body. Whatever its duration, it is distinguished by its will to spatial organization: to decide what is within and what is a violation of the body and its feelings, what is admissible and what is to be left out, all the while refusing contact that might well be unavoidable.

Joyce's essays anticipate his notorious complication of the inside and the outside, the avoidable and the ineluctable, as well the processes of

DOI: 10.4324/9781003009894-5

negotiating objects and experience within the conscious and unconscious mind. Such spatial and experiential complication resonates strongly with Menninghaus's discussion of disgust in spatial terms. Some scholarly arguments maintain that the scandalous and much-noted intimacy of perspective and characters' actions in all of Joyce's novels provokes (or even that it should provoke) varieties of outrage, repulsion, and disgust.[2] We can trace such intimacy back to some of his earliest published works, including his essays "The Day of the Rabblement" and "Oscar Wilde: The Poet of 'Salomé,'" with the latter's embrace of the "unclean spirit," in particular (148). This embrace of "uncleanness" and, implicitly, of contamination has an analogue in an openness to unclean relations that bring contamination. Emphasizing the importance of such openness in "The Day of the Rabblement" with his declaration about an aesthete's "floating will," Joyce argues that such openness and willing drift provide artistic and intellectual fuel, for which the artist who lacks local inspiration "must look abroad" (OCP, 51, 50). A will that "floats" abroad to seek what is locally unavailable, the strange, or the "foreign" is, of course, one that welcomes what is not already present, comfortably accepted, or perhaps even acceptable, in local circumstances. Its view of the unfamiliar and of cultural otherness as an aesthetic asset obviously contrasts the view of otherness in a disgusted response. As Sara Ahmed argues in her commentary on disgust in *The Cultural Politics of Emotion*, within the matrices of disgust, the "other is already seen as dirt, as the carrier of dirt"—dirt of the unwanted kind (82).

Joyce's work critically transforms, welcomes, and revels in the experience of "a thousand sordid images" that horrify the speaker in Eliot's "Preludes." If disgust forbids entry to unfamiliar, "unclean," and uncomfortable experience, impelling its restriction and removal beyond our affective fences, then the "floating will" that Joyce admires precisely seeks and sees the validity of such unsanitary experience.[3]

Drawn and Flung: *A Portrait of the Artist as a Young Man*

An openness of feeling fertilizes such a "floating will" in Joyce's novels, as the sensitivity in their characters and their narration (such as it is in *Ulysses* and *Finnegans Wake*) expands associative emotions at several moments when a single emotion, or a focus on one event, may dominate a character's or a narrator's attention. Such an expansion marks the narrative about midway in *A Portrait of the Artist as a Young Man*, as Davin disarms Stephen Dedalus by calling him "Stevie" and inviting Stephen to "[c]all me what you will" (195). The novel's narrator traces the effect of Davin's words on Stephen as follows:

> The homely version of his christian name on the lips of his friend had touched Stephen pleasantly when first heard for he was as formal in speech with others as they were with him. Often, as he sat in Davin's

> rooms[,] repeating for his friend's simple ear the verses and cadences of others which were the veils of his own longing and dejection, the rude Firbolg mind of his listener had drawn his mind towards it and flung it back again, drawing it by a quiet inbred courtesy of attention or by a quaint turn of old English speech or by the force of its delight in rude bodily skill—for Davin had sat at the feet of Michael Cusack, the Gael—repelling swiftly and suddenly by a grossness of intelligence or by a bluntness of feeling or by a dull stare of terror in the eyes, the terror of soul of a starving Irish village in which the curfew was still a nightly fear. (195)

Davin's informality contrasts Stephen's habitual interactions with friends ("he was as formal in speech with others as they were with him"), even as it precipitates Stephen's affection and melancholy. This melancholy is a response not only towards Davin's presumably unconscious and undisguised expression ("a quiet inbred courtesy of attention or by a quaint turn of old English speech or by the force of its delight in rude bodily skill"), but to the colonization of Ireland.

Before we reach the quoted passage, Stephen has followed a train of distracted thought to memories of Davin while contemplating a statue of Thomas Moore ("Ireland's national poet"). His thoughts take a hyper-associative, morbid path as he contemplates "wellmade boots that flanked the wall pair by pair" at the home of his friend (195). The affective welter associated with this moment, as well as the writhing turns in the long sentence, point to the complexities that provoke and qualify Stephen's disgust here. Simultaneously attracted and repulsed ("the rude Firbolg mind of his listener had drawn his mind towards it and flung it back again"), Stephen's melancholy imagination at this moment is sympathetic, nonetheless. His formalized aestheticism is already dented by a pleasure in the informal, but he is not at ease with it. The ambivalent rush of attraction and repulsion points to a confusion and uncontrollable derangement of emotional space that Jean-Michel Rabaté has read as signs of the modernist "pathos of distance."[4] Strong, unfamiliar feelings in personal interaction intensify the sympathy that Stephen experiences for Irish political and historical pathos. Such feelings accompany a sense of disgusted recoil at the same (or almost the same) time, "repelling" by what Stephen himself presumably deems "a grossness of intelligence," "a bluntness of feeling," or "a dull stare of terror in the eyes, the terror of soul of a starving Irish village in which the curfew was still a nightly fear."[5] Joyce's subtle narrative intricately links recognition of historical "terror" in a nationally specific "soul" and in physical starvation under British colonial rule with a personal moment that distresses Stephen through its emotional indices (grossness, bluntness, and dullness). It thus fuses sympathetic approval and aesthetic dismissal. Stephen's coincident and contrasting emotions here point to the instability of judgment that informality brings and that Joyce's later works will render even more challenging.

Joyce embeds various subtle contradictions for absolute judgments, and especially absolutely damning judgments, within the novel. In his oration at the spiritual "retreat" around the novel's middle, Father Arnall describes a corpse as "a jelly-like mass of liquid corruption" (133). With this striking metaphor, his rhetoric seems to succumb to the lure of the language of disgust that Arnall himself warns against, later in his morbid address: Such is the language of those fiendish tormentors, words of taunting and of reproach, of hatred and of disgust. Of disgust, yes! For even they, the very devils ... must turn away, revolted and disgusted, from the contemplation of those unspeakable sins by which degraded man ... defiles and pollutes himself[—the contemplation that the language of hatred and disgust itself provokes] (133). Even before Arnall evokes the "awful stench" of hell, Stephen experiences such disgust and defilement through olfactory humiliation: "The sordid details of his orgies stank under his very nostrils ... as the foul memories condensed within his brain" (129, 124).[6] Stephen's disgust is overdetermined by the initial exhortations and threats of his mother and nurse, by religious rhetoric, and by interpellations into nationalism, among other prominent factors. The overdetermination continues as he mortifies his senses, later in the book. However, even during this self-mortification, he is distant from the shaming force of smell and its power to disgust, as his doubts over religion increase:

> Each of his senses was brought under a rigorous discipline ... He found in the end that the only odour against which his sense of smell revolted was a certain stale fishy stink like that of longstanding urine; and whenever it was possible he subjected himself to this unpleasant odour.
>
> (162–3)

Menninghaus identifies "stinking as the cardinal experience of disgust," and yet, given the wide currency of this claim, it is especially striking that most kinds of stench do not induce Stephen Dedalus's disgust (374). The ability to bear, if not affirm, odour is linked to the doubts that initiate Stephen's rejection of hieratic life, as well as to humour. Stephen's first major *break* from disgust privileges humour, as is evident when he rejects the priest's invitation to the life of the church: "Smiling at the trivial air he raised his eyes to the priest's face and, seeing in it a *mirthless* reflection of the sunken day, detached his hand slowly which had acquiesced faintly in the companionship" (173; italics mine).

In the novel's first half, Stephen's failed attempts at order represent the bounded life that expels disgust:

> He had tried to build a breakwater ... against the sordid tide of life without him and to dam up, by rules of conduct and active interest and new filial relations, the powerful recurrence of the tides within him.

> Useless. From without as from within the water had flowed over his barriers.
>
> (104)

After Stephen has declined the ecclesiastical life, however, cues for disgust and disorderly informality give him cause for amused affirmation:

> Then, bending to the left, he followed the lane which led up to his house. The faint sour stink of rotted cabbages came towards him from the kitchen gardens ... He smiled to think that it was this disorder, the misrule and confusion of his father's house and the stagnation of vegetable life, which was to win the day in his soul.
>
> (176)

Immediately after this, Stephen laughs, twice.

In his brief commentary, "Yes, Laughter," Jacques Derrida stresses the relations of these affirmative moments of contemplation related with humour: "Throughout Joyce's oeuvre, the yes and laughter are intertwined. They form one and the same condition of possibility, a kind of transcendental that for once provokes laughter while making one think" (19). This conjunction of laughter and philosophical nuance is always true for Stephen after he exchanges his goal of religious office for a kind of aesthetic hieratism and then for aesthetic engagement.

At the point when he abandons his wish for priesthood, he decides that his "destiny was to be elusive of social or religious orders" (175). (This elusiveness announces the informality that Joyce's subsequent novels will assert with even more sophistication.) Even when Stephen seems disgusted with himself or his surroundings, his hostile response is to the demands for, or obstructions of, the exclusion of experience that he faces. We could indeed take his description of Ireland as "an old sow that eats her farrow" as a statement of disgust, but, as Joyce has shown plentifully earlier in the novel, Stephen's remark is a response to the exclusions and prohibitions that he sees Irish culture as demanding of him (220). A richly emblematic term for Stephen's definition of his own destiny is "wayward," a word that recurs at several important junctures in *A Portrait...*, decisively so as Stephen contemplates his own rejection of the priesthood: "All through his boyhood he had mused upon that which he had so often thought to be his destiny and when the moment had come for him to obey the call he had turned aside, obeying a wayward instinct" (179). Joseph Valente has famously argued that there is as much fear as defiance in this waywardness from social and religious strictures (*Quare Joyce*, 62). Anxiety and defiance do indeed influence Stephen to make a choice that swerves—as he consciously seeks to swerve—from the formal rigidity of society and religion to elusiveness: To put it in different words, he opts for informality as a counter to fear.

Such informality is evident even at the linguistic level when, feeling himself "near to the wild heart of life" at the seashore, Stephen gazes ecstatically at a girl wading in the water, and we read the following: "Heavenly God! cried Stephen's soul, in an outburst of profane joy" (186). The flexing and reconstitution of language here shifts its valences from obedient religious belief and relocates it to the "dirt" of erotic profanity. This largely liberating move to dirt reflects a crucial aspect of the novel's own linguistic, as well as formal, dimensions from its very beginning: the mutual influence of the inside and the outside. With Stephen's father's story of the "moocow" and "baby tuckoo," *A Portrait...* begins at a moment of intimate narration that works, simultaneously, as a distancing move, entwining the inside and the outside, and suggesting that the narratives of others shape our perspective from our very beginnings. Moreover, being both inside and outside the narratives of one's identity, the self is never textually pure. This insight lets us read one of the main strategies that Joyce sets up to question disgust in his novels: The fact of being *narrated* is already a fact of being contaminated by the world, in violation of the self-controlled boundaries that the disgusted self wants. Echoing the idea of a textually constructed self, Colin MacCabe reads the infinitive "to forge" in the welcome to life within Stephen's penultimate journal entry as signifying "forgery" in the sense of faking or "forging" the self (*James Joyce & the Revolution of the Word*, 39). In MacCabe's view, "the forger understands writing as continuous production rather than natural representation" (*P*, 276; MacCabe, 39). If being a "natural representation" signifies something unsullied by mediation or construction, then "continuous production" conveys something that requires new relations of the self for its variation.

Joyce's subsequent novels sustain the argument: Instead of claiming the right to make or maintain a sealed existence, *Ulysses* clarifies that the self we forge is neither completely false nor absolutely authentic. Nor is it *entirely* self-produced or "made not begotten," as Stephen Dedalus believes he indeed is, early in the novel (38). Rather, the self is a function of our choices, of our influences, and of our contact with others, their perceptions of us, and their names for us. In *Finnegans Wake*, these relations and influences establish an ethical network that denies anyone a claim to sensory invulnerability or detached morality or other engines for disgust, as I will proceed to argue. In short, these works endorse finely sensitive versions of informal contact and receptivity.

Ulysses: Dethroning Secret Tyrants

The first utterance from Molly Bloom to Leopold Bloom in *Ulysses* is informal to the extent of escaping formalized language altogether: Molly answers her husband's question about what she wants for breakfast with a "soft grunt"—"Mn" (56). Informal expression signals the conditions of a personal relationship here, as it does variously in Joyce's writings. If Davin's use of an informal name for Stephen produces a melancholic churn of political and aesthetic associations in *A Portrait*..., then, early in *Ulysses*, the employment of nicknames suggests different kinds of melancholy alongside familiar affection: "Poldy" signals both Molly's affection for Bloom *and* Bloom's possible sadness at the qualification of this affection through Molly's "infidelity"; when Bloom dotingly thinks of Milly as "Silly Milly," the reference has a melancholic note of distance and separation from his daughter. In the second instance, however, the melancholy in this moment grows murkier, as Bloom hums out for the absent Milly a perhaps casually, but nonetheless incestuously, reworded version of the composer Samuel Lover's tune "O Thady Brady you are my darlin'" before thinking of Milly as a "[p]ert little piece" (62, 63). Joyce gives the inadmissible or unspeakable half in each of these connections a relatively simple, but crucial, affective counterweight in Bloom's sorrow and melancholy, respectively. This does not excuse or wish away problematic aspects of Bloom's thoughts, but neither does it condemn them with the immediacy of disgust. As at various other moments in *Ulysses*, the text invites an associative interpretive generosity from its readers here: The semiotic complexity of the spoken and the unspoken—of *both* the sadness and the scandal—that Joyce compacts into these scenes emerges only through the joint consideration of factors that offset apparently affectionate informal names with other sadder or more provocative aspects of the novel. As it cross-connects overt action and spoken words with unspoken thoughts that might be judged "disgusting," the novel gives us access to psychological secrets with an implicit call for the deceleration of such judgment.

Suggesting the toll that normative pressures take on consciousness near the beginning of "Nestor," Stephen Dedalus thinks of the tyranny of secrets as "tyrants" willing to be "dethroned": "Secrets, silent, stony sit in the dark palaces of both our hearts: secrets weary of their tyranny: tyrants, willing to be dethroned" (28). Knowledge of this tyranny's fatigue—of secrets near their breaking point—shapes a change in Stephen: The long inner roil that he experiences in his moments of disgust through much of *A Portrait*... changes, at times, to more analytical disappointment and amusement in *Ulysses*. In the latter work, his consideration of his distance from his own ambitions ends in slightly bemused, humorous questions to the self: "Reading two pages apiece of seven books every night, eh?" and "You were going to do wonders, what? (40, 42). Later, as he imagines a woman clinging to her lover, he returns to colloquial questioning, "Now where the blue hell am I bringing her beyond the veil?" (48). Colloquialism at such moments signals a greater ease with the self than disgust permits. As a rhetorical reflection of lighter affect, colloquialism here collaborates with humour to counter disgust directed *against*, rather than from, the self. This is manifest in Stephen's humorous dismissal of self-loathing (and its close adjunct, shame) in "Scylla and Charybdis," when Buck Mulligan reminds him of "the night in the Camden hall when the daughters of Erin had to lift their skirts to step over you as you lay in your mulberrycoloured, multicoloured, multitudinous vomit!" (217). Stephen's reply deflects disgust into provocative lightness: "The most innocent son of Erin, Stephen said, for whom they ever lifted them" (217). Freud writes in *Jokes and Their Relation to the Unconscious*, "[H]umour is a means of obtaining pleasure in spite of the distressing affects that interfere with it; it acts as a substitute for the generation of these affects, it puts itself in their place" (284). Under pressure to show shame or regret at Buck's reminder, Stephen replaces those emotions with humour. His choice saves him the agonized negotiation of disgust at the memory of his drunken impropriety, substantiating Freud's claim that the "pleasure of humour ... comes about ... at the cost of a release of affect that does not occur: it arises from *an economy in the expenditure of affect*" (284). Freud notes explicitly that such economy achieves humour "at the cost of horror and disgust" and that humour's non-normative functions spare us "the cost of an economy of the feelings of piety" (*Jokes*, 288, 286). As the affective negative of disgust in Stephen's ironic reply to Buck, humour shows us by contrast the important role of disgust in an economy of piety. If Freud sees the liberated expenditure of emotions in humour as countering piety and disgust, then the substitutive mechanics of humour apply to the resistance of disgust. Joyce substitutes piety with relish and gusto that may well be unconscious on the part of characters who enjoy them in Joyce's texts, but that the texts report with knowing irony.

Piety is clearly absent at Leopold Bloom's famous breakfast at the beginning of "Calypso." The meal is, of course, replete with signs of sensuous indulgence, its oleaginousness (various fried items feature prominently) and pungency, which might easily attract a disgusted response. The grilled kidneys Bloom eats give "his palate a fine tang of faintly scented urine"—but he eats them "with relish," his palate turning any expected disgust into gusto, instead (55). The next sentence reads: "Kidneys were in his mind as he moved about the kitchen softly, righting her breakfast things on the humpy tray" (55). Joyce's syntax permits us to read the "tang" as influencing Bloom's very thoughts and thereby shaping a relish for gustatory deviance in thought, as much as in food: Kidneys were *in*—rather than "on"—Bloom's mind.

The novel complicates Bloom's appetitive gusto by relating it with memory in the following passage from "Lestrygonians" (my apologies for another long quotation):

> Stuck on the pane two flies buzzed, stuck.
>
> Glowing wine on his palate lingered swallowed. Crushing in the winepress grapes of Burgundy. Sun's heat it is. Seems to a secret touch telling me memory. Touched his sense moistened remembered. Hidden under wild ferns on Howth below us bay sleeping: sky. No sound. The sky. The bay purple by the Lion's head ... Pillowed on my coat she had her hair ... Coolsoft with ointments her hand touched me, caressed: her eyes upon me did not turn away. Ravished over her I lay, full lips

> full open, kissed her mouth. Yum. Softly she gave me in my mouth the seedcake warm and chewed. Mawkish pulp her mouth had mumbled sweet and sour with spittle. Joy: I ate it: joy. Young life, her lips that gave me pouting. Soft warm sticky gumjelly lips ... Pebbles fell. She lay still. A goat. No-one. High on Ben Howth rhododendrons a nannygoat walking surefooted, dropping currants. Screened under ferns she laughed warmfolded. Wildly I lay on her, kissed her: eyes, her lips, her stretched neck beating, woman's breasts full in her blouse of nun's veiling, fat nipples upright. Hot I tongued her. She kissed me. I was kissed. All yielding she tossed my hair. Kissed, she kissed me.
>
> Me. And me now.
>
> Stuck, the flies buzzed.
>
> (175–6)[7]

Gerald Gillespie's essay "Swallowing the Androgyne and Baptizing Mother" credits Gian Balsamo's view that, in this scene from Bloom's memory, possible generation and fruition are implied in the masculine coloration (seed) of the otherwise feminine nourishment (cake). Gillespie himself adds that, "in terms of substitution, Molly's 'spittle' containing the '[m]awkish pulp' which Bloom ingests with joy is the sacramental liquifaction in place of an older masculine or Dionysian blood or wine" (69).[8] While the passage does indeed play with Eucharistic tropes, the transfer of the masticated seedcake from mouth to mouth could also be read as disgusting, but is, instead, an act that Joyce imbues with passionate vivacity and even humour (with the text's evocation of the goat). Refusing to sanitize or euphemize, the text augments its scandalous, sexual, and even scatological aspects with poetic syntax in its descriptions of Molly's spittle, evocation of "pulp," and its mention of the defecating nannygoat "dropping currants." However, framing this memory with notes on the flies' being "stuck" on the pane, the novel indicates stickiness as a condition of captivity, but also as one of abjection, reflecting Bloom, as he compares his vibrant sexual past to his being unable to escape humiliation in his possibly cuckolded present, which, in a further humiliation, lacks the sticky, passionate contact that he recalls.

The condition of adherence or adhesiveness suggested by the word "stuck" differs obviously from that suggested by the word "sticky" as it describes Molly's lips in the passage. The difference reinforces Sara Ahmed's theorization of "stickiness" as disgusting, an attribution that, according to Ahmed, "can be questioned" because "the attribution of a quality to a substance ... relies on [its] figurability as disgusting" (90). In other words, if a substance can effectively be *described* as disgusting, it qualifies as the disgusting. Ahmed adds that "the very necessity of figuring that quality ... suggests its deferral along the chain of signification" that, in turn, suggests variability in the attribution of qualities to substances and to their functions (90). She cautions that "stickiness itself might not be a quality that always 'adheres' to an object. Rather[,] we can think of stickiness as an effect of surfacing, as an effect of the histories of contact between bodies, objects, and signs" (90). If stickiness, as Ahmed argues, is consistently viewed as a signature quality of the disgusting, then the figurative variability of the sticky might suggest the variability of what is (or indeed could be) seen as deserving disgust or a very different response. This is clear in the difference between Ahmed's instances of the sticky and Joyce's more complex instantiation of stickiness.

Where Ahmed's discussion dwells on the threatening or unwanted aspects of "stickiness," Joyce often turns to stickiness as a metonym for *pleasure*—and always in situations of uninhibited informality or intimacy. In his fascination with paradox, Joyce distances stickiness from its frequent links with disgust, tracing, instead, the confluence of "sticky" disgust and pleasure—in the lingering olfactory persistence of the "faint tang of urine" perfuming the kidneys at Bloom's breakfast, in the sweet "stickiness" of lozenges and the memory of Molly's "gumjelly lips" in "Lestrygonians," and in Bloom's viscous ejaculation in "Nausica'a." As evident in the long passage from "Lestrygonians" quoted here, Joyce gives his characters' physical excitement at such pleasures lively syntactical analogues ("her stretched neck beating, woman's breasts full in her blouse of nun's veiling, fat nipples upright. Hot I tongued her. She kissed me."). Enda Duffy observes, "Joyce is the practitioner par excellence of a modernist adrenaline aesthetics [who produces] seismographically accurate writing that tracks somatic variation as evidence in changes of intensity" ("High-Energy Modernism," 86). This sharp insight applies widely to Joyce's work, but, in a telling sign of *Ulysses*'s critical distance from disgust (except at one moment when Bloom's "gorge" rises at the Burton Hotel), the book does not show those somatic energies in high agitation at moments that might conventionally be linked more with disgust and hardly at all with pleasure (169). At such moments, the text does not specify any signs of recoil, blushes, bodily heaving, or other somatic shifts. Bloom relishes his breakfast without the slightest wince at the tang of urine, Stephen laughs about lying in vomit, and (in a passage that I will soon discuss here) Molly recalls walking past men who exposed their penises to her. As Tyrus Miller notes in *Late Modernism*, late modernist writers "Taking their stance upon the shifting seismic plates of European society between two catastrophic wars, confronted no less an issue than the survival of individual selves in a world of technological culture, mass politics, and shock experience" (24). Miller asserts that, in response to the depersonalizing and mechanizing effects of such a world, laughter, "itself a kind of spasmodic automatism only marginally distinct from, the laughable mechanism of our embodied existence, can help ... to convince us that a self, however minimal, is still there" (25). In its laughter at experiences that could be expected to numb, shame, or shock, *Ulysses* practises such persuasion lightly. The novel's resistance to disgusted agitation is even clearer when, in deadpan irony, it flouts expected deference to restraint from appetitive contamination (through alcohol and sex with the prostitutes of nighttown, in this instance) in "Eumeus":

> *En route* to his taciturn and, not to put too fine a point on it, not yet perfectly sober companion Mr Bloom who at all events was in complete possession of his faculties, never more so, in fact *disgustingly sober*, spoke a word of caution *re* the dangers of nighttown...
>
> (614; italics mine)

Further, the passage's subversiveness clarifies that, when *Ulysses* adopts a euphemistic tone, it does so to undercut euphemism itself, as well as its rhetorical concomitants, such as forgetting, obliviousness, and rationalization. As the narrative turns to its subversively wistful description of the idyllic realm in Inisfail, early in "Cyclops," it refers to "the eugenic eucalyptus" among other "lofty trees" that grow in this land (294). A related annotation by Don Gifford informs us that the Australian eucalyptus ("not native to Ireland") is "'eugenic' because a tincture made from opium, cinnamon, and kino, an exudation of the eucalyptus, was widely used a douche in the early twentieth century" (317). The scatological undercurrent in Joyce's irony here is not only a sceptical astringent against the wistfulness that the narrative simulates, but also a rebuttal via the connotation of impurity that the reference to the douche brings to the purity desired in eugenics. Beyond parodic hyperbole as evident in the description of Inisfail, the chapter displays the absurdity of racist rhetoric by adopting the flaws of that very rhetoric in its own syntax. When we first meet "the citizen" in the novel, he is "having a great confab with himself and that bloody mangy mongrel, Garryowen" (295). The short sentence mischievously evokes the paradoxes in what it describes: Having a "confab" with *yourself* or an analogue for yourself (in the citizen's case, Garryowen) is, of course, not having a confab at all; nor is a "mongrel" a representative sign of the politics of ethnic purity that the citizen espouses. The novel sets the grounds to demonstrate that the disgust and hatred of the citizen's political agenda are solipsistic disengagements—as the phrase "confab with himself" suggests, they are escapes into the self. In other words, they are restrictions that we place upon the possibilities of our own experience, in fear of pollution to our self-definition by those who disgust us and those we hate, often without even the small excuse of a basis in personal experience.

The anonymous narrator of "Cyclops" displays such a swerve into disgust without personal experience of what he deems disgusting, when he states, "I'm told those Jewies does have a sort of a queer odour coming off them for dogs" (304). Analyzing such a response in *The Anatomy of Disgust*, William Miller observes:

> These kinds of group stenches come with group membership … And to the extent that one could distance oneself from the group or adopt a special status one's stench would proportionally subside. The stench of Jews, as noted earlier, could thus be washed away by baptism; that of women by chastity, and so on.
>
> (246)

Here, one kind of restriction brings another kind of restriction, where each restriction is a benefit-by-disavowal. The first restriction barricades us, in the instances that Miller offers, against what is seen as a problem rising out of religious affiliation: a "Jewish stench"; the second, against a gender-specific vulnerability to the "dirty" or "dirtying" practice of sex.

The "dirt" of sex is abundant among the hallucinations of the "Circe" chapter, which are, themselves, often driven by self-disgust that Joyce unravels through their status as hallucination. Duffy suggests that "'Circe' is perceived as the most 'difficult' and incomprehensible episode in [*Ulysses*] precisely because it generates and blatantly flaunts contradictions, forcing them further into the reader's field of perception" (*The Subaltern Ulysses*, 133). Playing with contradictions in a pungent moment, the chapter displays the coalescence of sticky disgust, eroticism, and even comic exuberance, when "warbling" and "twittering" kisses evoke sticky disgust in their call to Bloom, saying, "Icky licky micky sticky for Leo!" (475). That gestures closely associated with loving tenderness taunt Bloom resonates strongly with Bloom's own disappointment with love as he remembers what he now lacks in "Lestrygonians." If we take this reading, then the moment of the taunting kisses is a moment of sympathy, rather than insult, for Bloom, swelling the chapter's parade of contradictions that underscore its ambivalence, rather than merely its rage or cruelty. And indeed, after the chapter's long trawl through fetishized objects and the disgust of humiliating, contemptuous, and sadomasochistic rhetoric in its second half, Joyce replaces self-loathing with anticipations of the energetic and multiple valences of *Finnegans Wake*, neither merely boisterous (especially given the appearance of Bloom's dead son at the chapter's ending) nor (keeping in mind much of the chapter's hallucinatory hyperenergy) only melancholy. In short, the chaotic excess of "Circe" confounds the easy demarcation of "clean" and "dirty" space that a disgusted response claims.

Playing Pigglywiggly: The Ethics of Ambivalence in *Ulysses* and *Finnegans Wake*

Informality invites discomfort when it knowingly manifests as an "excessive" intimacy—an unwanted or unsanctioned familiarity, which draws censure or repulsion or even censorship. Modernism's history of such excess has perhaps its most notorious instances in *Ulysses* and *Lady Chatterley's Lover*, but not so much in *Finnegans Wake*, perhaps because of the famously limited readership of the latter. However, Joyce's last novel often asserts a vertiginous form of excess by performing or taking on the attributes of excessive intimacy, and thereby aligning itself with their capacities to disgust. Ahmed points to the relation between our naming of a disgusting object and our claim to distinction from that object:

> The disgust reaction creates an object, which we can describe as a border or fetish object, insofar as it admits to a prior contamination. The

> very "pulling away" from the event is what allows it to acquire this fetish quality. At the same time, the generation of the object also creates the subject. By naming the event as disgusting, the subject "stands out" in the "standing apart" or "pulling away" from the event.
>
> (96)

To discuss such "standing apart" as part of disgust's spatial dynamics, let me focus on the sensation of unwanted nearness that is prominent in two moments of attention to male genitals, ostensibly forced upon women, within Joyce's novels: the first, from Molly Bloom's soliloquy in *Ulysses*; the other, from *Finnegans Wake*, as Shaun/Jaun gives Issy a sermon on alchemy through the metaphor of sexual desire between brother and sister.

Considering her time in Gibraltar in the "Penelope" chapter, Molly recalls:

> that disgusting Cameron highlander behind the meat market or that other wretch with the red head behind the tree ... when I was passing pretending he was pissing standing out for me to see it with his baby clothes up to one side ... theyre always trying to show it to you every time nearly I passed outside the mens greenhouse near the Harcourt street station *just to try some fellow or other trying to catch my eye* as if it was 1 of the 7 wonders of the world.
>
> (753; my italics)[9]

The novel eases Molly's disgust with a humorous acknowledgement that her own curiosity or promiscuous impulse propels the excursions on which she sees these unwelcome sights: She recognizes that she deliberately passed the "mens greenhouse" "just to try some fellow or other trying to catch my eye." Doing so, at least involuntarily, she acknowledges that, through her own choice to "try some fellow," she is implicated in the experience that produced her sense of disgust. This stands in sharp contrast with the kind of "standing apart" in the response of the disgusted subject who has neither Molly's ironic honesty nor her alertness.

Although Joyce's work takes sides with intimacy that does not involve the manipulation or oppression of another over that which does, he complicates conventional assumptions distinguishing such forms of intimacy. The men forcing themselves on Molly's attention do not receive any significant sympathy in *Ulysses*, of course. By the time such forced attention is reprised in *Finnegans Wake*, Joyce does not condemn even it without substantial qualification.

Indicating both her husband HCE's and her son Jaun's incestuous attraction to her daughter Issy near the novel's ending, ALP notes the change in her "sonhusband" who is "turning ... for a daughterwife" (627). Joyce's language in *Finnegans Wake* often supplements such overtly scandalous truths about male–female relations with infantile intimacy. The novel's disfigurement and overt contamination of normative languages take its words into the even riskier territory of vivid verbal filth, transgressive fantasy, and incest. As Jaun gives Issy his sermon on alchemy, he describes his penis as

> the calfloving selfseeker, under the influence of woman, including up to you, disarranging your modesties and fumbling with forte paws after your billy does twy as a first go off ... and going on with his idiot every time you gave him his chance to get thick and play pigglywiggly.
> (III.2, 438)

Jaun's infantile, intimate language augments, rather than leavens, the obvious ugliness of what he describes. The quoted passage starts with an evocation of bestiality or fetishism (we can read "calfloving" as both "indulging in bestiality" and "fetishizing calves as synecdochic human-images") before moving on to the obvious evocation of a penis (the "billy"—"billy-goat" or "billy-club"). The latter takes a bizarre—and, in orthodox terms, disgusting—turn when the penis mentioned in the passage seems to acquire autonomous life as an "idiot" who, either through its own will or that of the person of whom it is a part, takes "his chance to get thick and play pigglywiggly." Joyce's idiosyncratic deployment of synecdoche frequently conveys an analogous informality, both in its rearrangements of grammar and in the reassignment of agency to body parts, rather than a centralized consciousness.[10]

For Immanuel Kant, in the *Critique of Judgment*, there is "only one kind of ugliness which cannot be represented in accordance with nature without destroying all aesthetical satisfaction[:] that which excites *disgust*" (155; italics Kant's). Our experience of the disgusting is one of aesthetic perversity because, as Kant notes, "in this singular sensation, *which rests on mere imagination*, the object is represented as it were obtruding itself for our enjoyment, while we strive against it with all our might" (155; my italics). According to this logic, the unwanted nearness of disgust overwhelmingly signals a weakness in affective geometry, if you will—a lack of *formal* control—as the disgusting object obtrudes itself into sensory space that itself, in affective terms, seeks to expel it, but lacks the requisite boundaries or protective casing in our *imaginative will* to do so. The passage on the "idiot" penis in Jaun's sermon is itself clearly an instance of such obtrusion, because, in its insistent, infantile speech ("your billy does twy," "play pigglywiggly"), it mirrors the wilful idiocy of the penis that it describes. This further reflects Kant's view of the disgusting: As Kant puts it, "the artistic representation of the object is no longer distinguished from the nature of the object itself in our sensation, and thus it is impossible that it can be regarded as beautiful" (155). The playful shock that Joyce's image of the penis administers clearly conflicts with the object of a universal satisfaction that is the Kantian beautiful—but not only so. At odds with the sanctioned generalizations of a universalist aesthetics, it is also the object of a peculiar, complex, mischievous, and particular aesthetic recognition—a qualified pleasure that provokes revision of the very notion of a continuous satisfaction. Jaun's overblown and ironically "innocent," babyish sermon to Issy elicits uneasy laughter, as its words suggest aberrant possibilities. These words thereby turn simultaneously into linguistic discrepancies, swerving from mimesis.

Analyzing disgust in *Ugly Feelings*, Sianne Ngai incisively sees "the negative aesthetic already latent in Kant's definition of the disgusting as the endpoint of mimetic art" (348). Mimesis, of course, posits an ideal that must be endlessly followed and imitated (at whatever remove) in representation. In contrast with such representation, the disgusting stalls mimesis, repelling desired imitative fidelity, and privileging aberration with its shocks. While their provocations might earn them a place in Kant's definition of the disgusting, *Ulysses* and *Finnegans Wake* employ lightness and play that keep them from morbid obscenity, even in their most flagrant moments. However, these works assert a self-conscious self-implication in manifest perversity.[11] They do so through their exploration of scandalous thoughts or actions, through their notorious formal gymnastics, and through their intense attention on the senses and the sensuous.

Alison Pease observes, however, that "the sensuous content of *Ulysses*'s narrative is rendered impotent by form" (89–90). Taking a more moderate view, Laura Frost thinks that "Joyce invokes but contains sensuous pleasures[:] he contorts and pushes them beyond their limits through language" (62). If this is an effect because Joyce's formal cross-connections and contortions complicate sensations that please us, what about his treatment of *sensations that do not please*—of which disgust is among the strongest? The paradox that Frost bemoans—where Joyce "contains sensuous pleasures" because he "pushes them beyond their limits"—involuntarily signals Joyce's fascination with the shuttling boundaries of the inside and the outside in the play of language and sensation, as each influences the other. This stands in obvious contrast to the immobilization of such boundaries that a disgusted response desires. Ostensibly disavowing condemnation of the obscene, and expecting the clear division of versatile form and sensuous content, Pease observes the mobile boundaries in Joyce's work through a binary logic. However involuntary such a binary may be, her dismissal of the novel's sensuous content steers her towards a clear distinction between pleasure-giving obscenity and its more qualified iterations that, in her apparent logic, cannot give pleasure *at all* because they are qualified.

The qualification of pleasure in Joyce's work, as I have tried to show, frequently accompanies his repudiation of shame, but not an unconditional one. In his response to Leo Bersani's views on intimacy, Adam Phillips likens shame to

> a threshold from the personal to the impersonal, from consent to abandonment, from cherished and horrifying self-images to those images of oneself that one could never have before the experience ... Guilt is what

> we feel about the forbidden, shame is what we feel on the verge of the unknown and unknowable.
>
> (*Intimacies*, 111)

So the former evokes the prohibited; the latter, what *should not be* known. Having linked HCE and ALP with all his male and female characters as character-clusters through (among other moves) resonant repetitions of the letters "HCE" and "ALP," and through his siglia for *Finnegans Wake*, earlier in the novel, Joyce reflects a collective production and reception of the culturally forbidden moment in Jaun's lewdness in *Finnegans Wake*. He thus produces characters who are, by virtue of their interconnectedness in thought and discourse, party to Jaun's gleeful negligence of his own guilt (much less shame) at this moment. Stallybrass and White point to the reflection of a social logic in the instinct to condemn the exuberance in such gleeful display, noting that

> a convincing map of the transformation of carnival involves tracing migrations, concealment, metamorphoses, fragmentations, internalization and neurotic sublimations. The *disjecta membra* of the grotesque body of carnival found curious lodgement throughout the whole social order of late nineteenth- and early twentieth-century Europe. These dispersed carnivalesque elements represent more than the insignificant nomadic residues of the ritual tradition ... In the long process of disowning carnival and rejecting its periodical inversions of the body and the social hierarchy, bourgeois society problematized its own relation to the power of the "low," enclosing itself, indeed often defining itself, by its suppression of the "base" languages of carnival.
>
> (180–1)

While Joyce's strategies in conveying Jaun's crude display in *Finnegans Wake* do indeed involve such dynamics, they do not erase the oppressiveness in his display. Joyce points not to an easy disappearance of responsibility, but to its *radiation without a single centre* and its diffuse circuits that suggest sympathy (in its etymological sense: Gk. *sym* + *pathos*: "concerted feeling" or "feeling with") amid disturbing laughter, at the same time. The joining of sympathy and criticism (the implied ignition for the uneasiness in the novel's laughter) dismantles the conventional division of wanted nearness and unwanted nearness that Menninghaus describes as schemas for experience with disgust and experience with love, desire, and appetite, respectively. *Finnegans Wake* does not adumbrate any moral aloofness, neither does its writer: Given the writer's own implication within the work's meshed perspectives and putative outrageousness, his is not an elevated vantage here, nor is it a self-exculpation. Instead, it is an admission of his own corruption and self-endangerment. This is manifest when, with cheerfully mordant irony, a voice ventriloquizing the writer of *Finnegans Wake* announces the act of "scribicide" (14). The announcement confirms, as Sam Slote has shown in *Joyce's Nietzschean Ethics*, that Joyce's work vivifies a Nietzschean insight: "an artist is only worthy 'when he knows how to laugh at himself'" (Nietzsche, quoted in Slote, 133). Such laughter in Joyce's novels evokes Nietzsche's conception of *amor fati*. The Latin phrase *amor fati* may be loosely translated as "love of fate" or "love of one's fate"—but, in Nietzsche's hands, it is a "Yes-saying" to the world. As Nietzsche famously declares in *The Gay Science*:

> I want to learn more and more to see what is necessary in things as what is beautiful in them—thus I will be one of those who make things beautiful. *Amor fati*: let that be my love from now on! I do not want to wage war against ugliness. I do not want to accuse; I do not even want to accuse the accusers. Let *looking away* be my only negation! And, all in all and on the whole: some day I wish to be only a Yes-sayer!
>
> (157)

The vantage that such an ambition demands cannot be one of moral detachment from ugliness (the perceived form of the disgusting).[12] It cannot claim inviolable separation from the unwanted facts of the world. Part of the denial in disgust is a refusal to acknowledge that many of these unwanted facts influence us already and have shaped what we might consider to be our integral selves. Ahmed reminds us, "We might recall here that vomiting involves expelling something that has already been digested, and hence incorporated into the body of the one who feels disgust" (94). Various moments of "deviant" thought and expression in Joyce's novels draw attention to personal histories of "ingesting" and "polluting" the world (in the sense of consuming, absorbing, and expanding its "unclean" material and influences). Seeing such ingestion as a process that precedes or exceeds our registration of it, they recognize the futility of trying to build, like the Stephen Dedalus of *A Portrait*..., a "breakwater ... against the sordid tide of life." The recognition affords an index of our own implication in and relations with what we claim to despise when we attempt the expulsion of that which we deem disgusting. The transmission of this insight underscores an *amor fati*.

Disgust involves a will to forget and, at times, ignorance of such prior engagement with the world in its will to instant rejection. While the "Yes-saying" of Nietzschean *amor fati* might seem to be the simple opposite of such rejection, its will to *learn*—to engage in a process and to analyze the "necessary" and the "beautiful" in things—keeps it from instant acceptance. As Nietzsche presents it, and as Joyce practises it, *amor fati* is not critical surrender, it does not trade resistance or examination for quietism or analytical abeyance. Ahmed contends, "The speech act, 'That's disgusting!', can work as a form of vomiting, as an attempt to expel something whose proximity is felt to be threatening and contaminating[,]" and so "to designate something as disgusting is also to create a distance from the thing, which paradoxically becomes a thing only in the act of distantiation" (94).

Joyce makes us aware of our self-distancing, and thus enriches (or, if you like, *ethicizes*) the paradox. Engaging the disappointment, candour, anxiety, humour, abjection, ambiguity, and even the gusto of the ugly or the supposedly disgusting, *Ulysses* and *Finnegans Wake* employ the mobile frames of Nietzschean lightness to observe what Menninghaus calls a "hell of insight" (167). In Menninghaus's words:

> As the effect of a "strict discipline" in the field of language, the condition, path, and signature of cognition, the *affect* of disgust is always already in contact with that disgusting object which the philosopher engages ... in his descent into the hell of insight.
>
> (167)

Joyce's engagement with this hell is liberating, but, of course, conditional. *Ulysses* and *Finnegans Wake* unshackle language, not from some minimal readability, but from the strictly disciplined condition, path, and signature of cognition that Menninghaus sees as preconditions for the affect of disgust. Doing so, they thwart the quick *assignation* or aesthetic banishment of the disgusting object. As these novels call for non-linear (even retrospective) reading, and for agile interpretation of textual relations through the disordering of strict syntactical sequence or standardized words, their formal peculiarities have behavioural analogues in an easing and reconstitution of normative action and interaction. Informality, in this sense, destabilizes hierarchies of "wanted" or "unwanted" nearness, and of prescribed expression through the relations of form and behaviour in Joyce's work.

Asserting such informality as aesthetics and ethics, Joycean informality also destabilizes disgust's "paradoxical temporality," to borrow a phrase from Sara Ahmed. According to Ahmed, the temporal operation on which disgust depends is paradoxical because, in the sequence of its encounter with its object, the disgusted response "both 'lags behind' the object from which it recoils, and generates the object in the very event of recoiling" (92–3). That is: The response does not exist before the object, but the response *defines* the object, nonetheless, and through repetition and circulation, *makes* the object as what it is seen to be. Through the power of such definition, Ahmed argues, "disgust can generate effects by 'binding' signs to bodies as a binding that 'blocks' new meanings" (92). Joyce does not permit his reader to be complicit in this self-contradictory temporality. Inviting the reader to dwell on and in the disgusting moment, he resists disgust's hurry: He lets his reader reconsider that which is supposedly disgusting. He thereby violates a temporal pressure: to judge something quickly and be done with it, to dispatch it from the realm of our senses in a rush and thus render it an exile beyond the borders of our disgust. Ahmed speculates:

> [T]he limits of disgust as an affective response might be that disgust does not allow one the time to digest that which one designates as a 'bad thing'. I would argue that critique requires more time for digestion. *Disgust might not allow one to get close enough to an object before one is compelled to pull away.*
>
> (99; italics mine)

Ironically, then, in such circumstances, proximity or close consideration risks not disgust itself, but the transformation of disgust into something like sympathy or, at least, the alteration of hostility towards the supposedly disgusting object.

Joyce's novels linger upon the disgusting not only through imagery or through descriptions of the material world and events. As I have partly suggested above, they practise an informal engagement with the disgusting through the very consciousness of their characters. Examining Molly's narration in "Penelope," Margot Norris notes, "[N]othing has quite prepared us for her perfectly eloquent, if colloquial, sharp tongue" (*Virgin and Veteran Readings of Ulysses*, 238). For Norris, Molly's colloquial eloquence conveys undisguised feelings that, in turn, signal another asset for Molly's candour: "a sharp, critical intelligence that sees 'through' people's exteriors and into *their* attributes" (238). For evidence of this, Norris reminds us that the novel itself corroborates Molly's negative judgments on many "of the self-righteous[,] mean-spirited fellows Bloom encounters in the course of his day" (238; italics Norris's). This fact is crucial for the novel's implied stance on informality. Molly's informal speech wells in her thoughts to herself: As unmediated language, therefore, it is honest language. Further, it is a sign not only of the candour of the character thinking these thoughts, but also of her precise insights into others. Molly's indecorous language thus underscores that, more often than not in *Ulysses*, dispensing of the trappings of formality that disgust enforces is also dispensing of dishonesty and self-righteousness. The latter function as attempts to distance their practitioners from the lapses in conventional virtue that Molly's soliloquy displays intimately and that *Ulysses* offers its readers with obvious appreciation.[13]

Norris suggests that, despite Molly's ostensible complaints against Bloom and Mrs. Riordan in "Penelope," "Molly quickly turns around and makes concessions to Bloom … and grants excuses to Mrs. Riordan ('I suppose she was pious'[)—both] gestures that Marilyn French considered a propensity for contradiction … But they could also signify a sense of justice" (239). Norris leaves out the qualification immediately after the latter quoted thought from Molly: The full phrase reads "I suppose she was pious *because no man would look at her twice*" (738; my emphasis). Norris's omission, whether intended or otherwise, obscures the humorous scepticism of both Molly and *Ulysses*—neither Molly nor the novel leaves ostensible virtue unqualified. If, either through attitude or direct statement, a character (such as Father Arnall or the dean of studies in *A Portrait of the*

Artist as a Young Man) claims transparency or invulnerability or absolute moral consistency, then Joyce's work disturbs that claim, often by suggestion, rather than direct statement. The ambiguation of virtue provides not only a riposte to the presumed or actual power of authoritative characters in Joyce's fiction, but also an implicit argument against claims to absolute knowledge, whether of another's psychology or these characters' own. As Vicki Mahaffey has argued, Joyce, among other modernist writers, is "in passionate revolt against the widespread optimistic view that we *understand* the vagaries of human nature" (191–2).

Joyce's Ethics of Ambiguity

Echoing Nietzsche's "On Truth and Lying in a Non-Moral Sense" in the closing arguments of *The Ethics of Ambiguity*, Simone de Beauvoir writes of conformity:

> [Our] whole ethics does nothing but encourage it in this lying enterprise since we are asking each one to confirm existence as a value for all others; isn't it simply a matter of organizing among men a complicity which allows them to substitute a game of illusions for the given world? (157)

Against the illusory uniformity of normalized values and meaning, ambiguity augments the qualification of virtue in Joyce's writings, abetted by the manifest distance from semblance that these works often display. In his essay fragment "The Significance of Beautiful Semblance," Walter Benjamin observes that beautiful semblance (*Schein*) was "given its last formulation by German Idealism" in the tenet that "beauty is semblance—the sensuous appearance [*Erscheinung*] of an idea or the sensuous appearance of the true" (137). Within German idealist logic, Benjamin writes, "Semblance and play form an aesthetic polarity," because play, by definition, deviates from the true sensual appearance in semblance—the playful object is, at its mildest, a variation on normative or "true" semblance (137). By refusing the very protocols of mimesis, *Ulysses* and *Finnegans Wake* evade the semblance/play polarity: In Molly's recollection, the playful irruption of her apparently unconscious admission of her curiosity to "try some fellow or other trying to catch my eye" disorients blame for the *cause* of her encounters with putatively "disgusting" sights; in Jaun's sermon, the image of the penis asserts an uncanny simultaneity: It is disgusting *and* playful in its baby talk. The informality of Jaun's manner suggests possible menace in his words to Issy, but it also makes it impossible for us to decide if Jaun's is either uncontrollable lust that is *not disguisable* because it is so childishly candid and exuberant, or if it is *disguised oppression* because it is so manipulatively ironic.

This is an engine for Joyce's *refusal in form* to semiotic domination, despite the risks of revulsion, persecution, or derisive neglect. On the one hand, *Finnegans Wake* imperils its own legitimacy as an artefact of "high culture" by entering such simultaneously frivolous and fraught conceptual space, but, on the other, its coagulated words undo the binary choice of either absolute distinction or all-subsuming unity of form. Of courses, this involves a tension between (and confounding of) the absolutely non-mimetic idiosyncrasy often attributed to *Finnegans Wake* and mimetic fidelity that adumbrates no idiosyncrasy at all.

As Jacques Derrida observes in "Two Words for Joyce":

> Some minimal readability, an element of univocity or an analyzable equivocality, must resist the Joycean overload and condensation for a reading *to begin to take place* ... something of the meaning of *He war* [the two words from *Finnegans Wake* on which Derrida's essay famously dwells] must cross the threshold of intelligibility, through the thousand and one meanings of the expression.
>
> (27)

While the language of Joyce's later works suggests multiple meanings and makes itself vulnerable to disgust, it stages Stephen Dedalus's desire to "fly by those nets" that are flung upon the "soul of a man ... to hold it back from flight" (*P*, 220). It does so through its very destabilization of language. Stephen thinks of human souls in "Proteus" as "shame-wounded by our sins" (*U*, 48). *Ulysses*, however, intercepts and transforms the discursive weapons with which the notion of sins produces such wounds. Mirroring the "avid shameclosing eyes" of Leopold Bloom's cat in *Ulysses* and Molly, as well as the perverse play of Jaun's sermon on alchemy to Issy, Joyce's later works resist the outright affective condemnation that the stabilization of *both* form and morality enables (*U*, 55). They playfully demand respect for what Derek Attridge has termed the "force of the new," an interpretive openness to a "suspension of my habits [and] a willingness to rethink old positions in order to apprehend the text's inaugural power" (25). Resistance to the moral or aesthetic cues for disgust pivots on such an imperative to reconsider or appreciate (rather than dismiss), and to revise energetically one's assumptions in the face of affective or aesthetic challenges. Joyce's works, of course, perform such revision by showing things through their parrhesiastic modernism with unflinching frankness. As they invite consideration of other readings through ambiguous *non-prescription*, they also invite consideration—rather than condemnation—of otherness. They, thus, employ ambiguity and paradox as fertile, if shifting, ethical grounds. Benjamin Boysen has described *Finnegans Wake* as "the result of an endeavor to stage a certain intimate sympathy between the ego and the other, in which 'You'll feel [rather than see] what I mean'" (314). The quotation at the end of the sentence clarifies that the text seeks to stage the sympathy that Boysen describes in the realm of feeling, even more than visibility. Through this effort, *Finnegans Wake* extends the attempts in Joyce's earlier novels to link things that might seem incommensurable, or even undesirable, but whose actual and possible relations we cannot *immediately* foresee. As such, they are relations that we cannot immediately foreclose. That generosity and openness to risk make Joyce's works an exercise against disgust.

Notes

1 Disgust poses a signature *spatial* problem for some strains of modernism—such as Eliot's—where disgusted or anxious responses appear as a signature problem of aesthetics, especially in depictions of unease about "other" places and conditions: Cf. Edward Said's observation that, in modernism, "[s]patiality becomes, ironically, the characteristic of an aesthetic rather than of political domination" (190).

2 Works voicing such a view include Robert R. Wilson's *The Hydra's Tale* and, more recently, an essay on the insensitivity and self-absorption of Leopold Bloom's unspoken thoughts: Paul Marchbanks's "The Ineluctable Modality of the Visibly Disabled in James Joyce's *Ulysses*." For a reading of ideological dubiety within the intimacy that Joyce depicts, see Georg Lukács's screed upon *Ulysses* within "The Ideology of Modernism" in *The Meaning of Contemporary Realism*.

3 Cf. Joyce's acknowledgment of the mingling of spiritual "elevation" and vulgarity in a comment, from his conversations recorded by Arthur Power, that Ireland and *Ulysses* itself retain versions of a "mediaeval" perspective because they seem to him reflections of "those mediaeval taverns in which the sacred and the obscene jostle shoulders" (107). This recognition of the coalescence of presumed opposites complements Joyce's admiring note about Giordano Bruno in his essay "The Universal Literary Influence of the Renaissance" (written in 1912), where he credits Bruno for noting that "every power, whether in nature or in the spirit, must create an opposite power, without which it cannot fulfill itself, and he adds that in each such separation there is a tendency toward reunion" (20, *JJP*).

4 For a subtle gloss on how such pathos pertains to Joyce, see especially the chapter "The Birth of Modernism from the Spirit of Nietzscheanism (Yeats, Joyce, and Beckett)" in Rabaté's *The Pathos of Distance* (pp. 51–67).

5 Seamus Deane informs us that one hundred and five Coercion Acts were passed in Westminster for the administration of Ireland between 1800 and 1921 (*Portrait*..., n. 309). Here, they provoke in Stephen both a sense of their material horrors and his own snobbery.

6 The importance of the olfactory in Joyce's works is well-documented. For agile analyses of it, see the opening chapter, "James Joyce and the Scent of Modernity," in Laura Frost's *The Problem with Pleasure* and Crispian Neill's excellent essay "The Afflatus of Flatus: James Joyce and the Writing of Odor."

7 Richard Ellman describes what he calls Joyce's "experiment" with a prostitute, declaring that the experience "helped to fix his image of the sexual act as shameful, an image suppressed but never quite abandoned later" (48). In light of the above-quoted passage from "Lestrygonians," I'm not so sure about the latter part of Ellman's claim.

8 In his essay, "Epiphanic *Ulysses*: Joyce's Trail of Breadcrumbs," Michael Opest, too, reads the scene for its Biblical echoes, linking it with transubstantiation and epiphany, but without comment on its humour (160).

9 "According to the Gibraltar Directory and Guide Book, the 79th Queen's Own Cameron Highlanders were stationed at Gibraltar from June 1849 to August 1882" (Gifford, 616).

10 For a brilliant discussion of these idiosyncrasies, see Derek Attridge's study of them in *Peculiar Language*, esp. pp. 160–71.

11 In a summary of Theodor Adorno's commentary on the origins of the avant-garde in the transgression of taboos, Rachel Potter notes that, for Adorno, the avant-garde's "formal freedoms are created in a historical context in which there is no freedom ... This conflict between artistic freedom and worldly constraint is constitutive of the autonomous nature of modern art" (194). The implication of the world and itself in transgression that *Finnegans Wake* rehearses, however, cancels any illusion of aesthetic autonomy.

12 As Nietzsche contends in *Beyond Good and Evil*, "Disgust at filth can be so great that it prevents us from cleaning ourselves—from 'justifying' ourselves" (65). To put it differently, disgust forecloses introspection, keeping us from critical self-evaluation that might help the improvement or refinement (the "justifying") of the self.

13 Cf. Stephen Dedalus's decision that "[h]e would fall" in *A Portrait of the Artist as a Young Man*.

5 "Inverted Hypocrisy"
Auden's Informal Pedagogy

Fondly appraising Auden's poetry and character after his death, Hannah Arendt offers a brilliant insight into both with a short phrase: "inverted hypocrisy" (529). If hypocrisy is the concealment of what might generically be called "faults" or "vices," then the inverted hypocrisy that Arendt records is the concealment of what might generically be called "moral excellence" or "virtues."[1] She relates this concealment with a modern reluctance to arrogate virtue, and, by implication, to make oneself appear more informal or deviant or *louche* than one is in practice. Such self-performance, of course, exposes its practitioner to disapprobation, as well as disappointment. Calling Auden "an expert in the infinite varieties of unrequited love," Arendt connects her intuition of Auden's sadness with the advice in his poem "Death's Echo" that we should respond vibrantly to life's rhythms in the brief time we have to do so: "I think it was this *tristesse* and its 'dance while you can' that made Auden feel so much attracted to … Berlin of the [']twenties where *carpe diem* was practiced constantly in many variations" (528). According to Arendt, Auden's association with Bertolt Brecht in Berlin catalyzed his "inverted hypocrisy":

> What made this influence possible was that they both belonged to the post-First World War generation, with its curious mixture of despair and *joie de vivre*, its contempt for conventional codes of behavior, and its penchant for "playing it cool," which expressed itself in England, I suspect, in the wearing of the mask of the snob, while it expressed itself in Germany in a widespread pretense of wickedness, somewhat in the vein of Brecht's *The Threepenny Opera*. In Berlin, one joked about this fashionable inverted hypocrisy, as one joked about everything: "*Er geht böse über den Kurfürstendamm*"—meaning, "That is probably all the wickedness he is capable of."
>
> (529)

The function of such an attitude in Auden's and Brecht's work, Arendt speculates:

DOI: 10.4324/9781003009894-6

> was to hide an irresistible inclination toward being good and doing good—something that both were ashamed to admit, let alone proclaim ... What drove these profoundly apolitical poets into the chaotic political scene of our century was Robespierre's *zèle compatissant*, the powerful urge toward *les malheureux*.
>
> (529–30)

Rather than see this inclination as a source of *shame*, like Arendt does, or even as embarrassment, we can read it as the practice of a strenuous, astringent ethics—a practice of ethical restraint and introspective self-revision, but not of castigation, repression, or moral advertisement for the self. The *zèle compatissant*—the "compassionate zeal" for "the unfortunate" or "the sad"—that Arendt describes keeps Auden not only from pontification and domineering formality, but from certainty. In a kind of ethical self-discipline that made him ethically (or, if you will, compulsively) reconsider the very forms he had chosen earlier, he rendered his own work informal by repeatedly revising it. Reflecting upon his turn from Marxist politics, Arendt recalls Auden's self-admonishment in his foreword to his *Collected Shorter Poems* (1965), when he rejects his lines "History to the defeated / may say alas but cannot nor pardon" on the grounds that to say so was "to equate goodness with success. It would have been bad enough if I had ever held this wicked doctrine, but that I should have stated it simply because it sounded to me rhetorically effective is quite inexcusable" (xxvi, *Collected Poems*). Commenting on such introspection that made Auden vulnerable to compulsive revision, Arendt writes:

> What ... made him a great poet was the unprotesting willingness with which he yielded to the "curse" of vulnerability to "human *un*success" on all levels of human existence—vulnerability to the crookedness of the desires, to the infidelities of the heart, to the injustices of the world.
>
> (532; italics Arendt's)

Standardized "success" itself is, for Auden, an anaesthetizing act or condition. As such, it is an aid for alienation and historical disengagement, which, in his case, would mean breaking his relationship with modernity, one that he sustained intensely, though in different degrees and guises, in his work. In a piece on Auden's early poetry in the *Oxford Outlook*, Louis MacNeice describes Auden as using "an up-to-date technique to express an up-to-date mood" (86). MacNeice clarifies that "Mr. Auden's mood is that notorious disillusionment of our time which yet goes forward to realize itself" (87). Auden's capacities for disillusionment produced in his early work an impatience with "humbug" closely allied with that which Gottlieb finds in Arendt. Especially in the first two decades of his poetic career, he trained his impatience on manifestations of unquestioned ideology in speech, ethics, self-fashioning, and mechanical loyalties.

The practice honed an eye for disingenuousness and obfuscation from the self and from others. As Susannah Young-ah Gottlieb notes in *Regions of Sorrow*, Arendt herself viewed "humbug" as "an extreme version of nonsense, [which] does not rise to the level of a point of view but remains immersed in the opacity of its own interiority" (55). The insight resonates strongly with Auden's own unveiling of humbug in various forms, including historical and political matters, even after he rejected Marxism.[2] Such unveiling was the obverse of a will to praise that is abundantly evident in his elegies for W. B. Yeats, Sigmund Freud, and Ernst Toller. Quoting the last pair of lines from Auden's poem for Yeats ("In the prison of his days / Teach the free man how to praise."), Arendt writes,

> Praise is the key word of these lines, not praise of "the best of all possible worlds"—as though it were up to the poet (or the philosopher) to justify God's creation—but praise that pitches itself against all that is most unsatisfactory in man's condition on this earth and sucks its own strength from the wound: somehow convinced, as the bards of ancient Greece were, that the gods spin unhappiness and evil things toward mortals so that they may be able to tell the tales and sing the songs. (533)

"Half-Watt Hypnotism": Formal Education and Ideological Masks

A teacher for most of his adult life, Auden retains a pedagogical dimension in his poetry. His concern with education, moreover, lasts as an unoppressive pedagogical impulse across his writing life. Instead of evincing even an implicitly pedantic pedagogy, his scepticism about dogmatism and normative success shape the pedagogy of informality in his work. The young Auden issues a plea for such informality in a short essay titled "Private Pleasure" (1932; *Prose*, Volume I). Early in the piece, which was commissioned as a review of three books about English school education (*The Year Book of Education 1932*, edited by Eustace Percy; *The Triumph of the Dalton Plan* by C. W. Kimmins and Belle Rennie; and *Reminiscences of a Public Schoolboy* by W. Nichols Marcy), Auden gives us a montage of responses to schooling in England:

> Folk-dancer, remembering a once-sore behind, thinks, "Ah, had the masters loved, I should have expanded like a flower." Old boy in the club, having another, solemn as a clergyman declares[,] "You can't get away with it. A good school stamps a man" ... [T]eacher vigorously pursues the logic of his tiny department. "How many pupils can I get?" "What is the optimum method for getting the greatest number of them through school certificate?" No one can afford to stop and ask what is the bearing of his work on the rest of the world ... Education, all

> smoothly say, is the production of useful citizens. But, good God, what on earth is a useful citizen just now?
>
> (25)

These vignettes could have been excerpted from *The Waste Land*, if not for their levity and resistance to a surrender of connections, as established by the writer's concern for neglected consideration of work for its bearing on "the rest of the world." Detailing the forms of lives overdetermined by uniform bourgeois aspirations, starting with educational priorities, Auden hypothesizes, "Like everything else in our civilisation, the system we have made is becoming too much for us; we can't stop the boat and we can't get out into the cold sea. The snail is obeying its shell" (25). The comment bears a prominent scepticism that shapes Auden's poetry throughout his career, even after his conversion to the Anglican church. In Auden's work, the snail keeps questioning the necessity of the shell. But it does so without self-exculpation: the pronoun "our" before "civilization" announces awareness of one's inevitable participation in the structures of liberal "civilization" its title puts under question and that shape the young Auden's protest. Auden calls the liberal morality of current English schooling "a dope to allay irritation" (26). He unpacks its top-down organizational formulas, as follows:

> If he's rich, your sort, then segregate him with the other young of your sort, let him year by year through his school-days feel all the excitement of a social climber, and make him so afraid of the opinions of your sort, that you may be sure he'll never do anything silly, like forgetting his class.
>
> (26)

Auden is aware that, for ideology to succeed, it needs to guarantee its own perpetuation. He is, to put it differently, alert to processes that, several decades later, Louis Althusser was to theorize in "Ideology and Ideological State Apparatuses." For this purpose, Althusser reminds us, "a social formation which did not reproduce the conditions of production at the same time as it produced would not last a year. The ultimate condition of production is therefore the reproduction of the conditions of production" (85). Further, "Ideology represents the *imaginary relationship* of individuals to their *real conditions* of existence" (109). From the outset of his essayistic work, Auden is conscious of this relationship as an imaginary one. Ideology disseminates itself, perhaps most successfully, through what Althusser calls "interpellation." Interpellation is a process of "hailing" (and a condition of being "hailed" or conscripted) into ideological strictures and assumptions. Althusser explains that "those who are in ideology believe themselves by definition outside ideology," or in other words, "ideology never says 'I am ideological'" (118). In the latter half of "Private Pleasure," as Auden outlines the preemption of questioning in such a system, he ventriloquizes the makers of vague, manipulative shows of kindness that safeguard the system from initiative and dissent: "It's all so very diffy [*sic*]. Let's go and ask the children ... Now remember; no slapping. The most wonderful thing in the world is love" (26). Auden retorts, "Every child responds to the love smarm—for a bit. But emotionally it withers" because "[s]tupidity which is a natural defence against living beyond one's means collapses under the intense fire of [such] kindness" (26). Auden contrasts such perfunctory kindness in private schools complemented by a self-absorption born of deprivation in English public schools, whose students, after they are removed from their "intense social field," "like bees taken from a colony ... spiritually die" (26). The harsh challenges of fending for themselves after they graduate guarantee other forms of social damage, according to Auden: They will not attempt to produce a more inclusive society, "because that would mean admitting the others, those who have frizzed hair, or eat peas with a knife" (26).

What is the alternative? Auden's narrator answers sardonically, "Dearie, you can't do anything for the children till you've done something for the grown-ups"—that is, re-educate them out of their habituated ways of thinking and overhaul society, including its system of education (27). The tactical deployment of the single word "Dearie" in Auden's conclusion shows an important difference between informality and intimacy: Informality does not assume or declare familiarity—it can reorient terms of familiarity for *disagreement*. Informality, in Auden's use of "Dearie," employs a term of familiarity to voice ideological criticism: It distances its employer's perspective critically from that of the interlocutor that it ironically addresses. The absence of such a differential perspective is what he considers to be a generalized crisis in his essay "The Liberal Fascist (Honour)" (1934; *Prose*, Volume I). Amplifying a Mansfieldian attack on liberalism in the essay, Auden begins this narrative of his memories of his own school—the Gresham School, Holt—with a note on the frequency of conflicting impressions of one's schooldays. As apparent proof, he concedes that he was "never bullied or molested" while at the school, but, in a less affirmative explanation for that fact later in the essay, he notes that schools such as his have "the mass-production of gentlemen" as "their *raison d'être*" (55, 56). Holt's education about morals was based on an "Honours System" activated in the headmaster and housemaster's interview with every new boy at the school—"half-watt hypnotism we used to call it," Auden quips—which was based on a promise to honour three conditions: not to swear, not to smoke, and "not to say or do anything indecent" (58, 59). As the schoolboys at Holt receive instructions to surveil under the guise of morality, their views of morality itself are interpellated into maintaining the circuits of formality on which a hierarchized society depends. As Auden notes in "Private Pleasure," "And so unconsciously the liberal becomes the secret service of the ruling class, its most powerful weapon against social revolution" (26). Such camouflaged maintenance of hierarchies (where the preservation of ideology offers itself as morals) indicates an important aspect of ideology: It disguises itself while trying to ensure its future manifestations. With such a goal, schools breed uniformity not only in the minds of students, but even into the aesthetic performances that code institutional morality: Auden suggests that "the staff might give up wearing those ridiculous black clothes (if they still do) which made them look like unsuccessful insurance agents" (56). Through this suggestion, Auden slyly suggests that the spectacle of drab solemnity itself stages an aesthetic politics: It affectively reproduces the agenda of perpetuating formality and conformity in the school (if not beyond) without recognizing or identifying itself as an ideological exercise. According to Althusser, nothing is more ideological than the practical denial or "denegation" of ideology (118). Here, "denegation" signifies not only the belief that one is outside ideology, but also that one transcends it. That is to say, the state tries rhetorically to mask its ideological violence by claiming to be non-ideological, rather than admitting it. (This is a vivid reflection of Marx's observation in *Die Rheinische Zeitung* that the state *presupposes* itself as realized reason, as I discuss in the introduction, here.) In his book *For Marx*, Althusser argues, "In truth, ideology has very little to do with 'consciousness', even supposing this term to have an unambiguous meaning. It is profoundly *unconscious*, even when it presents itself in a reflected form (as in pre-Marxist 'philosophy')" (233; italics Althusser's). He asks, "But what do we mean, then, when we say that ideology is a matter of men's 'consciousness'?" (233). His reply to his own question resonates strongly with more sceptical strains of modernism:

> First, that ideology is distinct from other social instances, but also that men live their actions, usually referred to [as] freedom and "consciousness" by the classical tradition, in ideology, *by and through ideology;* in short, that the "lived" relation between men and the world, including History (in political action or inaction), passes through ideology, or better, *is ideology itself.*
>
> (233)

The obvious implication here is that we *cannot* be free of ideology—that there is no such thing as absolute freedom. More sceptical strains of modernism suggest that we can have something like *illegitimate* freedom within ideology, however, by remaining self-conscious, critical, and wary of habituation, another term for which might be "ideological reflex." Resistance to habituation will not remove us from ideology, but it could ease psychic entrenchment made by routine.

When the voices of authority in Auden's "Private Pleasure" say, "The most wonderful thing in the world is love" in the service of ideological training, the double denegation of ideology persuades them that interpellation is, indeed, love. There are two kinds of denial that denegation offers itself as, seeking to avoid the two categories into which Althusser divides a state's normalizing gestures. It is neither fully a "Repressive State Apparatus," which "functions 'by violence'" nor an Ideological State Apparatus," which functions "*by ideology*" (97; italics Althusser's). These two kinds of state apparatus manifest themselves in many types of combinations that Althusser notes or anticipates, writing, "very subtle explicit or tacit combinations may be woven from the interplay of [the two]" (98). Auden disentangles some of these combinations in his remarks on his own school.

"Half-watt hypnotism" at Gresham used the Honours System for two major consequences, according to Auden: If anyone broke the promises it demanded, they were expected to confess the breach and, if they did not, their schoolmates were expected to report them to school authorities (59). For Auden, these effects also shaped his future political stances:

> Of the two consequences of our promises, the second, the obligation to interfere with one's neighbour, is of course much the most serious. It meant that the whole of our moral life was based on fear, on fear of the community ... It makes one furtive, dishonest, and unadventurous. The best reason I have for opposing Fascism is that at school I lived in a Fascist state.
>
> (59)

Gesturing to attitudes in his poetic writing against surveillance (as in "The Unknown Citizen"—1939), Auden goes on to argue against the teaching of the Honours System's ideals to school students, because ideals

> are the conclusions drawn from a man of experience, not the data: they are ... for the mature ... For the young without experience, ideals are as grave a danger in the moral sphere as book learning is in the intellectual, the danger of becoming a purely mental concept, mechanizing the soul.
>
> (60)

Ideals circulated in this way crystallize psychology into beliefs and tendencies before they are experienced critically or put to the test. Auden urges a replacement of the Honours System not so much with changes in administrative structures and policies as in attitudes. Offering what amounts to a pedagogical theory compacted into a brief list of assets for an educator, he argues:

> For a teacher to be of real value to his pupils, he must be a mature and above all a happy person, giving the young the feeling that adult life is infinitely more exciting and interesting than theirs; he must be prepared to give them all his powers of affection and imaginative understanding when they want them, yet to forget them completely the moment they are gone[,] and lastly he must have no moral bees-in-his-bonnet, no

> preconceptions of what the good child should be; he must be shocked or alarmed at nothing...
>
> (60)

In the closing clause, Auden defines the good teacher as one who, at least, does not drive students at odds with norms into preconceived behavioural standards, and, further, one whose ethical capacities accommodate, rather than try to foreclose, outrage through an ethical awareness that all behaviour that shocks or alarms is cause for pedagogical care, rather than quick censure or rejection. He urges critical self-consciousness from teachers, in the sense that they liberate their students by, at minimum, giving them room for behavioural reconsideration, maturity, and change.

Masks and Scepticism

Displaying such self-consciousness while considering changing selves in "A Modern Use of Masks; An Apologia" (1936; *Prose*, Volume I), Auden reminds his reader, "Everything we do, everything we think or feel modifies our bodies" (157). Auden adds to this Paterian view of selves in constant flux through a recognition of physical and gestural fluidity in self-performance, arguing, "Furthermore, we all possess, to a greater or lesser degree, the power of posing, the power of adopting another character, and the greater the power to do this, the more power we have to change our faces" (157). The importance of chosen poses and self-fashioning in Auden's work is particularly vivid in works where narrative or speech transmits itself overtly as other than its writer's. "Letter to a Wound" from *The Orators* functions as an apostrophic address to a wound that is alive and that, initially, seems hostile to its bearer, its inimical agency evident in its "resentment" of the joy experienced by the person it inhabits (*The English Auden*, pp. 71–2). But the narrator comes to see the wound as a source of refinement and maturity for himself, addressing it repeatedly as "my dear" in the letter's second half. The intimate form of address here changes the valences of the word "dear" from something costly or displaying self-absorption—a precious attitude towards others or complacent will to ignorance (as implicated in Auden's use of the word "Dearie")—to something cherished or precious for oneself. The figure of a wound is something precious to the letter writer as a source for maturity or conductor of consideration, here. Such recognition for the intellectually and ethically refining capacities of pain is crucial to the informal pedagogy that Auden's elegies offer.

Auden embeds this pedagogy in what Arendt terms his "inverted hypocrisy," the flippant or impudent veneer of which drew charges of frivolity for Auden's poetry, especially at the beginning of his career. In a piece on Auden published in the *New Statesman and Nation* in 1940, T. C. Worsley (who wrote a tract on education with Auden) defines Auden as "a very uneven poet," firstly because, in Worsley's opinion, Auden cannot "resist the small boy's impulse to throw a stone at Solemnity's window" (*Critical Heritage*, 305). This putative flaw, however, is not mere prank or vandalization. Auden's shrewd exercises in impudence differ from Joyce's. He extends Joyce's resistance to disgust, but he leavens Joyce's portrayals of the disgusting with a sanity in Phillips's sense: Manifestly sympathetic to abjection, his work, nevertheless, does not dwell in humiliation as much as Joyce's. He is more invested in mapping human hypocrisy than in swerving to its openly scandalous antitheses.[3] Worsley's pronouncement inadvertently highlights the political irreverence in Auden's work that partly mirrors the insouciance of Dadaism and other strains of modernism. Scrutinizing such irreverence at length in *Destruction Was My Beatrice*, Jed Rasula notes that, in George Grosz's Dadaist works, "calculated puerile art had a distinctly political edge," defying "the notion of art as 'an aesthetic harmonization of bourgeois ideas of ownership'" (66). Later in his study, Rasula sees a less-noted concomitant of Dadaism, as he credits, "beyond all the smoke and mirrors, the pranks and hoaxes—some quest for a better outcome, a more humane disposition, something like Hugo Ball's sage advice: 'Let us be thoroughly new and inventive. Let us rewrite life every day'" (309). Intense respect for a disposition to "rewrite" life shapes Auden's early poetry, including his celebrated elegies of 1939. He extends this respect through a demanding self-criticism that is evident in his compulsive, even notorious, rewriting of his own poems, especially through qualifications of their ethical arguments and messianic or dogmatic potential. Amplifying their "inverted hypocrisy" especially for the latter kind of change, his inclusion of everyday speech in his poetry draws aspersions of literary vandalism or perversity: As Bonnie Costello discusses Auden's idiom in "Journal of an Airman" from *The Orators* (1932), she notes, "The voice is that of an antipoet who uses slang and crude imagery" (50).

The Elegiac Night

Auden's informality marks even his poems of mourning for various prominent intellectual figures, its critical and ironic sympathies responding as much to their demise as to their cultivation of personae and masks. Let me turn to its operations, especially in the elegiac poetry that Auden writes till his formal taking of the Anglican Communion in 1940. I will focus mostly on the importance of informality in Auden's sympathy for the unanticipated, the invisible, and the forgotten in his elegies for Yeats, Freud, and Toller (all from 1939). These works intensify the mood of disillusionment, with the "up-to-date" scepticism that MacNeice saw as a feature of Auden's work, as well as a staging of temporal disorientation: As the poems for Yeats and Toller apostrophize the dead, they interrogate conventional notions of presence and memory. This eccentric use of apostrophe signals not only the intimacy of a personal conversation with the dead, but also the urgency compelling us to converse informally with the dead. Diana Fuss's book, *Dying Modern*, addresses these questions by investigating three different voices in the poetry of modern death: the dying voice, the reviving voice, and the surviving voice, which, taken together, Fuss sees as constituting a modern *ars moriendi* (3). The elegy for Toller works as informal dialogue: Its speaker's "reviving voice" invites responses it knows it will not receive, other than through its own personal searching and provisional inferences—through intense relations with memory and textual investigation. The speaker asks:

> What was it, Ernst, that your shadow unwittingly said?
> O did the child see something horrid in the woodshed
> Long ago?
>
> (ll. 7–9)

The queries request answers that they cannot get, but can speculate upon by guesswork based on careful recall of someone with whom the speaker's tone suggests informal—though not necessarily intimate—relations. (The questions suggest informality through their colloquial manner, but also convey the absence of intimate knowledge.)

Each of Auden's elegies employs a speaking voice that multiplies its capacities, personae, and addressees by means of articulative postures very much like those that Auden attributes to theatrical masks in his apologia, "A Modern Use of Masks" (1936). His strategy for this is a subtle, rapid, and—at times—seamless prosopopoeia or "mask-wearing" that is adopted frequently in poems where corpses speak in the voice of the dead, as Fuss notes in *Dying Modern*. Linking prosopopoeia to death, Fuss observes that the Holocaust "appears to mark the historical limit beyond which the corpse poem hesitates to venture" (64). In this exercise, the "few Holocaust poets who do employ the voice of the dead tend to adopt neither an individual nor a collective persona but a unique voice that is both at once" (Fuss, 64–5). Fuss reads a unique-but-double voice in Jacob Glatstein's line "'"I am I"— / thousands of slaughtered I's,' [from] a poem that reveals not the poet's desire to revive the dead but rather his own profound identification with the dead" (65). Further mapping such identification, she notes:

> Recent trauma theory reminds us that one might survive an unthinkable atrocity like the Holocaust and yet still not feel alive, a point made particularly eloquently by Charlotte Delbo in *Auschwitz and After*: "I died in Auschwitz, but no one knows it."
>
> (65)

Fuss extends her discussion of such a condition through a generous reading of Yevgeny Yevtushenko's "Babii Yar." After quoting the poem's speaker (who claims, "I am each old man here shot dead"), Fuss asserts, "Allowing the dead to speak through them, each poet tentatively seeks to reverse the de-personalization of mass murder by lending to the unmourned victims of genocide his own individual voice" (65). These are not tentative instances of poets allowing the dead to speak through them, however; they are, instead, examples of poets allowing themselves to speak as the dead while their poems make clear that their speakers are alive. Fuss sympathetically endorses the poets' choice in these words: "These singular poems do not presume to resurrect the dead, only to memorialize them from the respectful position of writers confronting the enigma of their own uncertain survivals" (65). The line that I have quoted from Yevtushenko's poem, however, clearly shows an incorporating voice that identifies with and assumes the identities of the dead—as, in different ways, do the speakers in the quotations from Glatstein and Delbo. These speakers offer obvious solidarity with the dead, but there is some diminution in their appreciation of another's particular experience of death in a holocaust if they choose to speak *as*, rather than even *for*, these dead.

Fuss large-heartedly argues, "If modern elegists frequently ventriloquize the dead, they do so to keep the call alive, sending their own voices out into the wilderness" (110). This is almost inarguably so, but to equate your voice with that of the dead, with no apparent prosopopoeic move, borders on or performs a perhaps-unconscious appropriation of voice. When one takes the obviously and overwhelmingly higher moral ground to speak *as a victim who is another or also another*, do the cultural and ethical mitigations of empathy turn into a moral license for merging identities or appropriating voices? In Fuss's words, "Through the rhetorical animation of the dead made possible by the trope of prosopopoeia, the corpse poem seeks instead to redress the historical erasure of the corpse that even literary criticism has at times promoted" (68). Prosopopoeia seeks to redress this erasure by injecting a masked or imaginary or illusory—as opposed to an unmediated or "real" or "fully alive"—speaker into a work. However, Fuss's commentaries on the quoted works by Yevtushenko, Glatstein, and Delbo obscure the recognition of this difference, seeing the speech in their poetry as, in Paul de Man's words, "the screen of a language that controls its own representational mastery" (*Allegories of Reading*, 22). Here, Fuss evokes de Man's essay "Hypogram and Inscription," in which de Man gives the following etymological explanation for prosopopoeia: "*prosopon-poiein* means to *give* a face and therefore implies that the original face can be missing or nonexistent" (30). To "give" a face is, of course, to mediate, but the identification of the living with the dead does not offer the mediated voice of the dead in Fuss's selection of poems by Yevtushenko, Glatstein, and Delbo. These poems offer, instead, the voice of the living who identify themselves with and as the dead *while not speaking as the dead*. It is the imposition of identification in these poems that seems to escape *Dying Modern*.

Although she evokes the modernist elegy several times, Fuss's commentary does not consider Auden's elegiac works, perhaps because these are prominent instances of the modern elegy that have received substantial critical attention already. However, some attention to Auden's elegies might add some necessary nuance to Fuss repeated charge of melancholia against the modernist elegy. Her views on the corpse-poem have manifest affinities with "In Memory of W. B. Yeats," which reminds us that the "words of a dead man / Are modified in the guts of the living" (247). As the words of the dead percolate in the world, the poem suggests, they leave traces of ethical lessons for which the poem's two closing verses call in these famous words:

> With the farming of a verse / Make a vineyard of the curse, / Sing of human un- success / In a rapture of distress; // In the deserts of the heart / Let the healing fountain start, / In the prison of his days / Teach the free man how to praise.
>
> (249)

In an urgent iteration of its educational dimensions, Auden's poem sees critical appreciation as the antidote to the horrors of the world it addresses. The astringent challenge for the poet is to teach such appreciation to someone who has already achieved freedom within the prison of time. In light of the global war that haunts the elegy, such freedom is a privilege, whether racial, national, or economic. For Auden, global memory, particularized in the memory of readers, is the means for the metaphorical attainment of such freedom and the medium for its extension.

Part of the last line of its third stanza ("he became his admirers") and the last pair of lines in its fourth stanza (The words of a dead man / Are modified in the guts of the living") reconfigure the elegy's title to "W. B. Yeats in Memory," in effect—the poet exists through memory. Auden extends such memory, in significant part, through quotation of a textual past in his elegies. Quotation or citation itself is an act of informal relation of a text with another, or of a quote-maker with a textual precursor. When "In Memory of W. B. Yeats" echoes *Lycidas* (Among the ivy "never sere" ran "the grim wolf w/ privy paws" with a further inversion and echo in section III, stanza 5), Auden's evocation of Milton to describe current circumstances both enlarges textual memory and links the literary past to the present. Through its reflexive modification the words of the dead in the guts of the living, Auden's poem performs the dialogics of "Tradition and the Individual Talent" that *The Waste Land* stifles. Unlike *The Waste Land*, which uses quotation of the textual past to suggest horrified, contemptuous comparisons with the present, Auden relates the present to the past in the hope of reconstituting it (or, rather, the past and the present, together) for the making of a future "vineyard" in the "prison" of our days.

This prison is also the locus for "the nightmare of the dark"; its terrors, partly are those of imminent war, but (within the elegy for Freud) also of the pain that haunts those cast out of bright "normalcy" into social darkness, "where the injured / lead the ugly life of the rejected" (274). The temporal metaphor for the shelter, the detention, and the articulations of the ostracized is the night. The Yeats elegy's request for practice in "how to praise" is a call that Auden's elegy for Sigmund Freud seems to answer partially, but significantly, with its reminder "to be enthusiastic about the night" (249, 276). This night deserves such appreciation, the poem tells us, "not only for the sense of wonder / it alone has to offer, but also // because it needs our love" (276). The latter is an argument for, among other things, acknowledging what the night reveals, and so for dismantling the politicized hierarchies of what can and cannot be put on display; for permitting visibility to the unseen; for respecting and taking pleasure in the forbidden; and (perhaps most important) for respecting a resistance to exposure.[4] The latter offers a persuasive rebuttal to the need for certitude symptomatic in Fuss's presumed exposure of intentions and closure.

The third part of elegy on Yeats *is* prosopopoeic in Fuss's sense of adopting "neither an individual nor a collective persona but a unique voice that is both at once"—the poem's third part is an address from both the living and the dead poet (64–5). Auden mobilizes such prosopopoeic strategies to render reading itself an act of informal transmission, intimate indeed, but also informal, estranging and rearranging the terms of intimacy through the irreverent scepticism that Auden's elegies perform. Consolation constructs something like this terminus—a presumed place of affective closure or suspension for one's grief—and, as Fuss herself suggests, the violence of modernity puts consolation at a premium. However, Fuss's conclusion stresses that "it may be too soon to foreclose on consolation" (107). Fuss reproaches what she terms "current critical thinking" which "holds that it is only in the refusal of consolation that we find ethics; only by resisting an established literary mode like traditional elegy can a poet truly do justice to the unsettling and unsparing truth of dying modern" (108). Fuss's conflation of refusal and resistance is telling. Is it in *refusal* of consolation entirely, or in resistance to consolation—or, more precisely, in resistance to an *expectation* of it—that we find ethics?

If "In Memory of W. B. Yeats" imagines the start of "healing fountains," the elegy for Freud nonetheless begins in consciously confounded questioning:

> When there are so many we shall have to mourn,
> when grief has been made so public, and exposed
> to the critique of a whole epoch
> the frailty of our conscience and anguish,
>
> of whom shall we speak? For every day they die
> among us, those who were doing us some good...
>
> (273)

The poem's opening stanza is aware of the *absence* of an apt selection for an elegy in the face of the enormousness and enormity of daily deaths on a massive scale not only in the field of battle or other conventional theatres of violence, but "among us." The vertiginous conjunction of the proximity and pervasiveness of death during a global crisis, whether a world war or pandemic, unveils the absurdity of evoking "aptness" as a criterion for memorialization. Ethical loss for the world (the loss of "those who were doing us *some good*") accompanies the annihilation of form in the name of the maintenance of form (of the nation-state, empire, race, and so on) during war. In Auden's elegies the questioning of such loss accompanies the questioning of *conventions as bearers of form*. In part, this is because Auden is aware of the threateningly non-nuanced effects and aims of war, which, in rash interpretations, could be read as informality taken to its logical extreme: The brutality of violence brings the destruction of form—rather than remaking, revision, and easing of formality. What Auden calls "the concupiscence of the oppressor" in the elegy to Freud is not only a lust for violence, but for obedience—it is interpellation as appetite (274).

Tyranny demands the literalization of loyalty and love, self-exposure, and unanimity that tyrants demand, respectively, as obedience, consent to surveillance, and alignment of desires with the tyrant's own. Given Freud's resistance to the literal, especially through his emphases on the importance of invisible or unregistered psychological processes, Auden elegizes Freud by adopting a Freudian signature: The elegy for Freud was Auden's first syllabic poem, using syllabic congruity, rather than obvious rhyme. This shift gives formal arguments, as a constellation of less overt and more elusive statements (mirroring psychology), greater semiotic significance in a poem on Freud. Further, such concealment expands the liberatory capacities in informal self-fashioning that Auden defends near the beginning of "A Modern Use of Masks," and that Auden addresses informally but sympathetically as an important aspect of the personae of Yeats, Freud, and Toller in his elegies. Explicitly noting that Freud assumed "traces of the autocratic pose" of "the paternal structures he distrusted" as a "protective coloration," Auden famously declares, "To us, [Freud,] is no more a person / Now but a whole climate of opinion" (275). How does a person become a whole climate of revised opinion, overhauling previous such climates? Extrapolating from the poem's logic: He does so, because his persuasive distrust of patriarchy has spread into a culture-wide questioning of patriarchal norms. And this kind of rebellion is what artistic and intellectual culture has now internalized. The relations between revisions of formality and self-fashioning are crucial for this argument.

In each of the elegies under consideration, Auden makes poignant but informal reference to self-fashioning as some form of defence, desired or not, for the elegized: Mixing affectionate irreverence with self-implication by calling Yeats "silly like us," Auden points to Yeats's anxieties about "physical decay" prominently as a sign of Yeats's silliness; in an admiringly paradoxical pairing, he notes that Toller was "egotistical and brave"; and, again, voicing admiration disguised as an insult, he declares that Freud "wasn't clever at all" before the elegy produces a caesura:

He wasn't clever at all: he merely told
the unhappy Present to recite the Past
like a poetry lesson till sooner
or later it faltered at the line where

long ago the accusations had begun,
and suddenly knew by whom it had been judged...

(274)

The lines suggest (without literalizing their argument) that the sceptical elegy—like the *talking* in the "talking-cure"—brings us to the fault-lines of our stories. Further, the caesura leads to an insight and, thereby, performs an appreciative doubling of the pause of recognition in psychoanalysis. But recognition itself is not a cure—Freud notoriously offers recognitions and not "cures," strictly speaking.[5] (In that sense, psychoanalysis, like poetry, "makes nothing happen.") The poem for Freud withholds solace for itself and its reader. It ends, more somberly than the tributes to Yeats or Toller, as a record of grief, with no gesture to consolation. Even when Auden's elegies promise the *possibility* of consolation, they do not offer it as an erasure of, or equivalent counterweight to, loss, resisting the formality of a closure to loss. In his resistance to the very notion of sufficient restoration, Auden resists presumptions about the possibilities of restoring *prior* cultural order and plenitude. As he asks Toller in his apostrophic address: "Or had the Europe which took refuge in your head // Already been too injured to get well?" (249). The question suggests that things may be too injured to be restored or fully cured, but (as his making a vineyard from a curse suggests) not to see the world's conditions as the "way the world ends" *while it still exists*.

What each of Auden's elegies tries to reclaim is capacities for illegitimate freedom, with the realization that such freedom might not bring a cure. Instead of a cure, it might well entail solitude: As he writes in the elegy for Freud, "to be free / Is often to be lonely" (275). Sensitive to both emotional and ethical isolation here, he seems informally to include the arguments of another thinker as he elegizes Freud, that thinker being Friedrich Nietzsche.[6] Within the ambit of Auden's and Freud's thought (less so, within Nietzsche's), this link between loneliness and freedom can also haunts the normatively rejected—those deemed "abnormal" and therefore outcast or ostracized. Seen as radical, unassimilable difference when (in the poem's clearly implied arguments and Freud's more famous versions of them) their "abnormality" is often a manifest version of tendencies, desires, and traits that normative society represses or disavows, rather than a *lack*. The very definition of abnormality in such society is, then, a consequence of attitudes. As Auden argues in his essay "Psychology and Art To-Day" (1935), "The importance of Freud to art is greater than his language, technique or the truth of theoretical details. He is the most typical but not the only representative of a certain attitude to life and living relationships" (61). Citing a much-debated passage from

Freud's introductory lectures on psychoanalysis in an essay on Freud titled "Psychology and Art To-day," Auden notes that it has "infuriated artists, not altogether unjustly," with the following claims:

> There is, in fact, a path from phantasy back again to reality, and that is—art … [L]ike any other with an unsatisfied longing, [the artist] turns away from reality and transfers all his interest, and all his Libido, too, on to the creation of his wishes in life … it is well known how often artists in particular suffer from partial inhibition of their capacities through neurosis … Further, [the artist] possesses the mysterious ability to mould his particular material until it expresses the idea of his phantasy faithfully; and then he knows how to attach to this reflection of his phantasy-life so strong a stream of pleasure that, for a time at least, the repressions are out-balanced and dispelled by it.
>
> (*The English Auden*, 333–4)

Striving to disrupt the social repression of the vulnerable or outcast in his poem for Freud, Auden maintains a dissatisfaction that he finds in Freud's arguments to be another major aspect of artistic psychology: "We only think when we are prevented from feeling or acting as we should like. Perfect satisfaction would be complete unconsciousness" (63). Discounting that we might like to be in continuous or sustained thought, Auden's definition of perfect unconsciousness is accurate, all the same. Such dissatisfaction fuels much of Auden's early work and his arguments in the elegies under discussion, here. Further, it keeps his elegies from both surrendering to norms and offering facile consolation, at the same time.

Fuss argues, "Elegies speak to both audiences, forced to negotiate the impossible ethical demands of a genre that strives neither to disrespect the dead nor to ignore the needs of the living" (5). The swirling negatives of that claim aside, why are these demands "impossible"? Auden carries out both tasks with subtlety and considerable success by dissolving orthodox notions and the ceremonial poetry of respect. These are signs of Auden's "inverted hypocrisy," indeed; but they are also signatures of the fertility of paradox for his poetics of informality in the face of crises. This poetics invites a reimagining of the present that is, itself, a function of the reorganization of past (and so a better rehearsal of the arguments in "Tradition and the Individual Talent" than *The Waste Land*): It involves modifying "the words of the dead"—the human archive of thought—into an appreciation of the unfamiliar, the non-formulaic, the unprescribed, and, perhaps, even the disorienting in imagined *potential* experience. This latter quality—a necessary imagined disorientation—is a sign of the intoxication that the wine from the "curse" (historical crises) transformed into a vineyard would produce. It is through critical irreverence for, even defiance of the literally given—of *evident form*—in hostile circumstances that we can reimagine the world, or, in other words, learn how to make a vineyard of a curse.[7] At such moments of the defiance of evident or prescribed form, appreciation emerges as a function of *informality*. Auden's stone-throwing attitude towards "Solemnity," which provoked T. C. Worsley's disapproval, gives Auden scepticism to fertilize the respect that he conveys in his elegiac writings.

The pedagogy in Auden's poems escapes pedantry by replacing it with urgent argument—it is an encouraging pedagogical call that conflates hope and sorrow, as well as rage and protest, with a more overt investment in rationality than in Joyce's work. Auden does not presume moral elevation; instead, he calls for a logical resistance to presumptions of such elevation in the apocalyptic or the "concupiscence of the oppressor." It is in their issuance of appeals that Auden's elegies are especially subtle, ethical, and appreciative of both relations and difference. Jahan Ramazani notes that, in their "skeptical intelligence," these poems employ a dialectical pattern, through which "the poet first challenges the paternal figure before melting into him" (176, 178). But, in Auden's poems, the solidarity with dead figures operates more as solidarity than a complete "melting into." The implicit or overt critiques of such figures in Auden's elegies marks and modulates the ostensible praise for them, as well as identification with them. As Ramazani himself notes, "Auden's imitative cathexis of his oedipal heroes is all the more powerful because it breaks through the dam of an earlier defiance" (178). Auden's protests in his elegies do not assume that the ethics he sees the dead as modelling will guarantee stable solutions. The ethical imperatives in his works are not to see pain and pleasure, opportunity and challenge, mourning and meditation, or criticism and praise as extricable, especially in crises. Instead, he sees as imperative that, amid "human unsuccess," the ethicist or the ethical elegist negotiate such crises in "a rapture of distress," where pain and ethical clarity, as well as hope and respect for difference *as* ethical clarity, churn to produce the arguments of "In Memory of W. B. Yeats" (249). This is not traumaphilia. To remain only in the rapture of distress, and thereby *not* to sing of human unsuccess, would be to remain in masochism. Auden explicitly resisted masochism, protesting, in his review of De la Mare's *Behold This Dreamer*, that people "are content masochistically *to be lived*" (*Prose* II, 38; italics Auden's).

His elegy for Ernst Toller rewords the thought: "We are lived by powers we pretend to understand / They arrange our lives." If informal appreciation is the aim of poetic pedagogy in the poem for Yeats, then it is an especially admired quality in the poem for Toller. Evoking the cultural forgetting of such appreciation in the rushed performances of culturally expected rituals, Auden writes in the poem's opening verses:

> And the friends who are sad and the enemies who rejoice
>
> Are chased by their shadows lightly away from the grave
> Of one who was egotistical and brave,
> Lest they should learn without suffering how to forgive.

(249)

Again, Auden constructs a counterintuitive solution for quick forgetting in the form of a suggested protest. The last line in the latter verse finds particularly appreciable the experience of suffering for an appreciation of suffering, of capacities to suspend condemnation *as well as* redemptive confidence in the absence of the experience of suffering. The latter would be the kind of confidence that lets us assume powers to redeem or resurrect to "normalcy" with our forgiveness.[8] However, the protest against normative processes of forgiveness built into the line is that interpellation or normative expectations numb us to deserved sympathies under the "half-watt hypnotism" of norms; that we cast aside possibilities to sympathize, appreciate, and forgive until we ourselves suffer the humiliation or pain of those for whom we delay or refuse forgiveness.

"In Memory of W. B. Yeats" gives us as a model of such forgiveness when it asks for lessons on how to praise. Extending critical elegiac ethics through its very mixture of admiration and irreverence, it declines abiding, predictable, discrete, or appropriately stable responses to crises. The intensities of its simultaneous hope and protesting distress are not gushing with some anticipatory triumphal exuberance, but they do stage a resistance to outright fatalism and melancholia.[9] Reflecting the mobility of the simultaneously vast and intimate scope of his concerns, the poem's speaker elegizes through a general voice, addressing an unidentified audience, first; then, the "Earth," both as place and as global population; and, in the poem's closing section, an unidentified audience, again, before it issues its closing plea to poets, at large (including the singular figure of Yeats, in particular). To do so, it employs something like the technique of informal sympathy that Rancière sees Faulkner and Woolf employ in prose fiction, while exposing itself to charges of presumed sympathies or evasion through sophisticated, but light, self-deprecation. The latter charge fuels Orwell's excoriation of Auden in "Inside the Whale":

> And of course the rather priggish note that is common to most of these writers is a symptom of release. By throwing "pure art" overboard they have freed themselves from the fear of being laughed at and vastly enlarged their scope...
>
> (232)[10]

Especially given Auden's sensitivity to his own implication within class, race, and nation, Orwell's objections have a touch of churlish prescriptiveness. In contrast, counter-prescriptive (and, arguably, counterintuitive) energy shapes Auden's elegies' self-conscious ethics and concern for global historical memory. John Bayley points to such self-consciousness in a tribute to Auden titled "Only Critics Can't Play": "In an essay on Walter De la Mare[,] he quoted Santayana's comment: 'Every artist is a moralist though he needn't preach'" (231). Bayley connects this warning against preaching with Auden's objections to art being governed by the rules of "family life" and "social amenity" (230, 231). Later in his essay, Bayley adds a pair of rapid qualifications, saying that, his objections to the rules of family life aside, "Auden's art really depends on something very like it. But it is, let me hasten to add, family life on an international scale—there is nothing provincial about it" (231).

Within this vast scale of concern, Auden builds room for unusual, confusing, and challenging considerations. A Joycean respect for paradox provides the grounds for a reorientation of thought that Lukács calls "vivid sensuous form," a precondition for revolution, in *History and Class Consciousness*. Lukács contends that:

> as the mere contradiction is raised to a consciously dialectical contradiction, as the act of becoming conscious turns into *a point of transition in practice*, we see once more in greater concreteness the character of proletarian dialectics as we have often described it: namely, since consciousness here is not the knowledge of an opposed object but is the self-consciousness of the object *the act of consciousness overthrows the objective form of its object.*
>
> (178; italics Lukács's)

Auden produces such reorientation through various aesthetic moves: shifts of location through dialectical montage (between the private and public, the uncontrolled natural and the hyperregulated urban, normatively, the individual body and the world); juxtapositions of calm, even ceremonious, speech and intensely seething and delirious—ostensibly nonsensical—utterance (when he speaks of "a rapture of distress," or of a man "free" within a "prison"); and a radical departure from elevated, elegiac tone (when he describes Yeats as "silly" or Freud as "not clever at all"). The latter version of rhetorical deviance violates classical expectations for *epideixis*, one of the three branches, or "species" (*eidē*), of rhetoric as outlined in Aristotle's *Rhetoric*. Epideictic oratory is ceremonial oratory that involves the rhetoric of praise or blame. Hans Ulrich Gumbrecht writes in *In Praise of Athletic Beauty*:

> [T]he only genre of speech for which Aristotle, in his *Rhetoric*, did not identify a specific function was the epideictic genre … In a move that we can today describe as antimetaphysical, he insisted that we should praise not just the virtues of those we admire but also, and above all, their achievements. In his clear warning against the tendency to let our attention go beyond the purely material world, is a desire to concentrate on the things that surround us and to work on our relation to them—and nothing else. Aristotle went on to observe that, through praise, we attribute "beauty and importance" to the objects of our praise, and he finished the passage on epideixis by pointing to the tropes of amplification as being appropriate for this genre—meaning that more words and

> more variations of certain descriptions were the best way to praise what we love.
>
> (33–4)

Unlike classical *epideixis*, however, the dynamics of praise and blame in Auden's elegiac poetry do not operate discretely: Auden inserts into his elegies a politics that mutually intensifies praise and blame for the elaboration of notions of success and failure. His experiments with "inverted hypocrisy" make paradox a rhetorical and political resource for him. They make his use of paradox not merely a counter to prescription, but a contrapuntal prescription: the collaboration of the public and the private, praise and irreverence, in the production of a politics of joint hope and scepticism (if you like, an optimism of the will and pessimism of the intellect, neither stable nor distinct). This politics compels us to read the imperatives in the elegy for Yeats not as assumptions of authority, but as uncertain injunctions of hope.

While some critical studies, such as Jahan Ramazani's *Poetry of Mourning*, contain brief commentary on Auden's weaving of classical poetic form, praise, and irreverence in his elegies, the connection between that irreverence and the political arguments in those elegiac works has not received substantial examination. The critique of Yeats's vanity in the second section of Auden's elegy ("You were silly like us") presages Auden's critique of the paranoid narcissism haunting nations on the verge of the Second World War (248–9). It thus extends the scope of the modern elegy from the personal to the political. The angry irreverence for "the dogs of Europe" in the poem's third section is very different than the affectionate irreverence the poem affords Yeats (248). The latter critique offers a serious delight in beauty and reconstitution of norms ("make a vineyard of a curse") as its solution to patriotic propriety before war. Poetry is not a motive *cause* for such reconstitution, but it is *a mode*, "[a] way of happening." Describing style over origin, the insight places means over causality, an instrument of possibility, rather than literalization—thus, it is, by its own logic, "unconstraining" (III, st. 4). After the sonorous invocation of the "Earth" to receive "an honoured guest," the poem presents its mournful injunction, "Let the Irish vessel lie / Emptied of its poetry" with the slant or imperfect rhyme of "lie" and "poetry" (248). This is both an enactment of pathos and a brief, informal embrace of imperfection: bad rhyme and bad puns—for which Auden claims good poets have a "weakness," many years later in "The Truest Poetry Is the Most Feigning" (619). The informal, imperfect rhyme stages a lack: a poetry facing *loss*. The acknowledgement and blurring of absence and presence at this moment—and, by definition, in elegies that evoke the absence and presence of a lost figure—refinethe modernist inquiry of the persistence of the supposedly absent within what is obvious or literally visible. Auden's practice of such inquiry amplifies into arguments for permitting visibility to the unseen.

A compassionate zeal (the *zèle compatissant* that Arendt attributes to Auden) for validating the forbidden—dismantling the politicized hierarchies of what can and cannot be put on display—drives Auden's elegy for Freud...[11] With its reminder of Freud's stress on the need to validate experience of the forbidden, the poem recognizes not only honesty about the psychically repressed but also *honesty about the socially repressed* as a sign of being "enthusiastic over the night." If the night is the morally precarious time of concealment and invisibility, it is a time of psychological contingency and potential for versions of community that our conscious, "daylight" selves might not acknowledge or even recognize as worthy of acknowledgement. A sensitivity to the time for the emergence of the absent and the invisible thus shapes Auden's conjoining of praise with protest. This very tendency also makes the night a stage and a metaphor for the unveiling of hostilities ("In the nightmare of the dark / All the dogs of Europe bark"). Noting the political production of cultural climates, Auden thematizes the overdetermination of historical conditions by the powerful in his protesting note here through variations of it in his other elegies. The discursive manufacture, invalidation, and expulsion of possibilities by those in power close his apostrophization of Toller:

> We are lived by powers we pretend to understand:
> They arrange our loves; it is they who direct at the end
> The enemy bullet, the sickness, or even our hand.
>
> It is their tomorrow hangs over the earth of the living
> And all that we wish for our friends; but existing is believing
> We know for whom we mourn and who is grieving.
>
> (250)

The verses see the intensity of grief and its deployment in imaging alternatives for its causes as the only possible (and likely, unsuccessful) counters to the powers that "arrange our loves." This fuses a questioning of socially surrendered agency with a protest against the formalization of love, which itself requires the making of yet another alternative to given reality in the "vineyard" of imagination. To offer a poetic vineyard while facing the curse of war is, in some obvious ways, an outrageous act, offering an ethics through aesthetics that welcomes—and is even intoxicated by—the possibilities of violent reconstitution at times of crisis.[12] Moreover, to do so is to undertake ethical and aesthetic criticism through the appreciation of art or complexities that undermine destructive militancy by seeking within violent circumstances the possibilities to *remake*, rather than destroy. Such poetic appreciation, simultaneously alerting and intoxicating, forms the antidotal vineyard in a time of war. It fuels the subtle and overt irreverence with which Auden's poems resist both the forces of war and the forces of propriety, instead urging strife against the silencing or foreclosure of unsanctioned expression. Their simultaneous scepticism and openness to unfamiliar relations thus work antidotally against the later Eliotic attempts to seal art in "right" attitudes to God or purely classical aesthetic realms. Linked from the start to "unsuccess" (rather than "failure"), Auden's kind assertions of informality in "In Memory of W. B. Yeats," "In Memory of Sigmund Freud," and "In Memory of Ernst Toller" engage the possibility and even the responsibility of conceding its incompleteness and insufficiency of response.

Notes

1 Let me stress my use of the term "virtue" as generic and idiomatically contemporary, here: I am not evoking, for instance, the distinction between *virtu* and *fortuna* in early modern Europe.

2 Auden's continued practice of demystifying, contrarian, and even impudent responses to world events rebuts Arendt's charge that, when Auden "became a Christian[,] he left the train of History altogether": See his address to the Indian Congress for Cultural Freedom (1953), his passionate disagreements with British colonial policy in "Partition" (1966), and his poem against triumphalist responses to the Apollo IX lunar mission, "Moon-Landing" (1969) (531).

3 In lines from "Letter to Lord Byron" that reflects both his admiration of, and distance from, Joyce's more informal flourishes, Auden concedes that Jane Austen was "not an unshockable blue-stocking"; but, given her sharp incisions into hypocritical furtiveness, Auden writes, "You could not shock her more than she shocks me; / Beside her Joyce seems innocent as grass" (84).

4 For an elegant discussion of the night as a psychoanalytic metaphor for the engines of artistic expression of what has been forbidden or repressed, see pp. 86–105 in Elisabeth Bronfen's *Night Passages*.

5 In a list distilling what he calls the "essence of Freud's teaching" in "Psychology and Art To-day," Auden notes:

> The task of psychology or art, for that matter, is not to tell people how to behave, but by drawing their attention to what the impersonal unconscious is trying to tell them, and by increasing their knowledge of good and evil, to render them better able to choose, to become increasingly morally responsible for their destiny.
>
> (*The English Auden*, 339, 340–1)

In her study of Auden's work habits "Still Doing It By Hand," Hannah Sullivan notes Auden's "measured impersonality" in his contrarian poem "Moon Landing"—which we can read as an attempt to *perform* what he calls "the impersonal unconscious" in his essay (20).

6 Nietzsche glosses the links between freedom and loneliness in various works; among them: his commentary on the "man of intuition" in *The Birth of Tragedy* (150–3); his gesture to the link again in *On the Genealogy of Morals* (41). Further, in "Nietzsche on Loneliness, Self-Transformation, and the Eternal Recurrence," Justin Remhof notes Nietzsche's conflation of loneliness and freedom: "[I]n the 1886 preface to *HH* [Nietzsche] writes, "Loneliness [*Einsamkeit*] encircles and embraces him [the free spirit], ever more threatening, suffocating, heart-tightening, that terrible goddess and *mater saeva cupidinum*" (196). Auden himself writes several poems on loneliness, including "Loneliness," "Their Lonely Betters," "Talking to Dogs," "Talking to Mice," "Talking to Myself," and "Two Don Quixote Lyrics," among several better-known others.

7 Auden himself contends in "Psychology and Art To-day," "Creation, like psycho-analysis, is a process of re-living in a new situation" (*The English Auden*, 337).

8 Gottlieb perceptively describes such nuanced generosity in Auden's "In Praise of Limestone" within the offset portion of her following claim: "[T]he grammar of the poem even suggests that with forgiveness comes the redemptive resumption that is—or perhaps is only figured as—resurrection" (194).

9 Vicki Mahaffey reads the closing lines of the poem as a restoration of equilibrium between imprisonment and freedom (202).

10 Auden's attitude to such self-deprecation takes different turns in his elegiac work. Commenting on "The Cave of Making," Auden's elegy for Louis MacNeice, Ramazani writes:

> In an earlier period [Auden] might have had to sit through feasts, improvising "a eulogy / of some beefy illiterate burner." Banishing all nostalgia for such a role, Auden frankly embraces the elitism of modern poetry [in his poem of mourning for MacNeice]. He is thankful
>
> to serve this unpopular art which cannot be turned into
> background noise for study
> or hung as a status trophy by rising executives,
> cannot be "done" like Venice
> or abridged like Tolstoy, but stubbornly still insists upon
> being read or ignored. (203)

While Auden's own assumptions are questionable in a period of rampant abridgement, like the current age of social media, I would also question Ramazani's reading, but only for its use of the term "elitism": Auden is certainly less accommodating in his sympathies within the address to MacNeice, but is an endorsement of rigour or careful reading elitism, precisely? Is the possession of interpretive cultural capital not more a function of labour than, say, the possession of material wealth?

11 Auden's poem memorializing Henry James (1941) has similar ethical investments in flexing formal purposes and permissions, seeing formality as a structure for games ("With what an innocence your hand submitted / To those formal rules that help a child to play") and questioning of proportion, propriety, or censorship during grief ("lest Proportion shed / The alpine chill of her shrugging editorial shoulder / On my loose impromptu song").

12 The proximity between the poem's publication and Auden's conversion to Anglicanism notwithstanding, the blurred epistemology and agency in Christian "rapture" are secularized here. This is so, if only because the poem issues a call for human action, asking the poet, rather than a divine agent, to remake or reconceive the world through the artistic imagination.

Conclusion

Openness to Misreading: The Risks of Informality

On her sea-voyage back to England from Turkey in Woolf's *Orlando*, Orlando, now a woman, is offered a slice of beef by her ship's captain Nicholas Bartolus. Woolf presents the moment that immediately follows, with Orlando's response to it, pungently, lacing the scene with almost-pornographic language:

> "A little of the fat, Ma'm?" he asked. "Let me cut you just the tiniest little slice the size of your fingernail." At those words a delicious tremor ran through her frame. Birds sang; the torrents rushed. It recalled the feeling of indescribable pleasure with which she had first seen Sasha, hundreds of years ago ... Which is the greater ecstasy? The man's or the woman's? And are they not perhaps the same? No, she thought, this is the most delicious (thanking the Captain but refusing), to refuse, and see him frown. Well, she would, if he wished it, have the very thinnest, smallest shiver in the world. This was the most delicious of all, to yield and see him smile. "For nothing," she thought, regaining her couch on deck, and continuing the argument, "is more heavenly than to resist and to yield; to yield and to resist. Surely it throws the spirit into such a rapture as nothing else can. So that I'm not sure," she continued, "that I won't throw myself overboard, for the mere pleasure of being rescued by a blue-jacket after all."
>
> (114–15)

The scene delights in a furtive license for insinuation in the informal through its play with promiscuous feeling, Orlando's own flirtatious fantasies, and ambiguity: "shiver" evoking the tremors of orgasm in a brief suggestion that is not exactly subtle with the specific sign of the carnal in Bartolus's offer of meat and fat. With its ambiguity, Woolf's language relinquishes or, at least, slackens its grip on propriety. Alongside, instead of a claim to ownership of meaning, there is a textual invitation to sociability—*to play with* meaning. This is not merely an endorsement of interpretive informality as easy literalism or casualness, but an invitation to consider alternatives, to respect the less obvious and unfamiliar possibilities in an utterance.

DOI: 10.4324/9781003009894-7

Inverted Dignity

Plying the scene with sexual gusto and various double entendres (with offers of flesh, and delight at prospective shivers), Woolf also suspends conventional dignity. The scene stresses Orlando's ambivalence about gender and erotic uncertainty, leaving playfully open the answer to her question about whether men or women have the greater ecstasy. The irrationality of the moment, with its indeterminacy and paradoxical pleasure ("to yield and to resist" *simultaneously* produce Orlando's sense of the moment's "deliciousness"), contrasts the decisive reason that shapes dignity for Immanuel Kant in the *Groundwork of the Metaphysics of Morals*. Arguing in the text that rational beings can select their own ends, Kant elaborates, "Rational nature is distinguished from the rest of nature by the fact that it sets itself an end" and that rational beings gain an "unconditional and incomparable worth" through this ability to establish their own ends (44, 43). Such worth is what Kant calls dignity. If decisive reason and its corollary capacities for determining ends are the qualifications for dignity, Woolf's (or Joyce's) adoption of open-ended ambiguity, playful indecision, and suspensions of rational behaviour altogether distance (or, if you will, liberate) their characters from Kantian dignity. Instead of asserting such dignity, parrhesiastic modernist texts often voice or imply a preference for informal behaviour that consciously or unconsciously risks the loss of normative currency and prestige *through a distance from rationality* (as, say, in Woolf's, Joyce's, Mansfield's, and Auden's clear sympathies for ambiguous—even nonsensical—flirtation, *amor fati*, stalled ratiocination, and raptures of distress, respectively). While they sustain a Kantian will against the instrumentalization of people—against seeing others as "merely means," to use a Kantian phrase—they do not see the adequacy of reason rendering people as *autonomous* ends in themselves, but as figures endlessly woven and unwoven through a series of relations with the world. In short, a character like Leopold Bloom or Orlando or Laura Sheridan or even W. B. Yeats in Auden's elegy is reshaped by unceasing relations with the world. None of these characters is either mere means or absolute ends, secluded from contingency in its autonomous dignity, even as the texts in which they feature resist the instrumentalization of people by institutions, morality, conventions, attitudes, and norms.

In her consideration of the vast culturally enforced disparities in opportunity for men and women, Simone de Beauvoir points to a striking reason for the scarcity of women's access to dignity in *The Second Sex* (1949). She observes, "[Man's] activity has another dimension that endows him with supreme dignity: it is often dangerous" (73). As Beauvoir notes the direct proportionality of risk and dignity in social conventions, a negative inference from her thought gives us an insight on the relations of modernist informality and dignity. Extending Beauvoir's logic and the logic in Arendt's explanation of Auden's "inverted hypocrisy," we can picture an "inverted dignity" in informality that declines proclamations of selves as ends for (or of) virtue. Such logics confirm claims to dignity precisely in acts or choices that defy the conventional appearance of dignity. Woolf's and Joyce's scurrilous or scandalous *parrhesia*, Mansfield's mapping of unacknowledged frustrations in bourgeois domesticity, and Auden's "inverted hypocrisy" enhance, rather than diminish, their candidacy for dignity. Refusing displays of valour and strength, their disavowals of social approval, censorship, ostracism, or even idolatry *risk* dignity that eschews and even repels validatory awe. With its lack of spectacular physical sacrifice or virtuous triumph, such dignity is easily unrecognized because it is normatively denied.

"Over-Familiarity" and Informality

Stephen Dedalus' journal entries in *A Portrait of the Artist as a Young Man* reflect various kinds of informality: vulnerability, intimate retrospection, unvoiced protest, and dependency. They also include an entry that evokes a scene of presumption, earlier in the novel: the moment when the dean of studies at Stephen's college condescendingly dismisses the word "tundish" as a non-English word, humiliating Stephen (205). Later, after Stephen records in his journal that, because the word had haunted him, he "looked it up and [found] it English and good old blunt English too. Damn the dean of studies ... !" (274). The moment restores dignity to Stephen through the informality of the candour in his journal entry and through the linked dispelling of the dean's presumption, adding piquancy to his earlier humiliation through the lingering pain evident in his cursing at the end of the quoted passage. This version of informal dignity is a very different form of modernism's resistance to casualness as presumption or an assumed *intimacy* than the textual resistance to literalism in the passage from *Orlando*, above. The scene from Joyce's novel calls for respect for the unfamiliar in a more overt way. Modernist literature often defamiliarizes and even criticizes the presumptions of familiarity—"over-familiarity"—through its depictions of behaviour that reflects the *appearance* of intimacy. In assuming or performing comprehensive knowledge of English, the dean of studies appears intimate with the language—he shows, but obviously does not have, such knowledge. Presumption obviously marks the transformation of *sociable* informality to overfamiliarity. Near the ending of Mansfield's "The Garden Party," Laurie Sheridan either assumes that he knows what Laura Sheridan wants to say or that her desired utterance is unimportant enough to elide in advance. Mansfield's text protests his complacency not only for its presumption, but also because it does not permit expression—it cancels, or, at minimum, suspends Laura's speech.

Offsetting overfamiliarity, the informality that more generous strains of modernism offer is attentive or inventive (and, thus, in a sense, *earned*) or playful or defiant or some combination of these qualities. Moreover, in their capacity for agile irony, the informality in such modernist works eludes, and refuses to make, rigid moral demands for unqualified sincerity and self-exposure. In this sense, such modernist informality aids resistance to social surveillance and definition by others through reminders of the limitations of perception and memory. It shows observation as a precarious mode of preservation. Woolf's *Jacob's Room* is alert not merely to fluctuating views of the self in such narration, but of narrative as provisionally organized semiotic flux. Woolf suggests this view when she writes, "One must do the best one can with her report. Anyhow, this was Jacob Flanders, aged nineteen. It is no use trying to sum people up. One must follow hints, not exactly what is said, nor yet entirely what is done—" (29). A *narrated* object, Jacob is a figure for a narrated object's—a text's—unstable production through relations with the world. The novel argues that such production can, in turn, only be a conglomerate of incomplete *suggestions* about the object's character, thereby thwarting notions of comprehensive familiarity. Commenting on Jacob as a figure, Kevin Bell makes a sharp point: "That this figural creation is a presence-ing of negativity, a purely verbal testimony to the absence for which it can never substitute, and yet must in every utterance, demonstrates the most shattering evidence of the text's principle of nonidentity" (107). If, for Auden's "In Memory of W. B. Yeats," the words of the dead are "modified in the guts of the living," *Jacob's Room* shows the living as imperfect conveyors of the dead making words. Its narrative operates as serial reminders that the forms of our selves are functions of stories made elsewhere.

Simultaneity, Influence, and Informal Contact

One of the commonplaces in scholarship on modernism is that, in modernist works, an insistent awareness of "elsewhere" shapes the affective conditions that they explore.[1] The unease, a sense of the uncanny, the deployments of montage, and radial feelings such as those in what Rancière and Auerbach call the "random occurrence," as well as critiques of global conditions, mark the work of Conrad, Joyce, Woolf, Forster, and even Eliot. The unease is a mark, as much of cultural diagnoses, as of self-critique: a textual introspection. Modernist responses to such introspection vary, as I have tried to show here. However, in more generous works, this introspection resists pontification while urging informality as a social preference. These works are aware that such a social mode not only risks harm to its practitioner, but also that its ethics contrast both euphemistic and hyperbolic cultures. After a discussion of Yeats's oracular cultural pronouncements in *The Struggle of the Modern*, Stephen Spender notes that the aftermath of the First World War saw "a withdrawal of artists into less apocalyptically great positions" (259). Noting that the withdrawal comes after the war, Spender views it as inevitable:

> Instead of sitting on the battlefield and "waiting for the end," which might either be a victory transforming the whole of history, or a defeat

> ending all history, the poets have had to take up positions, acquire dogmas and philosophies, consolidate technical innovations, simply in order to continue their own work.
>
> (260)

These realignments entailed a new relation with the world for poets and critics (the "New Critics," specifically), but it was couched as an absence of relation for texts with the world. Spender argues, "That the critics ... wrote 'new' criticism does not make their researches any less a withdrawal" (260). Reflecting Althusser's thesis that "[i]deology represents the imaginary relationship of individuals to their real conditions of existence," these theorists' promotion of the autotelic artwork produced their own philosophical retreat from politico-historical engagements. As they actively sought to argue against the world's influence on the text, their easy sociability with forms in the world was thwarted by their theorization of the separation of these forms from the world. Unravelling such assumptions, modernism repeatedly points to the registered and unregistered influences of the world.

Contemplating the itinerary of influences upon Florian Deleal in Pater's "The Child in the House," the text's narrator decides that they had "floated thither from who knows how far" (4). The moment records influence as a Derridean trace, which forms the constellation of not only outward markers but of internal or psychological tendencies, susceptibilities, and propellers of character that Pater sees as the "soul-stuff," shaping consciousness through eccentric relations (4). This "soul-stuff" in Pater's writing (and its dissemination through the massive impact on British and Irish modernism of his student, Oscar Wilde, and through the tutelage of his sister Clara to her most famous student, Virginia Woolf) is crucial for both the transmission and absorption of consciously uttered thoughts, as well as spirit and attitudes. The public and the private, the local and the exotic, personal and public spheres reflect and shape each other through conscious and unconscious influence, and so, by the fact of their unconsciously absorbed shaping force, their trajectories of influence cannot be made manifest—their movement escapes our conscious registration. However, especially given the technological and discursive acceleration of global communication since the years of "High Modernism," its marks are surely global. Fertilized further with the vibrancy of African American linguistic inventiveness, American literature is ripe for a study of informality.

Propriety as Property: Censorship and Ownership

There are rich philosophical connections of informality with evolving connotations of words that determine nuances and meanings as ignitions for behaviour and sociability in modernist literature. To both acknowledge and appreciate these, and to show fluctuating relations, varying philosophical nuances, and even ostensible opposition of connotations that coalesce in the histories of single words, let me examine some significant etymologies in this conclusion, shifting my focus to the tensions between what is "appropriate" versus what is "preferable." Here's the etymology for the adjective "appropriate" in the *OED*:

> < Old French aproprie-r < late Latin appropriāre, adpropriāre (c450), < ad to, with idea of "rendering" + proprius own. Two forms: one (from Anglo-Norman) suppressing -i- ; the other, used chiefly in past participle, preserving -i , -y . Superseded in 17th cent. by the Latinized equivalent appropriate adj. and n.

The first given meaning in the dictionary for the word points to a now-obsolete usage: "1. To assign as private property or possession to; to set apart for a special purpose; spec. in Ecclesiastical [terminology] to annex to a religious corporation." The etymology clarifies what is an often-unacknowledged action in evocations of appropriate words or action: "Appropriate" the adjective often serves "appropriate" the verb. That is to say, when claiming appropriateness, we use the notion of what is appropriate to appropriate (gather to themselves) what can be said—in effect, to censor others.

This links closely with the sense of appropriation in the word "propriety" in the *Oxford English Dictionary*:

> propriety, n.
>
> Etymology: < Anglo-Norman proprietie, Anglo-Norman and Middle French proprieté, propriété (French propriété) ownership, proprietorship (a1176 in Old French), personal property (1212), particular or individual character of a person or thing (c1265), landed property, lands (a1377) and its etymon classical Latin proprietāt-, proprietās ownership, special property or character, proper or specific meaning of a word, fitness, appropriateness, rightness, property (2nd cent. a.d.), in post-classical Latin also special character of a language, idiom (4th cent.), landed estate (7th cent.), possession of worldly goods, in violation of a vow of poverty (frequently 1234–1443 in British sources), correctness (c1363 in a British source) < proprius proper adj. + -tās

Both words, "appropriate" and "propriety," are therefore bound by notions of ownership in their very etymon. But whose ownership is this? Who owns the definition of what is appropriate and what is proper? If an appropriate joke is attached to ownership, who owns our jokes? With a gesture to the self-evident, let me offer this answer: Notions of "the appropriate" are the products of the powerful state and cultural machinery that determines what is normatively permissible and what is to be excluded, what we can say and what is unsayable, what we can laugh at and when our laughter should make us uncomfortable, and even when we should stifle our laughter. Such machinery works, on the one hand, through institutionalized forces such as state actions and policy, religious discourse, academic arguments, the media, and other mind-setting influences. There is a phantom ownership of humour in such cases. But the phantom quality of such ownership is what demands for appropriateness neglect: It is the assumption of such ownership that produces a will to silence another, as well as the self. Seeking to avoid a difficult dialogue or discomfiting topics, such an attitude chooses silence. Seeking to foreclose blame, it forecloses debate. It opts for withdrawal or refusal to engage as a form of propriety, and even victimhood, through the official's evocation of fear—of people being afraid to say the wrong thing. Alternatively, there is a veiling of the real object of protection in such cases of wary silence—the self, which is instead offered as acceptably "nice."[2] Ostensibly choosing not to hurt the feelings of touchy others who, in your eyes, are very quick to blame you, you avoid hurting yourself. Silence is clearly the more comfortable option in such cases. It is the will to withdrawal that produces a will to silence another, as well as the self, in the form of detachment. Such a will shapes retreats from the world through various rationalizations, whether those of New Critics or of Father Arnall in *A Portrait of the Artist as a Young Man*. The tracery of the world's less obvious kinds of influence—through reminders that the language of the dead lives on in "the guts of the living," that existence alone is a rehearsal of postlapsarianism, that bourgeois categories for bliss restrict rather than expand experience—is a reminder of the world's less obvious kinds of relations.

Transience

Modernist informality offers us glimpses of such association candidly, and so without the guarantees of amity, cooperation, and conviviality. But its drive for *parrhesia* is repressed in the service of conformity and euphemism. In the closing sentence of *Acrobatic Modernism*, Rasula poetically notes, "Looking at modernism, we're perennially haunted to find something looking back at us, while extending a hand in—what, is it a greeting?" (401). The uncertainty of this greeting marks modernist informality. Even in its more definitive instances, modernist literature offers precarious formal models. Its ironic candour leaves room for alternative readings and non-normative ways of seeing and showing that go against the grain of established morality, prescribed behaviour, or static versions of the truth. It, thus, opens interpretive space for misreading as fertile, if shifting, ethical grounds.

A crucial aspect of its ethics lies in the very importance it gives to the instability of these grounds through its emphasis on the incessant mobility of relations and of transience. As Woolf writes in *Jacob's Room*:

> In any case life is but a procession of shadows, and God knows why it is that we embrace them so eagerly, and see them depart with such anguish, being shadows. And why, if this—and much more than this is true, why are we yet surprised in the window corner by a sudden

> vision that the young man in the chair is of all things in the world the most real, the most solid, the best known to us—why indeed? For the moment after we know nothing about him.
>
> Such is the manner of our seeing. Such the conditions of our love. (72–3)

The statement underscores the transience in our perspectives and, thereby, our ownership of understanding as a flicker. Logically, then, it offers a paradox: the conventions that validate our very thoughts and views as exclusively our own. In its overt ambivalence, instability, and unconventionality, the informality of parrhesiastic modernism counters such legitimate ownership. Against abiding morality, virtuous self-valorization, and normalcy, it urges its readers against the embarrassment and shame enforced by habituated morals, subtly and overtly. It shows that the Paterian "perpetual weaving and unweaving of ourselves" brings changes to our interpretations of the world, and that those changes are the very conditions for the making of the preferable. Alongside, it requires the repeated, even strenuous, unlearning of habit to produce conditions of easier sociability, approaching those that Marcuse sees as the logical result of a Marxian "realm of freedom." In its affirmative and anxious depictions of informality, candid modernism gifts us prospects that do not have dominant sanction, but could ease interaction, refresh language, and offer unembarrassed, if unstable, alternatives to convention—an *ethics* of illegitimacy.

Notes

1 See Rabaté's *The Pathos of Distance*; Valente's "James Joyce and the Cosmopolitan Sublime"; Walkowitz's *Cosmopolitan Style*; Saikat Majumdar's *Prose of the World*; and Anthony Cuda's *The Passions of Modernism*.

2 In perhaps its widest use today, the word "nice" conveys that someone (or something) is "pleasant in manner, agreeable, good-natured; attractive" or "Kind or considerate in behaviour; friendly." But why do we have phrases like "nice as a nun's hen" or "more nice than wise"—phrases very common in the nineteenth century and even in the early twentieth century? Here is the origin of the word "nice," according to the *OED*:

> < Anglo-Norman *nice, nis, nise* and Old French *nice* (c1160; c1250 as niche; now French regional) < classical Latin *nescius* (see NESCIOUS a.). Cf. Old Occitan nesci (c1150; also attested as *neci, nesi, nessi*; Occitan *neci*), Spanish *necio* (1220–50), Catalan *neci, nici* (both 14th cent.), Portuguese *necio* (14th cent.; 15th cent. as *néscio*), Italian *nescio* (1321), *all conveying the sense of "foolish, simple, ignorant."* [italics, mine].

In a slightly startled note, the dictionary says, "The semantic development of this word from 'foolish, silly' to 'pleasing' is unparalleled in Latin or in the Romance languages. The precise sense [of its] development in English is unclear." So there are two main camps for the meaning of the word "nice": one conveying the sense of "silly, foolish, etc." and the other, "precise, carefully accurate, demanding close attention." How do we reconcile these two conflicting aspects of the word's meaning? We might consider the word "nicety" that, in its origins, was closely associated with "niceness" as "foolishness," but, in its contemporary usage, signifies "the quality of requiring close consideration; delicacy, intricacy, subtlety; or the point at which these qualities are required." Keeping these etymologies in mind, I want to argue that "nicety" needs not only an alertness to present conditions, but the need to remember: the need to be aware of the context of things. That alertness of memory helps us to negotiate situations that require intricacy and subtlety. On the other hand, "niceness" (of the generic kind) works as a kind of inadvisable condition, a condition of stupidity or forgetting—a kind of pleasantness that overlooks uncomfortable, disruptive details.

Works Cited

Ahmed, Sara. *The Cultural Politics of Emotion*. New York: Routledge, 2004.

———. *The Promise of Happiness*. Durham, NC: Duke University Press, 2010.

Althusser, Louis. *For Marx*. Trans. Ben Brewster. New York: Verso, 2006.

———. “Ideology and Ideological State Apparatuses.” *Lenin and Philosophy and Other Essays*. Trans. Ben Brewster. New York: Monthly Review Press, 2001.

Altieri, Charles. “Theorizing Emotions in Eliot’s Poetry and Poetics.” *Gender, Desire, and Sexuality in T. S. Eliot*. Ed. Cassandra Laity and Nancy Gish. Cambridge: Cambridge University Press, 2009. 150–72.

Anderson, Amanda, et al. *Character: Three Inquiries into Literary Studies*. Chicago, IL: University of Chicago Press, 2019.

Arendt, Hannah. “Remembering Wystan H. Auden, Who Died in the Night of the Twenty-Eighth of September, 1973.” *Thinking without a Banister*. New York: Schocken Books, 2018. 525–34.

Arnold, Matthew. *Culture and Anarchy and Other Writings*. Cambridge: Cambridge University Press, 2004.

Asher, Kenneth. *Literature, Ethics, and the Emotions*. Cambridge: Cambridge University Press, 2017.

———. *T. S. Eliot and Ideology*. Cambridge: Cambridge University Press, 1998.

Attridge, Derek. *Peculiar Language: Literature as Difference from the Renaissance to James Joyce*. Ithaca, NY: Cornell University Press, 1988.

Attridge, Derek, and Marjorie Howes, eds. *Semicolonial Joyce*. Cambridge, UK: Cambridge University Press, 2000.

Auden, W. H. *Collected Poems*. Ed. Edward Mendelson. New York: Vintage Books, 1991.

———. *The Complete Works of W. H. Auden: Prose, Volume I: 1926–1938*. Ed. Edward Mendelson. Princeton, NJ: Princeton University Press, 1996.

———. *The Complete Works of W. H. Auden: Prose, Volume II: 1939–1948*. Ed. Edward Mendelson. Princeton, NJ: Princeton University Press, 2002.

———. *The Complete Works of W. H. Auden: Prose, Volume III: 1949–1955*. Ed. Edward Mendelson. Princeton, NJ: Princeton University Press, 2007.

———. *The English Auden: Poems, Essays and Dramatic Writings, 1927–1939*. Ed. Edward Mendelson. London: Faber and Faber, 1986.

———. *Forewords and Afterwords*. New York: Vintage Books, 1989.

———. “Review of Walter de la Mare.” *New Republic*. 27 December, 1939.

Auerbach, Erich. *Mimesis: The Representations of Reality in Western Literature*. Trans. William Trask. New York: Doubleday Anchor Books, 1957.

Bayley, John. "Only Critics Can't Play." *W. H. Auden: A Tribute*. Ed. Stephen Spender. New York: Macmillan, 1975. 229–41.

Beauvoir, Simone de. *The Ethics of Ambiguity*. Trans. Bernard Frechtman. New York: Carol Publishing Group, 1991.

———. *The Second Sex*. Trans. Constance Borde and Sheila Malovany-Chevallier. Vintage Classics, 2011.

Bell, Duncan. *Reordering the World: Essays on Liberalism and Empire*. Princeton, NJ: Princeton University Press, 2016.

Bell, Kevin. *Ashes Taken for Fire*. Minneapolis, MN: University of Minnesota Press, 2007.

Benjamin, Walter. "The Significance of Beautiful Semblance." *Selected Writings: Vol. 3: 1935–1938*. Trans. Edmund Jephcott, et al. Cambridge, MA: Harvard University Press, 2002.

———. "The Work of Art in the Age of Mechanical Reproduction." *Illuminations*. Trans. Harry Zohn. New York: Schocken Books, 1969.

Berlant, Lauren. "Intimacy: A Special Issue." *Critical Inquiry* 24.2 (Winter 1998). 281–88.

Bersani, Leo, and Adam Phillips. *Intimacies*. Chicago, IL: University of Chicago Press, 2008.

Boysen, Benjamin. *The Ethics of Love: An Essay on James Joyce*. Odense: University Press of Southern Denmark, 2013.

Brennan, Teresa, and Carole Pateman. "Mere Auxiliaries to the Commonwealth: Women and the Origins of Liberalism." *Political Studies* 27.1 (1979). 183–200.

Bronfen, Elisabeth. *Night Passages: Philosophy, Literature, and Film*. Trans. Elisabeth Bronfen and David Brenner. New York: Columbia University Press, 2013.

Burke, Edmund. *A Philosophical Enquiry into the Origin of Our Ideas of the Sublime and Beautiful*. Oxford: Oxford University Press, 1998.

Butler, Melissa. "Early Roots of Feminism: John Locke's Attack on Patriarchy." *Feminist Interpretations of John Locke*. Ed. Nancy J. Hirschmann and Kirstie M. McClure. University Park, PA: Pennsylvania State University Press, 2007. 91–122.

Carlyle, Thomas. *Heroes, Hero-Worship, and the Heroic in History*. New York: Frederick A. Stokes Company, 1893. 123–30.

———. *Past and Present. The Works of Thomas Carlyle*. Vol. VI. New York: Peter Fenelon Collier, 1897.

———. *Past and Present. The Works of Thomas Carlyle*. Vol. XIII. London: Chapman and Hall, 1843.

Cather, Willa. "Katherine Mansfield." *Not Under Forty*. New York: Knopf, 1971.

Cavarero, Adriana. *Inclinations: A Critique of Rectitude*. Trans. Amanda Minervini and Adam Sitze. Stanford, CA: Stanford University Press, 2016.

Chakrabarty, Dipesh. *Provincializing Europe*. Princeton, NJ: Princeton University Press, 2000.

Cixous, Hélène. "The Laugh of the Medusa." Trans. Keith Cohen and Paula Cohen. *Signs* 1.4 (Summer 1976). 875–93.

Clark, T. J. *Farewell to an Idea: Episodes from a History of Modernism*. New Haven, CT: Yale University Press, 1999.

Clifford, James. "Travelling Cultures." *Cultural Studies*. Ed. Lawrence Grossberg, et al. New York: Routledge, 1992. 96–116.

Conrad, Joseph. *Heart of Darkness*. Oxford: Oxford World's Classics, 2008.
Conrad, Peter. *Modern Times, Modern Places*. New York: Knopf, 1998.
Costello, Bonnie. *The Plural of Us: Poetry and Community in Auden and Others*. Princeton, NJ: Princeton University Press, 2017.
Critchley, Simon. *Infinitely Demanding: Ethics of Commitment, Politics of Resistance*. London: Verso, 2007.
Cuda, Anthony. *The Passions of Modernism: Eliot, Yeats, Woolf, and Mann*. Columbia, SC: University of South Carolina Press, 2010.
Culler, Jonathan. "The Hertzian Sublime." *MLN* 120.5 (December 2005). 969–985.
Daley, Kenneth. *The Rescue of Romanticism: Walter Pater and John Ruskin*. Athens, OH: Ohio State University Press, 2001.
Dean, Tim. "T. S. Eliot, Famous Clairvoyante." *Gender, Desire, and Sexuality in T. S. Eliot*. Ed. Cassandra Laity and Nancy Gish. Cambridge: Cambridge University Press, 2009. 43–65.
de Man, Paul. *Allegories of Reading: Figural Language in Rousseau, Nietzsche, Rilke, and Proust*. New Haven, CT: Yale University Press, 1979.
———. "Hypogram and Inscription: Michael Riffaterre's Poetics of Reading." *Diacritics* 11.4 (Winter 1981). 17–35.
Derrida, Jacques. *Negotiations: Interventions and Interviews, 1971–2001*. Trans. Elizabeth Rottenberg. Stanford, CA: Stanford University Press, 2002.
———. "Two Words for Joyce." Trans. Geoffrey Bennington. *Derrida and Joyce: Texts and Contexts*. Ed. Mitchell, Andrew J., and Sam Slote. Albany, NY: SUNY Press, 2013a. 22–40.
———. "Yes, Laughter." Trans. François Raffoul. *Derrida and Joyce: Texts and Contexts*. Ed. Mitchell, Andrew J., and Sam Slote. Albany, NY: SUNY Press, 2013b. 19.
Duffy, Enda. "High-Energy Modernism." *Moving Modernisms: Motion, Technology, and Modernity*. Ed. David Bradshaw, Laura Marcus, and Rebecca Roach. Oxford: Oxford University Press, 2016. 83-96.
———. *The Subaltern Ulysses*. Minneapolis, MN: University of Minnesota Press, 1994.
Eagleton, Terry. *Walter Benjamin: Towards a Revolutionary Criticism*. London: Verso, 1981.
Elias, Norbert. *The Civilizing Process: The History of Manners and State Formation and Civilization*. Trans. Edmund Jephcott. Oxford: Blackwell, 1994.
Eliot, T. S. *After Strange Gods*. New York: Harcourt Brace, 1934.
———. *The Complete Poems and Plays*. London: Faber and Faber, 1985.
———. "Dante III: The *Vita Nuova*." (1929). *Dante*. London: Faber and Faber, 1965. 55–64.
———. "[The Feminine Voice]." *Katherine Mansfield's Selected Stories*. New York: W. W. Norton and Co., 2006. 343.
———. *The Idea of a Christian Society. Christianity and Culture (The Idea of a Christian Society and Notes towards the Definition of Culture)*. San Diego, CA: Harcourt, 1976.
———. *Inventions of the March Hare: Poems 1909–1917*. San Diego, CA: Harvest, 1998.
———. *John Dryden: The Poet, The Dramatist, The Critic*. New York: Terence and Elsa Holiday, 1932.
———. "Notes." *The Criterion*. I:IV. July, 1923. 421.

———. *The Sacred Wood*. London: Methuen, 1967.

———. "Tradition and the Individual Talent" (1919). *Selected Prose of T. S. Eliot*. Orlando, FL: Harcourt Brace Jovanovich, 1975.

Ellman, Richard. *James Joyce*. Oxford: Oxford University Press, 1983.

Engels, *The Origin of the Family, Private Property, and the State*. Revised trans. Alick West. October, 1884; New York: Penguin Classics, 2010.

Fine, Robert, and Robin Cohen. "Four Cosmopolitan Moments." *Conceiving Cosmopolitanism : Theory, Context and Practice*. Ed. Steven Vertovec and Robin Cohen New York: Oxford University Press, 2002.

Foucault, Michel. *Abnormal: Lectures at the Collège de France, 1974–1975*. Trans. Graham Burchell. New York: Picador, 2004.

———. *The Courage of Truth: The Government of Self and Others II: Lectures at the Collège de France, 1983–1984*. Ed. Frédéric Gros. Trans. Graham Burchell. New York: Picador, 2011.

———. *Fearless Speech*. Ed. Joseph Pearson. Los Angeles: Semiotext(e), 2001.

Freud, Sigmund. *Civilization and Its Discontents*. Trans. and ed. James Strachey. New York: W. W. Norton & Company, 1961.

———. "Humour." *Art and Literature*. Trans. Joan Riviere. London: Penguin, 1990.

———. *Jokes and Their Relation to the Unconscious*. Trans. and ed. James Strachey. New York: Penguin, 1989.

———. "Mourning and Melancholia." *General Psychological Theory*. Trans. Joan Riviere. Ed. Philip Rieff. New York: Macmillan Publishing, 1963. 164-79.

———. "On Narcissism: An Introduction." *General Psychology Theory*. Ed. Philip Rieff. New York: Macmillan Publishing, 1963. 56-82.

———. *An Outline of Psychoanalysis*. Trans. James Strachey. New York: Norton, 1989.

———. "The 'Uncanny.'" *Writings on Art and Literature*. Trans. James Strachey. Stanford, CA: Stanford University Press, 1997. 193-233.

Frost, Laura. *The Problem with Pleasure: Modernism and Its Discontents*. New York: Columbia University Press, 2013.

Froula, Christine. *Virginia Woolf and the Bloomsbury Avant-Garde: War, Civilization, Modernity*. New York: Columbia University Press, 2005.

Fuller, John. *W. H. Auden: A Commentary*. Princeton, NJ: Princeton University Press, 1998.

———. *A Reader's Guide to W. H. Auden*. London: Thames, 1970.

Fuss, Diana. *Dying Modern: A Meditation on Elegy*. Durham NC: Duke University Press, 2013.

Garnett, Angelica. *Deceived with Kindness*. Oxford: Oxford University Press, 1985.

Garver, Lee. "The Political Katherine Mansfield." *Modernism/Modernity* 8.2 (April 2001). 225–243.

Gifford, Don, and Robert J. Seidman. Ulysses *Annotated*. Berkeley, CA: University of California Press, 2008.

Gillespie, Gerald. "Swallowing the Androgyne and Baptizing Mother: Some Modernist Twists to Two Basic Sacraments." *The Comparatist*, vol. 33, 2009, pp. 63–85.

Goldman, Jonathan. *Modernism Is the Literature of Celebrity*. Austin, TX: University of Texas Press, 2011.

Gottlieb, Susannah Young-ah. *Regions of Sorrow: Anxiety and Messianism in Hannah Arendt and W. H. Auden*. Stanford, CA: Stanford University Press, 2003.
Graves, Robert. *Lars Porsena, or, The Future of Swearing and Improper Language*. Richmond: Oneworld Classics, 2008.
Gregg, Melissa, and Gregory Seigworth. *The Affect Theory Reader*. Durham, NC: Duke University Press, 2010.
Gumbrecht, Hans Ulrich. *In Praise of Athletic Beauty*. Cambridge, MA: Harvard University Press, 2006.
Hägglund, Martin. *Dying for Time*. Cambridge, MA: Harvard University Press, 2012.
———. *This Life: Secular Faith and Spiritual Freedom*. New York: Anchor Books, 2020.
Halliwell, Stephen. *Between Ecstasy and Truth: Interpretations of Greek Poetics from Homer to Longinus*. Oxford: Oxford University Press, 2012.
Hertz, Neil. *The End of the Line: Essays on Psychoanalysis and the Sublime*. New York: Columbia University Press, 1985.
Hebdige, Dick. *Subculture: The Meaning of Style*. London: Routledge, 1979.
Hext, Kate. *Walter Pater: Individualism and Aesthetic Philosophy*. Edinburgh: Edinburgh University Press, 2013.
Hildebrandt, Sabine. *The Anatomy of Murder: Ethical Transgressions and Anatomical Science during the Third Reich*. New York: Berghahn, 2016.
Hirschmann, Nancy J. *The Subject of Liberty: Toward a Feminist Theory of Freedom*. Princeton, NJ: Princeton University Press, 2003.
Hirschmann, Nancy J. and Kirstie M. McClure, eds. *Feminist Interpretations of John Locke*. University Park, PA: Pennsylvania State University Press, 2007.
Joyce, James. *Finnegans Wake*. New York: Penguin Books, 1976.
———. *James Joyce in Padua*. Ed. and trans. Louis Berrone. New York, 1977.
———. *Letters of James Joyce*. Ed. Stuart Gilbert. London: Faber and Faber, 1957.
———. *Occasional, Critical and Political Writing*. Ed. Kevin Barry. Oxford: Oxford University Press, 2000.
———. *A Portrait of the Artist as a Young Man*. Ed. Seamus Deane. New York: Penguin, 1992.
———. *Ulysses*. New York: Random House, 1962.
Kant, Immanuel. *Critique of Judgment*. Trans. J. H. Bernard. New York: Hafner, 1951.
———. *Groundwork of the Metaphysics of Morals*. Ed. and trans. Mary Gregor. Cambridge: Cambridge University Press, 1997.
Lacan, Jacques. "The Split between the Eye and the Gaze." *The Four Fundamental Concepts of Psychoanalysis*. Trans. Alan Sheridan. New York: Norton, 1978.
Lewis, Pericles. *Cambridge Introduction to Modernism*. Cambridge: Cambridge University Press, 2007.
Levine, Caroline. *Forms: Whole, Rhythm, Hierarchy, Network*. Princeton, NJ: Princeton University Press, 2017.
Locke, John. *An Essay Concerning Human Understanding*. London: Penguin Books, 2004.
———. "The Reasonableness of Christianity." *Writings on Religion*. Ed. Victor Nuovo. Oxford: Oxford University Press, 2002. 85–210.
———. *Two Treatises of Government*. Cambridge: Cambridge University Press, 1988.

Longinus. "On Sublimity." Trans. D. A. Russell. *Classical Literary Criticism*. Oxford: Oxford World's Classics, 2008.

———. "On the Sublime." Trans. T. S. Dorsch. Harmondsworth: Penguin, 1965.

———. "On the Sublime." Ed. and trans. W. Hamilton Fyfe, revised by Donald Russell. Cambridge, MA: Harvard University Press, 1995.

Lowe, Lisa. *The Intimacies of Four Continents*. Durham, NC: Duke University Press, 2015.

Lukács, Georg. *History and Class Consciousness*.

———. "The Ideology of Modernism." *The Meaning of Contemporary Realism*. Trans. John Mander and Necke Mander. London: Merlin Press, 1963. 17–46.

Lyotard, Jean-François. *The Postmodern Condition: A Report on Knowledge*. Trans. Geoff Bennington and Brian Massumi. Minneapolis, MN: University of Minnesota Press, 1989.

MacNeice, Louis. "Louis MacNeice on 'Up-to-Date' Auden (Untitled Review)." *Oxford Outlook*. Vol. XI. March, 1931. *W. H. Auden: The Critical Heritage*. Ed. John Haffenden. London: Routledge & Kegan Paul, 1983. 86–88.

Mahaffey, Vicki. *Modernist Literature: Challenging Fictions*. Malden, MA: Blackwell Publishing, 2007.

Majumdar, Gaurav. *Migrant Form: Anti-Colonial Aesthetics in Joyce, Rushdie, and Ray*. New York: Peter Lang, 2010.

Majumdar, Saikat. *Prose of the World: Modernism and the Banality of Empire*. New York: Columbia University Press, 2013.

Mansfield, Katherine. "Bliss." *Katherine Mansfield's Selected Stories*. New York: W. W. Norton and Co., 2006.

———. "The Daughters of the Late Colonel." *Katherine Mansfield's Selected Stories*. New York: W. W. Norton and Co., 2006.

———. "A Dill Pickle." *Katherine Mansfield's Selected Stories*. New York: W. W. Norton and Co., 2006.

———. "The Garden-Party." *Katherine Mansfield's Selected Stories*. New York: W. W. Norton and Co., 2006.

———. "How Pearl Button was Kidnapped." *Katherine Mansfield's Selected Stories*. New York: W. W. Norton and Co., 2006.

———. "In the Botanical Gardens." *Poems of Katherine Mansfield*. Oxford: Oxford University Press, 1988.

———. *The Katherine Mansfield Notebooks*, 2 vols. Ed. Margaret Scott. Minneapolis, MN: University of Minnesota Press, 2002.

———. "Prelude." *Katherine Mansfield's Selected Stories*. New York: W. W. Norton and Co., 2006.

Marchbanks, Paul. "The Ineluctable Modality of the Visibly Disabled in James Joyce's *Ulysses*." *Journal of Literary & Cultural Disability Studies* 12.1 (2018). 53–69.

Marcuse, Herbert. *An Essay on Liberation*. Boston, MA: Beacon Press, 1969.

Marshall, Ashley. "T. S. Eliot on the Limits of Criticism: The Anomalous 'Experiment' of 1929." *The Modern Language Review* 100.3 (July 2005). 609–620.

Marx, Karl. *Capital: A Critique of Political Economy*. Volume Three. Trans. David Fernbach. Penguin Books, 1981.

———. *Economic and Philosophical Manuscripts of 1844*. *Karl Marx: Selected Writings*. Trans. Loyd D. Easton and Kurt H. Guddat. Ed. Lawrence H. Simon. Indianapolis, IN: Hackett, 1994.

———. *Wage-Labour and Capital*. New York: International Publishers, 2006.

McHugh, Roland. *Annotations to Finnegans Wake*. Baltimore, MD: The Johns Hopkins University Press, 1991.

Mehta, Uday Singh. *Liberalism and Empire*. Chicago, IL: University of Chicago Press, 1999.

Meisel, Perry. *The Myth of the Modern: A Study in British Literature and Criticism after 1850*. New Haven, CT: Yale University Press, 1987.

Menninghaus, Winfried. *Disgust: The Theory and History of a Strong Sensation*. Trans. Howard Eiland and Joel Golb. Albany, NY: State University of New York Press, 2003.

Miller, Tyrus. *Late Modernism: Politics, Fiction, and the Arts Between the World Wars*. Berkeley, CA: University of California Press, 1999.

Miller, William Ian. *The Anatomy of Disgust*. Cambridge, MA: Harvard University Press, 1998.

Neill, Crispian. "The Afflatus of Flatus: James Joyce and the Writing of Odor." *James Joyce Quarterly* 53.3 (2016). 307–326. Project MUSE. doi:10.1353/jjq.2018.0010

Ngai, Sianne. *Ugly Feelings*. Cambridge, MA: Harvard University Press, 2005.

Nietzsche, Friedrich. *Beyond Good and Evil*. Trans. Judith Norman. Ed. Rolf-Peter Horstmann. Cambridge: Cambridge UP, 2002.

———. *The Birth of Tragedy*. Trans. Ronald Speirs. Ed. Raymond Geuss. Cambridge: Cambridge UP, 1999.

———. *The Gay Science*. Trans. Josefine Nauckhoff. Cambridge: Cambridge University Press, 2014.

———. *On the Genealogy of Morals*. Trans. Douglas Smith. New York: Oxford World's Classics, 2008.

Norris, Margot. *Virgin and Veteran Readings of Ulysses*. New York: Palgrave Macmillan, 2011.

Opest, Michael. "Epiphanic *Ulysses*: Joyce's Trail of Breadcrumbs." *Joyce Studies Annual*, vol. 2016, 2016, pp. 154–174. Project MUSE, muse.jhu.edu/article/650234.

Parsons, Deborah. *Streetwalking the Metropolis: Women, the City and Modernity*. Oxford: Oxford University Press, 2000.

Pater, Walter. *Appreciations. The Works of Walter Pater*. Vol. 5. Cambridge: Cambridge University Press, 2011.

———. *Imaginary Portraits, with The Child in the House and Gaston de Latour*. New York: Allworth Press, 1997.

———. *The Renaissance. The Works of Walter Pater*. Vol. 1. Cambridge: Cambridge University Press, 2011.

Pease, Allison. *Modernism, Mass Culture, and the Aesthetics of Obscenity*. Cambridge: Cambridge University Press, 2014.

Phillips, Adam. *Going Sane*. New York: Harper Perennial, 2007.

———. *On Flirtation*. Cambridge, MA: Harvard University Press, 1994.

Pitts, Jennifer. *A Turn to Empire: The Rise of Imperial Liberalism in Britain and France*. Princeton, NJ: Princeton University Press, 2005.

Plato, *The Republic*. Trans. Tom Griffith. Cambridge: Cambridge University Press, 2000.

Porter, Holly. "Moral Spaces and Sexual Transgression: Understanding Rape in War and Post Conflict." *Development and Change* 50.4 (July 2019). 1009–1032.

Power, Arthur. *Conversations with James Joyce*. Dublin: Lilliput Press, 1999.

Rabaté, Jean-Michel. *The Pathos of Distance: Affects of the Moderns*. New York: Bloomsbury Academic, 2016.

Ragg, Edward. "Apophatic Auden, Abstract Stevens: From Kierkegaard to Cézanne in 'The Sea and the Mirror' and 'The Figure of the Youth as Virile Poet.'" *Wallace Stevens Journal* 37.2 (Fall 2013). 199–223.

Ramazani, Jahan. *Poetry of Mourning: The Modern Elegy from Hardy to Heaney*. Chicago, IL: University of Chicago Press, 1994.

Rancière, Jacques. *The Edges of Fiction*. Trans. Steve Corcoran. New York Polity, 2020.

———. *The Politics of Aesthetics*. Ed. and trans. Gabriel Rockhill. New York: Bloomsbury Academic, 2004.

Rasula, Jed. *Acrobatic Modernism: From the Avant-Garde to Prehistory*. Oxford: Oxford University Press, 2020.

———. *Destruction Was My Beatrice: Dadaism and the Unmaking of the Twentieth Century*. New York: Basic Books, 2015.

———. *History of a Shiver: The Sublime Impudence of Modernism*. Oxford: Oxford University Press, 2016.

Remhof, Justin. "Nietzsche on Loneliness, Self-Transformation, and the Eternal Recurrence." *The Journal of Nietzsche Studies*. Volume 49, Issue 2, Autumn 2018. pp. 194–213.

Robbins, Bruce. "Comparative Cosmopolitanisms." *Cosmopolitics: Thinking and Feeling Beyond the Nation*. Ed. Pheng Cheah and Bruce Robbins. Minneapolis, MN: University of Minnesota Press, 1998.

Rose, Jacqueline. *On not Being Able to Sleep*. Princeton, NJ: Princeton University Press, 2003.

Ruskin, John. *The Two Paths*. Ed. Harold Bloom. New York: Chelsea House, 1983.

Said, Edward. *Culture and Imperialism*. London: Vintage, 1993.

———. *The World, the Text, and the Critic*. Cambridge, MA: Harvard University Press, 1983.

Schivelbusch, Wolfgang. *The Railway Journey: The Industrialization of Time and Space in the 19th Century*. Berkeley, CA: University of California Press, 1986.

Sedgwick, Eve. *Epistemology of the Closet*. Berkeley, CA: University of California Press, 2008.

Servotte, Herman. "Auden and Kierkegaard." *Multiple Worlds, Multiple Words: Essays in Honour of Irène Simon*. Ed. Hena Maes-Jelinek, Pierre Michel, and Paulette Michel-Michot. Liège: U of Liège, 1987. 275–82.

Shanley, Mary. "Marriage Contract and Social Contract in Seventeenth-Century English Political Thought." Ed. Nancy J. Hirschmann and Kirstie M. McClure. *Feminist Interpretations of John Locke*. University Park, PA: Pennsylvania State University Press, 2007. 17–38.

Sharpe, Tony. "'Always Present': T. S. Eliot and Re-cantation." *Modernism/modernity* 25.2 (April 2018). 369–387.

Simmel, Georg. "Freedom and the Individual." Trans. Richard P. Albares. *On Individuality and Social Forms*. Ed. Donald N. Levine. Chicago, IL: University of Chicago Press, 1971.

———. "The Metropolis and Mental Life." Trans. Edward A. Shils. *On Individuality and Social Forms*. Ed. Donald N. Levine. Chicago, IL: University of Chicago Press, 1971. 324-39.

Slote, Sam. *Joyce's Nietzschean Ethics*. New York: Palgrave, 2013.

Spears, Monroe K. *The Poetry of W. H. Auden: The Disenchanted Island*. Oxford: Oxford University Press, 1963.
Spender, Stephen. *The Struggle of the Modern*. Berkeley, CA: University of California Press, 1963.
Spender, Stephen, ed. *W. H. Auden: A Tribute*. London: Weidenfeld, 1975.
Spivak, Gayatri Chakravorty. *A Critique of Postcolonial Reason: Toward a History of the Vanishing Present*. Cambridge, MA: Harvard University Press, 1999.
Stallybrass, Peter, and Allon White. *The Politics and Poetics of Transgression*. Ithaca, NY: Cornell University Press, 1986.
Stivers, Richard. *The Illusion of Freedom and Equality*. Albany, NY: State University of New York Press, 2009.
Sullivan, Hannah. "'Still Doing It by Hand.'" *Auden at Work*. Ed. Bonnie Costello and Rachel Galvin. London: Palgrave Macmillan, 2015. 5-23.
Vogler, Candace. "Sex and Talk." *Critical Inquiry* 24.2 (Winter 1998). 328–65.
Valente, Joseph. "James Joyce and the Cosmopolitan Sublime." *Joyce and the Subject of History*. Ed. Mark Wollaeger, et al. Ann Arbor, MI: University of Michigan Press, 1996. 59-82.
Walkowitz, Rebecca. *Cosmopolitan Style: Modernism beyond the Nation*. New York: Columbia University Press, 2006.
Wellek, René, and Austin Warren. *Theory of Literature*. New York: Harcourt, Brace, and Co., 1949.
Whitehead, David. *The Ideology of the Athenian Metic*. Cambridge, UK: The Cambridge Philological Society, 1977.
West, Thomas G. "Nature and Happiness in Locke." *Claremont Review of Books* 2 (Spring 2004). 1–15.
Wilde, Oscar. *De Profundis*. New York: The Modern Library, 1992.
———. *The Picture of Dorian Gray*. Cambridge, MA: Harvard/Belknap, 2011.
Williams, Raymond. *The Long Revolution*. Harmondsworth: Penguin, 1965.
Wilson, Janet, and Janet Wilson, "Katherine Mansfield, Virginia Woolf, and the Nature Goddess Tradition." *Literature & Aesthetics* 27.1 (2017). 17–38.
———. "Mansfield as (Post)colonial Modernist: Rewriting the Contract with Death." *Katherine Mansfield and the (Post)colonial*. Ed. Janet Wilson, Gerri Kimber, and Delia Da Sousa Correa. Edinburgh, AB: Edinburgh University Press, 2013. 1-12.
Wilson, Robert R. *The Hydra's Tale: Imagining Disgust*. Edmonton, AB: University of Alberta Press, 2002.
Wolfe, Jesse. *Bloomsbury, Modernism, and the Reinvention of Intimacy*. New York: Cambridge University Press, 2011.
Woolf, Virginia. "Carlyle's House." *Carlyle's House and Other Sketches*. London: Hesperus Press, 2003.
———. "Character in Fiction." *The Essays of Virginia Woolf*, Vol. 4. Ed. Andrew McNeillie. Orlando, FL: Harcourt Brace Jovanovich, 1988.
———. "Craftsmanship." *The Death of the Moth and Other Essays*. Orlando, FL: Harcourt, 1970.
———. *The Diary of Virginia Woolf, Volume One, 1915–1919*. Ed. Anne Olivier Bell. London: Hogarth, 1977.
———. "How Should One Read a Book?" *The Second Common Reader*. Ed. Andrew McNeillie. San Diego, CA: Harvest Books, 1986.
———. *Jacob's Room*. Orlando, FL: Harcourt, 2008.

———. "The Leaning Tower." *Collected Essays*. Vol. 2. Ed. Leonard Woolf. New York: Harcourt, Brace and World, 1967. 153-61.

———. "The Mark on the Wall." *The Complete Shorter Fiction of Virginia Woolf*. Ed. Susan Dick. New York: Harcourt, 1989. 83-89.

———. "Modern Fiction." *The Essays of Virginia Woolf*, Vol. 4. Ed. Andrew McNeillie. Orlando, FL: Harcourt Brace Jovanovich, 1994. 157-65.

———. "The Modern Essay." *The Essays of Virginia Woolf*, Vol. 4. Ed. Andrew McNeillie. Orlando, FL: Harcourt Brace Jovanovich, 1994. 216-26.

———. *Moments of Being*. Ed. Jeanne Schulkind. New York: Harvest, 1985.

———. "The Narrow Bridge of Art." *Granite and Rainbow*. London: Penguin Books, 1998. 11-23.

———. "Mr. Bennett and Mrs. Brown." *The Virginia Woolf Reader*. Ed. Mitchell A. Leaska. Orlando, FL: Harcourt, 1984. 192-212.

———. "The Perfect Language." *The Essays of Virginia Woolf*, Vol. 2. Ed. Andrew McNeillie. San Diego, CA: Harcourt Brace Jovanovich, 1987. 114-19.

———. *To the Lighthouse*. San Diego, CA: Harcourt Brace Jovanovich, 1981.

———. "The War from the Street." *The Crowded Dance of Modern Life*. 3–4.

Wolfe, Jesse. *Bloomsbury, Modernism, and the Reinvention of Intimacy*. New York: Cambridge University Press, 2011.

Worsley, T. C. "Major Poet." *New Statesman and Nation*. July, 1940. *W. H. Auden: The Critical Heritage*. Ed. John Haffenden. London: Routledge & Kegan Paul, 1983. 303–306.

Zwerdling, Alex. *Virginia Woolf and the Real World*. Berkeley, CA: University of California Press, 1986.

Index

Made in the USA
Las Vegas, NV
30 October 2024

dd271857-9df3-40da-abb0-8889b5c0e4f8R01